INC 2012

Nelson Mandela Metropolitan University, South Africa
11-12 July 2012

Proceedings of the 9th International Network Conference

Editors

Reinhardt A Botha
Paul S Dowland
Steven M Furnell

ISBN: 978-1-84102-315-1

Preface

This book presents the proceedings of the Ninth International Network Conference (INC 2012), hosted by the Nelson Mandela Metropolitan University, South Africa, from 11th to 12th July 2012.

A continuing aim of the INC series is to provide an opportunity for those involved in the design, development and use of network systems and applications to meet, share their ideas and exchange opinions. The 2012 event again succeeds in this aim by bringing together leading specialists from academia and industry, and enabling the presentation and discussion of the latest advances in research.

INC 2012 has attracted authors from 8 countries and these proceedings contain a total of 20 papers, organised into four thematic chapters. The papers cover many aspects of modern networking, including web technologies, network protocols and performance, security and privacy, mobile and wireless systems, and the applications and impacts of network technology. As such, it is hoped that all readers will find a variety of material of interest. Each paper was subjected to double-blind review by at least two members of the International Programme Committee with a 66% acceptance rate. We would like to thank all of the reviewers for their efforts, as well as the authors for their willingness to share their ideas and findings.

The conference team is also most grateful to our keynotes speakers for accepting our invitation to share their expertise in the keynote lectures and in particular to SANReN for sponsoring Simeon Miteff's keynote presentation.

We hope that all of our delegates enjoy the conference, and that other readers of these proceedings will be able to join us on a future occasion.

Prof. Reinhardt Botha & Prof. Steven Furnell
Conference Co-Chairs, INC 2012

Port Elizabeth, July 2012

About the Institute for ICT Advancement

The Institute for ICT Advancement (IICTA) is proud to host INC 2012 in Port Elizabeth, South Africa. IICTA is a formal research institute in the Faculty of Engineering, the Built Environment and Information Technology at the Nelson Mandela Metropolitan University in Port Elizabeth, South Africa.

The aim of IICTA is to; teach, educate, research, consult and to provide services in the discipline of ICT to academia, commerce, industry and the community in the Nelson Mandela Metropolitan Area, the region, Southern Africa and in some cases internationally.

IICTA consists of five research groups. These are:

1. Information Security Management and Governance
2. Health Informatics
3. Usability and User Experience
4. End-to-end service design
5. Enterprise Knowledge Engineering

IICTA has successfully delivered fourteen (14) PhD students and fourteen (14) master's students over the last three years. In addition, nineteen (19) journal articles and ninety-five (95) conference articles stemmed from IICTA during this period.

Address Institute for ICT Advancement
P.O. Box 77000
NMMU
Port Elizabeth 6031
South Africa

Telephone +27 (0)41 504 3646
Fax +27 (0)41 504 9604
Email rossouw@nmmu.ac.za

About the Centre for Security, Communications and Network Research

The INC conference series is organised by the Centre for Security, Communications and Network Research (CSCAN) at Plymouth University, UK.

CSCAN is a specialist technology and networking research facility at Plymouth University. Originally established in 1985 (under the original name of the Network Research Group), the Centre conducts research in the areas of IT Security, Internet & WWW technologies and Mobility, and has a proven pedigree including projects conducted for, and in collaboration with, commercial companies, as well as participation in European research initiatives. Over the years, our research activities have led to numerous successful projects, along with associated publications and patents.

At the time of writing, the Centre has fourteen affiliated full-time academic staff and fifty-two research degree projects (at PhD and MPhil levels). The Centre also supports Masters programmes in Communication Engineering and Signal Processing, Computer and Information Security, Computer Science and Network Systems Engineering, and hosts a significant number of research-related projects from these programmes.

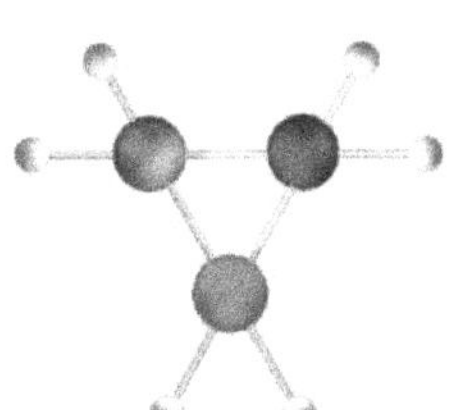

Address Centre for Security, Communications
and Network Research
Plymouth University
Drake Circus
Plymouth
PL4 8AA
United Kingdom

Telephone +44 (0) 1752 586 234
Fax +44 (0) 1752 586 300
Email info@cscan.org
URL www.cscan.org

INC 2012 Committees

International Programme Committee

Krzysztof Amborski	University of Technology, Warsaw	Poland
Nikos Antonopoulos	University of Derby	United Kingdom
Harald Baier	Hochschule Darmstadt, Center for Advanced Security Research Darmstadt (CASED)	Germany
Frank Ball	Frank Ball Consulting	United Kingdom
Udo Bleimann	University of Applied Sciences Darmstadt	Germany
Reinhardt Botha	Nelson Mandela Metropolitan University	South Africa
Arslan Brömme	GI BIOSIG	Germany
Phil Brooke	Teesside University	United Kingdom
Nathan Clarke	Plymouth University	United Kingdom
Jeff Crume	IBM	USA
Paul Dowland	Plymouth University	United Kingdom
Mariki Eloff	University of South Africa	South Africa
Christophe Feltus	Public Research Centre Henri Tudor	Luxembourg
Klaus-Peter Fischer-Hellmann	Digamma Communications Consulting GmbH	Germany
Ulrich Flegel	HFT Stuttgart, University of Applied Sciences	Germany
Woldemar Fuhrmann	University of Applied Sciences, Darmstadt	Germany
Steven Furnell	Plymouth University	United Kingdom
Bogdan Ghita	Plymouth University	United Kingdom
Martin Gonzalez Rodriguez	University of Oviedo	Spain
Carsten Griwodz	University of Oslo	Norway
Vic Grout	Glyndwr University, Wales	United Kingdom
Bettina Harriehausen	University of Applied Sciences, Darmstadt	Germany
Holger Hofmann	Cooperative State University Baden-Wurttemberg Mannheim	Germany
Bernhard Humm	Hochschule Darmstadt - University of Applied Sciences	Germany
Vasilios Katos	Democritus University of Thrace	Greece
Sokratis Katsikas	University of Piraeus	Greece
Martin Knahl	Furtwangen University	Germany
George Magklaras	Plymouth University	United Kingdom
Dwight Makaroff	University of Saskatchewan	Canada
Andreas Meissner	Fraunhofer IOSB	Germany
Jacques Ophoff	University of Cape Town	South Africa
Vassillis Prevelakis	AEGIS Research Center	Greece
Andreas Rinkel	University of Applied Sciences Rapperswill	Switzerland
Angelos Rouskas	University of Piraeus	Greece
Ingo Stengel	Plymouth University	United Kingdom
Kerry-Lynn Thomson	Nelson Mandela Metropolitan University	South Africa
Ulrich Trick	University of Applied Sciences Frankfurt/M.	Germany
Dimitrios D. Vergados	University of Piraeus	Greece
Merrill Warkentin	Mississippi State University	USA

Organising Committee

Reinhardt Botha (co-chair)
Paul Dowland (co-chair)
Heloise Levack

Keynote Speakers

Prof. Martin Olivier
Professor: Computer Science
University of Pretoria

Martin Olivier is a professor at the Department of Computer Science in the School of Information Technology at the University of Pretoria. His current research interests include privacy and digital forensics as well as database, application and system security. Research Activities are carried out in the Information and Computer Security Architecture Research Group at the University of Pretoria.

He is author or co-author of more than 180 academic publications. More than 30 students have completed their Masters or Doctoral studies under his guidance. He is a member of the editorial board of Data & Knowledge Engineering. He is also member of IFIP working group 11.9 on digital forensics, the ACM, the Suid-Afrikaanse Akademie vir Wetenskap en Kuns (South African Academy for Science and Art) and an associate member of the American Academy of Forensic Sciences. He regularly acts on the programme committee or as a reviewer for various conferences.

Simeon Miteff
Council for Industrial and Scientific Research

Simeon Miteff is a technical specialist with the Council for Industrial and Scientific Research, where he manages the technical aspects for the roll-out of South Africa's research and education network: SANReN.

He graduated with a BSc degree in Computer Science from the University of Pretoria in 2003, and completed a Honours degree in Computer Science at the University of South Africa in 2007.

Simeon has a background in UNIX systems and network administration, network operations, design and architecture and has on occasion been involved with software development and high performance computing.

Contents

CHAPTER 4 Applications and Impacts

Chapter 1

Network Technologies

Design and Implementation of Lower Layers of Q3 Interface in Telecommunication Management Network

G.Farahani

Islamic Azad University Parand Branch, Computer and IT Department, Tehran, Iran
e-mail: farahani.gh@piau.ac.ir

Abstract

This paper presents a new method to design and implement lower layers of Q3 interface at internet mode profile and client-server in Telecommunication Management Network (TMN). Regards to functional and procedural requirements of internet mode profile, we develop software to implement and test lower layers with consideration of multithreading and critical section techniques to communicate between server and clients.

Because of growing up internet in worldwide and accessibility of it at most switch centers, internet mode profile against connection oriented mode profile and connectionless profile, will use as a world method for information interchange, which it includes TMN. In this paper Q3 interface in TMN has been implemented and tested in laboratory.

In this implementation, client computers simulate telecommunication switchs and control switch substitutes with server computer that makes a required instructions to control telecommunication switches. Test environment which made for program, simulate a functions that interchange between network element and operating system. In our implementation we found Q3 interface in comparison to ordinary telecommunication has an approximately 26.6% performance improvement of instruction interchange in TMN.

Keywords

Telecommunication Management Network, Q3 interface, TCP/IP protocol

1. Introduction

Variety of telecommunication networks and systems, causes different private interfaces in the networks, therefore management of each private network requires different interfaces for operation of protocols in the networks. To clarify the duty scope of each part, we should use management architecture with standard connection interface. Therefore standard institute ITU-T declared first standard for Telecommunication Management Network (TMN) in 1985. TMN in the concept is a discrete network, which has connection at different points. These connections are shown in figure 1 (ITU-T, M3010, 1996). According to figure 1, connection points are between telecommunication network and TMN at switches and transmission systems. The protocols which implement internet profile with required recommendation for implementation of those protocols are shown in Figure 2 (ITU-T, M3020, 2000). Internet profile is acceptable method which these days, utilizes for implementation of management information transmission network.

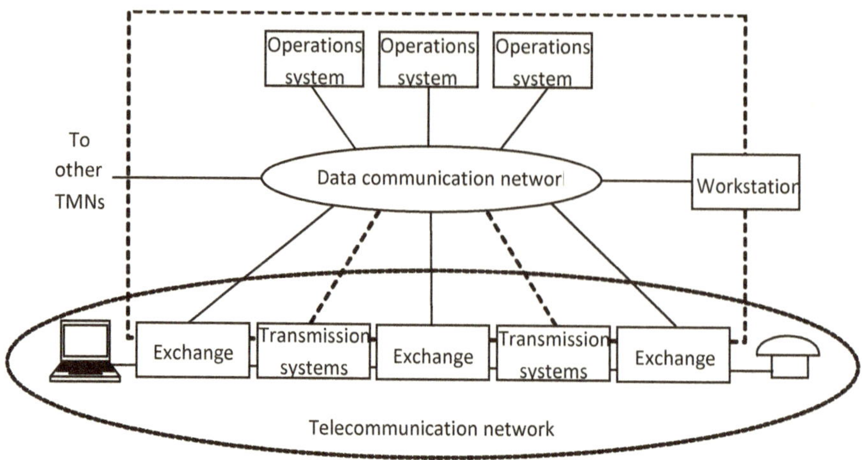

Figure 1: Relation between TMN and telecommunication network

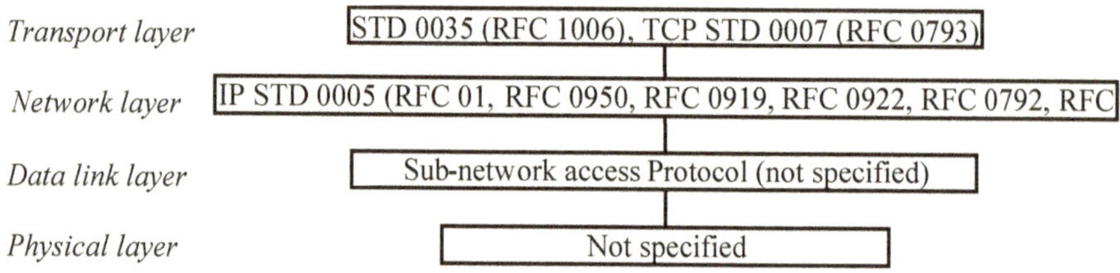

Figure 2: Internet profile protocols

Most producers of telecommunication equipment which are using other profiles except internet to manage information interchange, for compatibility with data transmission systems in the base of TCP/IP, currently are substituting their profiles with internet mode profile. In this paper we will simulate telecommunication switches which are implemented in Iranian Telecommunication Research Center (ITRC). In other countries especially European and American coutries, implementation according to their requirement has been carried out.

Now, studies on the other functionalities of telecommunication management network are carrying out which with association of Q3 interface program, we would be able to configure our network in the optimal condition (ITU-T, M.3000, 1995).

2. Telecommunication Management Network

In TMN there are three different architectures. We describe architectures briefly.

2.1. Functional architecture of TMN

In this architecture, five types of different functional architecture have been defined which in implementations of TMN, we don't require all of the functional blocks. Figure 3 shows different types of functional blocks of TMN.

In functional architecture of TMN we use references points to describe functional blocks. As a result, we have five set of reference points. Three of these reference points (Q, F and X) are defined completely with TMN recommendation but two other reference points (M and G reference points) are located at outside of TMN environment. In figure 4 reference points and their functional blocks are shown. At continuation, we will describe functional blocks of TMN briefly.

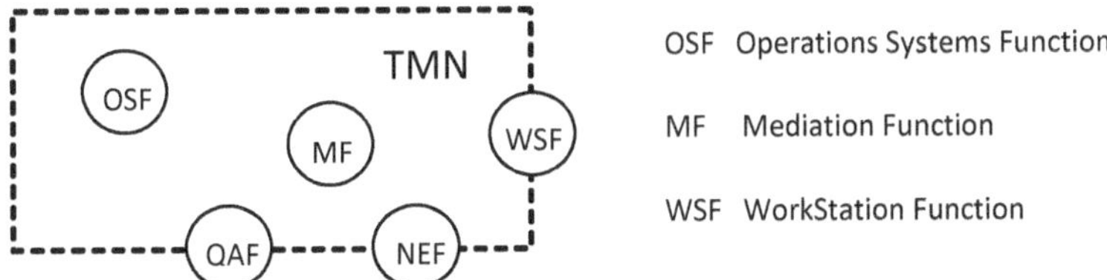

Figure 3: Functional Blocks of TMN

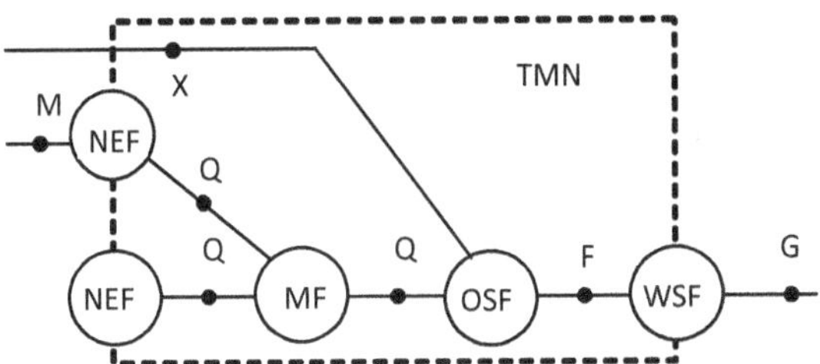

Figure 4: Different reference points in TMN

2.1.1. Network Element Function

A telecommunication network is made with switches and transmission systems. In TMN, these switches and transmission systems are examples of network elements.

2.1.2. Operation System Function

This function block is used for management operation initialization and receiving reports. An OSF will connect to NEF via Q3 reference point.

At primary standard in 1988, recommendation M.30 defined three reference points named Q1, Q2 and Q3 which reference point Q3 was used to interchange management information via management protocol of application layer and two other reference points defined for management information which should exchange via lower layers management protocol (e. g. data link layer) but after practical using of these two points, it was cleared that we can not make a difference between reference points. Therefore these two reference points replaced with reference point Qx. Generally services at reference point Q3 will consider as a Common Management Information Service (CMIS).

If require, it is possible TMN includes several OSF which in this condition OSFs communicated together via Q3 reference points and if OSFs are in the different environments of TMN, relation between them will carry out from X reference point.

2.1.3. Work Station Function

This function will prepare interpretation of management information for user.

2.1.4. Q Adaptor Function

It will use for connection of blocks that are not compatible with reference points of TMN.

2.1.5. Mediation Function

This block will operate on the transmitted information from NEF or QAF to OSF and will use to connect one or more NEF or QAF to OSF. The main duty of MF is storing and filtering management information and conversion of local format of information to the standard form (Lakshmi, 1999).

2.2. Information Architecture of TMN

This architecture describes the structure of information interchange between manager and agent which this information will use for management of information resources. In figure 5, common structure of relationship between manager, agent and information resources has been shown (Lakshmi, 1999).

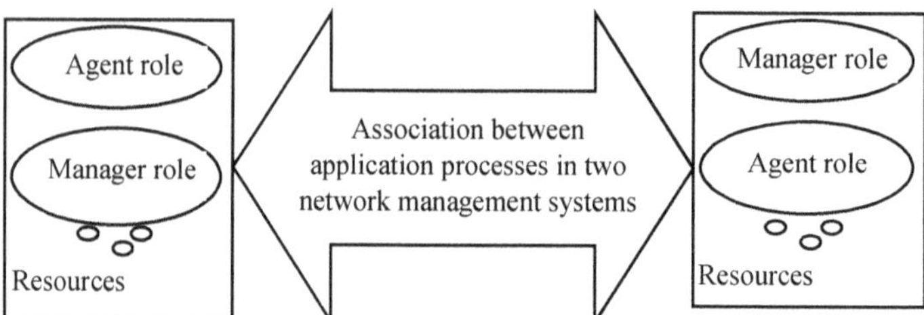

Figure 5: Common schematic of information architecture

2.3. Physical Architecture of TMN

Physical architecture of TMN will declare how we can implement functional block of TMN with physical equipments. Structural blocks usually will implement functional blocks of their names. Table 1 shows how to implement functional blocks in structural block (Lakshmi, 1999).

WSF	OSF	QAF	MF	NEF	
O*	O	O	O	M	**NE**
O	O	O	M		**MD**
		M			**QA**
O	M	O	O		**OS**
M					**WS**
					DCN

O: Optional; M: Mandatory; O*: May exist if OSF and MF exist

Table 1: Relation between functional blocks and structural blocks

3. Q3 Interface

In TMN, there are four different communication types which are shown in table 2.

Application	TMN interface
Between OS and NE, MD and NE Between OS and OS in a TMN environment	Q3
Between OS and OS in different TMN environment	X
Between MD and NE	Qx
Between WS and OS or WS and MD	F

Table 2: TMN interfaces

As shown in Table 2, Q3 interface includes all states which systems will enter in TMN environment. Although Q3 interface will use for interaction between function of different systems but type of interchanged management information in each different states that listed in front of Q3 in the table 2 is different because of logical layering or considered abstraction level. According to requirements of Q3 interface, three application classes are defined as below:

1. Interactive Class: In this class we deal with information that are received unexpectedly and should answer rapidly.

2. File-oriented Class: This class will use for applications that information are as management file.

3. Directory Class: This class will use to map application entity and its address for connection establishment.

3.1. Upper layers of Q3 interface

In this section necessary concepts for protocol requirements of upper layers will introduce, that upon to function supported with these layers, different services have been defined (ITU-T, Q.812, 1997).

3.1.1. Functional Unit

Functional unit is a method for services grouping in the designed sets. Upon to type of services and with using functional units, information interchange may perform.

3.1.1.1. Application Service Element (ASE)

It is a block which carries out specified function of application layer. Some of ASEs might be used in different applications. When several ASEs used at application layer, it is necessary to have coordination between them which in this situation we need a coordination unit that includes functions to organize between ASEs.

ASE includes Association Control Service Element (ACSE), Remote Operation Service Element (ROSE), Common Management Information Service Element (CMISE) and System Management Application Service Element (SMASE).

3.1.1.2. ACSE Functional Unit

ACSE will use at connection-oriented services and it use to establish and release the connection. This functional unit has four services which are A-Associate, A-Release, A-Abort and A-P-Abort. A-Associate service for connection establishment, A-Release service for gracefully disconnection, A-Abort service for suddenly disconnection by user of ACSE and A-P-Abort will use to suddenly disconnection by ACSE. Simply, ACSE services only have a task of connection and disconnection while data transmission will carry out with services of other three entities.

3.1.1.3. ROSE Functional Unit

After establishment of connection, management information should be send to destination with remote operation protocols and destination will send a response to source with these protocols. These requests and receiving related response will carry out in format of four services in ROSE functional unit that are RO-INVOKE, RO-RESULT, RO-ERROR and RO-REJECT.

RO-INVOKE service will use for sending initial request, RO-RESULT service will use to send positive response to request from side of receiver, RO-ERROR service will utilize for sending negative response to the request and RO-REJECT service employ to reject each of the three services mentioned before.

3.1.1.4. CMISE Functional Unit

This functional unit uses for common management information transmission between OS and NE. With use of services and protocols of this unit, all of the common management information will transfer to ROSE unit and will send as a request or response.

3.1.1.5. SMASE Functional Unit

This unit doesn't have obvious protocol and standard for implementation. It includes several system management functions which will use for more clearance and transparency of information and parameters of CMISE. Therefore SMASE with CMISE will deliver complete information to ROSE (ITU-T, Q.812, 1997).

3.2. TCP protocol in Q3 interface

TCP is a connection-oriented protocol which has little limitations for its lower layers to transmit secure data stream. Table 3 shows schematic of network layers at TCP protocol.

User or Upper layers
TCP
IP
Connected Network

Table 3: Schematic of network layers at TCP/IP protocol

From point of view of protocol's architecture, TCP layer will sit over IP, that IP layer will able TCP layer to send and receive information with fragments of different length (ITU-T, Q.811, 1997).

Internet Protocol will utilize to fragment TCP packets in source and adhesive them in destination and also data transmission and delivery between several networks and gateways. IP will transfer information between several networks according to priority and security. For implementation of TCP over IP, parameters such as reliability, data stream control, multiplexing, communication, priority and security should be considered (Thomas, 1996).

3.2.1. TCP/User Interface

After brief understanding of TCP protocol and functional units of application layer at internet mode profile, we will review interface between user and TCP. Because of each system has a different facility, therefore in implementation of TCP different interfaces for connection between TCP and user will be utilized, such that TCP could connect to application layer at Q3 interface and performs instructions of ACSE functional unit and return its answer. However, in all implementation of TCP, a minimum simple set of services should implement that are Open, Send, Receive, Close, Status, and Abort. Task of necessary services is as bellow:

Open service for connection establishment, Send service for sending of information, Receive service to receive information, Close service to graceful disconnection, Status service for monitoring of connection status (includes external socket, local connection name, receiving window, sending window, connection status, number of buffers which are waited to receive ACK, number of unknown buffers for urgent receiving, priority, security, fragmentation and data transmission time) and Abort for abruptly disconnection (Forouzan, 2009).

4. Comparison OSI and TCP/IP model

In table 4, network layers of two OSI and TCP/IP reference models are shown.

TCP/IP	OSI
Application	Application (Layer7)
	Presentation (Layer6)
	Session (Layer5)
Transport	Transport (Layer4)
Internet	Network (Layer3)
Subnet	Data Link (Layer2)
	Physical (Layer1)

Table 4: Comparison between OSI and TCP/IP reference models

At TCP model, session layer doesn't exist and related works to session layer carry out by transport layer. At TCP, presentation layer doesn't exist and related works to presentation layer carry out by application layer. Application layer exists in both reference model but their services are different. Transport layer at TCP/IP model, provide two standard protocol which named TCP and UDP.

At OSI model, network layer is like other OSI layers, that provides both connection-oriented and connectionless services while at TCP/IP model, internet layer is connectionless merely. At OSI model, Connectionless Network Protocol (CLNP) model is similar with IP protocol in performance and only their difference is variable address length at CLNP protocol while IP has a fix address length 32 bit (Pouffary, 1997).

Transport layer at TCP/IP doesn't have any limitation on the lower layers of TCP/IP but host must be able to connect to the network and send data with use of IP packet protocols. Because is not defined a standard protocol for sub network, this protocol will change from one host to other host and from one network to other network.

5. Implementation

Regards to client-server property which exits in TCP/IP protocol and because of using TCP/IP at lower layers of Q3 interface in our implementation, implemented software has a client-server property. On the other hand TCP/IP connection is connection-oriented, therefore if client connect to the server, fraction of server time will waste to receive information from client, even if client send it's information with short time gap. Therefore if server is answering or listening to the client, other requests should be in the queue till connection between first client and server released and another request answered. To prevent occurrence of problems like this, we have used multithreading property in the software (Duffy 2008). Multithreading has a property that will divide the time between different threads and upon to number of clients which have request for connection simultaneously with server, time will assign to them. In fact, Multithreading is combination of codes with special stacks which work as multitask. Thread is a best solution for queue of consecutive packets at management works such that manager will not wait to get a packet from network element and each time server receive a packet, it will process it and will send a suitable management answer. To create relation between application programs and TCP/IP protocol, we use a socket programming which each socket will get arguments and will return one or more results and will use as an end point for connection establishment in TCP/IP.

Implementation software of client-server, test program for send/receive functions, connection/disconnection and all of the function in TCP/IP protocol are written with C++ software on windows (Schildt, 2004). With respect to receiving information from application layer, connection establishment, connection release, clean and unaccepted data sending and different states of TCP are implemented (Petzold, 1998).

5.1. Proposed Algorithm

Regarding to three different approaches for transaction of information between threads named Semaphore, Deadlock and Critical Section, we have used Critical Section approach, it means if there is shared resource between threads and one thread use a shared resource, another thread doesn't have an ability of using shared resource till first thread finish its work with the shared resource. Proposed implemented algorithm for lower layers of Q3 interface is shown in figure 6. For implementation of our algorithm in the TMN, we used a processor core 7i with processor speed 3.2 GHz and bus speed 2400 MHz for server which simulate control center in TMN.

For 20 clients in the simulated TMN, we utilized processor Celeron dual core with processor speed 2.2 GHz and bus speed 800 MHz. Each instruction for ordinary approach in switching ordinary telecommunication networks with different protocols was 86 bit in average while when we use Q3 interface with proposed algorithm each instruction need 64 bit. Our management network was implemented in laboratory with RS232 network and maximum bit rate 11520 bps. Results of our implementation are shown in figure 7. Our proposed method with Q3 interface implementation has overcome to ordinary method in approximately 300 points in average with 26.6% performance improvement that performance was calculated as relative improvement of bit per second for each number of instructions per second.

6. Conclusions and the Future

Regarding to requirement of telecommunication networks to use worldwide protocols such as TCP/IP to manage and control whole telecommunication equipments such as switches with central processor, implementation of lower layers of Q3 interface is essential step. In this paper lower layers implementation was described. These layers were simulated and implemented on laboratory in simulated environment. We reached to 26.6% improvement in average for our proposed algorithm with Q3 interface in comparison to ordinary method in TMN to manage all telecommunication switches. Practical test of Q3 interface in TMN could be at continuation of our works.

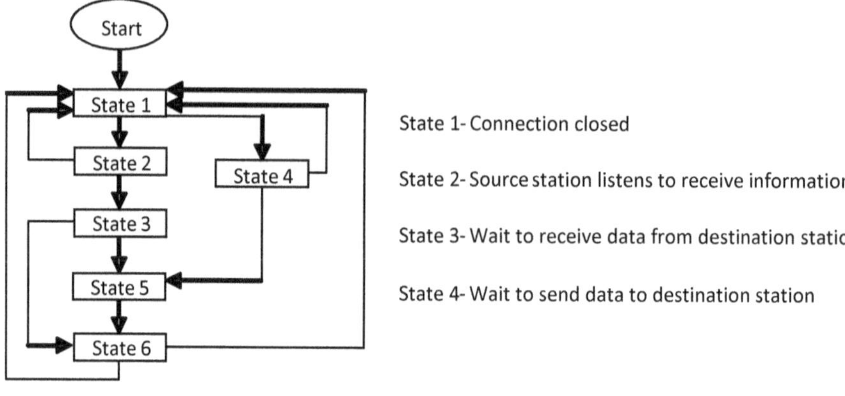

Figure 6: Proposed algorithm for connection between client and server

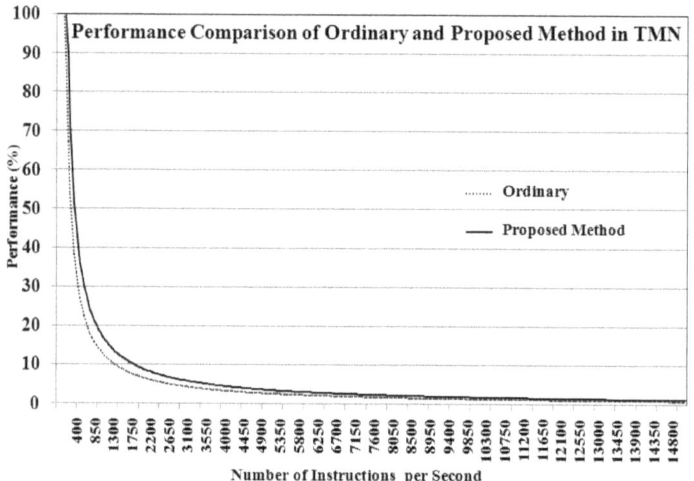

Figure 7: Comparison performance between ordinary and proposed method with Q3 interface in TMN

7. References

Duffy, J. (2008), *Concurrent Programming on Windows*, Addison-Wesley, ISBN: 9780321434821.

Forouzan, B. (2009), *TCP/IP Protocol Suite*, Mcgraw-Hill, 4th edition, ISBN: 9780073376042.

ITU-T, M.3000 (1995), "Maintenance Telecommunications Management Network: Overview of TMN Recommunications".

ITU-T, M3010 (1996), "Principles for a Telecommunications Management Network".

ITU-T, M3020 (2000), "TMN Interface Specification Methodology".

ITU-T, Q.811 (1997), "Lower Layer Protocol Profiles for the Q3 and X Interfaces".

ITU-T, Q.812 (1997), "Upper Layer Protocol Profiles for the Q3 and X Interfaces".

Lakshmi, G. R. (1999), *Fundamental of Telecommunication Network Management*, IEEE press, New York, ISBN: 9780780334663.

Petzold, C. (1998), *Programming Windows*, Microsoft Press, ISBN: 9781572319950.

Pouffary Y. (1997), *ISO Transport Service on top of TCP (ITOT)*, RFC2126, Digital Equipment Corporation.

RFC791 (1981), "Internet Protocol", Information Sciences Institute University of Southern California.

Schildt H. (2004), *The Art of C++*, McGraw-Hill/Osborne, ISBN: 978-0072255126.

Thomas, S. A. (1996), *Ipng and the TCP/IP protocols*, John Wiley & Sons Inc, ISBN: 9780471130888.

Performance Evaluation of On-Demand IP Address Assignment for Layer-2 Devices

R.Gad, D.Baulig, M.Kappes and R.Mueller-Bady

University of Applied Sciences Frankfurt am Main, Frankfurt am Main, Germany
e-mail: {rgad|dbaulig|kappes|mueller-bady}@fb2.fh-frankfurt.de

Abstract

While data link layer devices require no IP address for their operation, they often are run with an IP address assigned for configuration or monitoring purposes rendering the device potentially susceptible to attacks over the network. In this paper, we analyze the performance aspects of a prototypical implementation for assigning an IP address to such a device on demand analogous to port knocking on firewalls, allowing a safer IP-less operation when IP connectivity is not needed while retaining the possibility to connect to the device over IP at any time. Our results indicate that our technique can be employed with virtually no performance penalty.

Keywords

Network Security, Performance, Data Link Layer, Network Layer

1. Introduction

Data link layer devices such as bridges, switches, or bridging firewalls (Eggendorfer & Weber 2007), by definition, operate in a manner that is transparent to higher level protocols like IP, TCP, or UDP. Thus, such devices are fully capable of fulfilling their tasks without the need to run protocols above and beyond the data link layer. Consequently, there is no need to assign an IP address to these devices during regular operation.

However, many modern data link layer devices feature additional functionality that needs to be configured, maintained, and monitored. These tasks are typically performed remotely over the network using application-layer protocols such as SNMP, SSH, or HTTP(S) that are based on UDP or TCP respectively and, in turn, on IP. Thus, such managed data link layer devices are often configured with IP addresses and have services running that listen on publicly accessible ports in order to enable connections for management tasks.

A device with a permanently assigned IP address can be detected much easier by an attacker; furthermore, the device becomes susceptible to multiple attack vectors which can be used in order to, e.g., conduct denial of service attacks or gain access to services or sensible data. This problem is well known and has lead to approaches such as the creation of dedicated management networks disjoint from other "business" networks for such purposes. While this concept may mitigate some security threats, management networks are difficult to set up and maintain as they need to be completely separated from the business networks. The isolation between the networks can easily fail, e.g., due to configuration errors. In practice, to guarantee the separation of networks within a complex network setup, e.g., with large numbers of VLANs or even virtualized environments is an intricate and costly task requiring specialized and highly qualified personnel.

In small to medium sized business (SMB) environments, however, IT-Security is constrained by the human and financial resources at hand (Kappes & Happel 2009). Sophisticated security measures like dedicated management networks often do not exist in these environments at all or are not maintained properly leading to numerous security threats. The approach presented and analyzed here was developed in the context of a project targeted at SMB environments and aims at providing a pragmatic and cost-efficient solution to significantly mitigate risks while keeping deployment and management simple. The goal of our method is to provide an additional layer of security by operating data link layer devices with an IP address only when needed, if other solutions are not viable.

In many cases, data link layer devices such as managed switches do not need to be permanently accessible via services that operate on top of IP. Most use cases such as configuring a device or downloading log data only require access to such devices for very short time spans. Thus, IP addresses and services can be disabled for most of the time without affecting the regular operation of these devices. By disabling IP addresses and services that operate on top of IP a data link layer device remains hidden for the most part and the number of possible attacks against the device, its services, and operating system can be significantly reduced. While it is beneficial if IP addresses and the according services were only active for the duration of these maintenance periods, a method for securely triggering the assignment of an IP address when needed is required.

For services on the transport layer there are established techniques like port knocking (Krzywinski 2003) or more modern variants (deGraaf et al. 2005) (Al-Bahadili & Hadi 2010) that make it possible to enable access to services on demand, but hide or close the service ports during normal operation. The current implementations of these approaches have the limitation that network devices need to be accessible via IP and hence need to have configured IP addresses or provide out-of-band channels (Liew et al. 2010) for port knocking and similar approaches to work.

In order to provide an additional layer of security and to significantly reduce the number of possible attacks in a network we implemented a solution for operating data link layer network devices without configured IP addresses during regular operation and a way for securely activating and configuring IP addresses and services on demand for these devices that only allows authorized persons to activate and configure the higher layer functionalities. The authentication as sketched in our approach is performed via a mechanism that ensures only authorized people are permitted and that is resilient against attacks. This way data link layer devices and administrative services can be effectively hidden from an attacker during normal operation but are still accessible for administrators.

The remainder of this paper is organized as follows: in the next section, we outline our general approach for IP-less operation and a secure and authenticated on-demand IP address and service configuration. Then, we give an overview of the prototypical implementation we used for evaluation. In the main part, we present the procedures and results of performance and load tests that were conducted using our prototypical implementation in order to assess the reliability and robustness of our approach. Finally, we conclude our work and give an outlook on possible further research topics.

2. IP-less Operation and Secure On-demand IP Address Assignment

In the following, we propose a mechanism for the network layer that works somewhat analogously to port knocking on the transport layer. The requirements for our approach can be summarized as follows:

1. The target device does not possess any IP addresses beforehand.
2. An IP address can be assigned to the target device on demand.
3. IP address assignment must be possible from an arbitrary computer within the same subnet.
4. Only authorized entities can trigger IP address assignment.
5. The solution is resilient against different types of attacks such as, e.g., replay or denial of service attacks.
6. Device performance is not significantly impacted by the technique.
7. After IP address assignment, the device behaves like any IP device, i.e., any IP-based service may be used.

In our scenario the device in question is a bridge/switch that forwards packets (please note that in the context of this paper, we do not distinguish between packets and frames) between the connected Ethernet segments (see Figure 1) that are each connected to one of its network interfaces.

Our proposed approach is not cognate to existing device discovery mechanisms as we propose a method for concealing the presence of a device instead of publicly announcing it. Our approach presumes that the legitimate administrator is aware of the presence of the device. The aim of our approach is to hide a device in a network that can only be activated (assigned with an IP address) by its legal operator.

In order to meet the specification above, the device analyzes packets arriving on its interfaces and checks for specific cryptographically protected "Wake-Up" packets as depicted in Figure 1. Via these "Wake-Up" packets the IP address assignment is triggered and information about IP addresses or possibly other management data is securely sent to the device. While specific details are beyond the scope of this paper, we would like to point out that a multitude of possible management and configuration options further improving the security of the device exist including, but not limited to, restricting communications to particular IP addresses, assigning a specific IP address and enabling specific services on the device. For authentication and replay protection our prototype uses pre-shared one-time tokens. Other, standard cryptographic one-way designs can be easily employed as well.

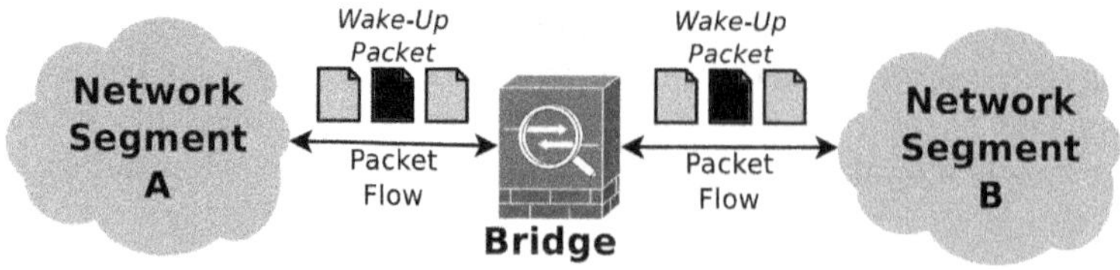

Figure 1: Transparent layer 2 device looking for "Wake-Up" packets

Another problem to tackle is how "Wake-Up" packets are actually sent to the device. Since the device does not possess an IP address it will not respond to any TCP/IP-based protocols including ARP and hence cannot be addressed on the network layer. Moreover, the MAC address of the device cannot be detected unless further protocols on the data link layer such as the IEEE 802.1D Spanning Tree Protocol (IEEE 2004) are active; thus, it cannot be addressed on the data link layer as well. However, as a layer 2 connectivity device, it is an integral part of the network structure and can processes all packets that reach one of its interfaces no matter if these will then be forwarded or not as shown in Figure 1.The task, however, is to ensure that “Wake-Up” packets reach the device independent of its position in the network structure. Our experiments showed that this can be most easily ensured for broadcast packets. The suitability of multicast packets depends on the installed network equipment; in our experiments we encountered situations in which multicast packets were not forwarded by certain layer-2 equipment like some switches. Finally, unicast packets are only suitable for being used as “Wake-Up” packets if it can be guaranteed that our “IP-less” device is located on the path in the network between the source and destination as otherwise these packets won't reach our device at all. More sophisticated approaches could utilize steganography for concealing authentication messages, e.g., in DHCP or other commonly used protocols which rely on broadcasts. However, such approaches are still subject to further research and are not covered in this paper.

3. Prototypical Implementation

We implemented a prototype for our method on an embedded, x86 Linux-based device configured as switch. As network layer protocol we used IPv4. In the following, we present some details of our prototypical implementation. We also outline possible alternatives where indicated. For other types of devices, additional implementation options may exist.

In order to check for "Wake-Up" packets while no IP address is assigned, we employ a sniffer to capture packets. For packet capturing we use jNetPcap (Sly Technologies, Inc. 2012), which builds on top of the libpcap (Tcpdump/Libpcap 2012) library. For analysis, the captured packets are copied into user-space and processed.

Promiscuously analyzing packets in user-space may result in performance issues such as high CPU load, skipped packets, or other negative side-effects, e.g., when the device is exposed to a high network load. Hence, we do not capture the whole network traffic but selectively capture only packets that are likely to be "Wake-Up" packets using kernel level filtering. This way, the number of packets getting passed to user-space is significantly reduced, keeping processing time low and allowing a high detection rate. This is particularly important as otherwise attack vectors for denial-of-service attacks might open up. In the performance evaluation in the next section we will analyze the effects of such flooding attacks in detail.

In our prototypical implementation, "Wake-Up" packets use IP broadcast addresses in conjunction with UDP and a specified port. We use this combination of properties as filter criterion at kernel-level to preselect potential "Wake-Up" packets within the regular network traffic. Clearly, for efficient filtering it is paramount to choose a combination of filtering properties such that only very few of the common network traffic packets match these criteria.

Using broadcasts ensures that the packets are sent to all endpoints on the data link layer level network segment including our device. Using single- or multicast would require us to make assumptions about the network topology and capabilities, which we neither can nor want to make. Since the focus here is on analyzing the performance characteristics of our method, which is not affected by the distribution method, we opted for the straight forward broadcast approach. However, broadcasts can be detected by any other host in the broadcast domain; thus, we are currently developing alternatives for further concealing the presence of our hidden device.

Figure 2: "Wake-Up" Packet Format

In our implementation, the device cannot respond to any wake-up calls until it has acquired an IP address. This necessitates the use of a replay-safe, one-way authorization method such as Single Packet Authorization (SPA) (Rash 2006). SPA allows cryptographically secured authentication by a single, one-way communication channel. In our prototype we use random one-time tokens for authentication as depicted in Figure 2. These randomly created one-time tokens are essentially shared secrets that are stored on both the administration computer and the hidden device. After each successful "Wake-Up" operation once an IP address had been assigned new, randomly generated one-time tokens are exchanged between the formerly hidden device and the administration system via an encrypted connection. Other cryptographic methods like S/KEY are also possible (Haller 1995) (Worth 2004) and the respective data would be placed at the beginning of the "Wake-Up" payload at the same position as the one-time token. Generally, every form of secured authentication is possible that enables authentication via a single, one-way message from the administration system to the hidden device. In our scenario the hidden device will be shipped with pre-generated one-time tokens that get replaced on the first successful “Wake-Up” using a sort of “bootstrap”. From there on only the legit administrator will be able to trigger the on demand IP address assignment as he will be the only one in possession of the required one-time keys.

4. Performance Evaluation

We measured the performance characteristics of our prototype with respect to the following dimensions critical for the practical usability of the mechanism: performance during regular operation, reliability of capturing and identifying "Wake-Up" packets, and performance during flooding-attacks such as brute force or denial of service (DoS) attacks.

First, the network performance of the device itself during regular operation with our proposed technique enabled should be similar to its performance without the secure IP on-demand assignment mechanism. This means in terms of measurable characteristics that, e.g., the throughput should not decrease and round-trip times should remain similar. Factors that could negatively affect these performance characteristics may be, amongst others, the system load caused by running the authentication software, the packet capturing itself, or the kernel-level traffic filtering. We assessed this aspect by performing benchmarks on our test hardware with and without running our prototypical software implementation and comparing the results. We repeatedly performed throughput measurements via UDP and TCP using different IP packet sizes. Ten measurements had been made for each packet size and protocol. Furthermore, we also measured the round trip time via UDP. The test setup was made up of two computers that were directly connected to one of the bridge ports each. The benchmarks were run from these computers in both directions across the bridge.

Our results show that the device performed equally in both cases; the network performance was not affected significantly by running our prototypical implementation (compare Table 1 and Figure 3). In Figure 3 the average UDP throughput for different IP packet sizes during regular operation and while running our prototypical implementation is shown. Some of the depicted values show a slightly higher throughput while running our prototype. These differences are due to common variation in throughput caused by the used embedded x86 Linux platform. For an IP packet size of 1500 byte the average throughput reached about 96.5% of the theoretically achievable throughput in both cases.

	Regular	**With Method**
Mean [ms]	0.3679	0.3705
Standard Deviation	0.02538	0.02581

Table 1: Results of UDP RTT Measurements

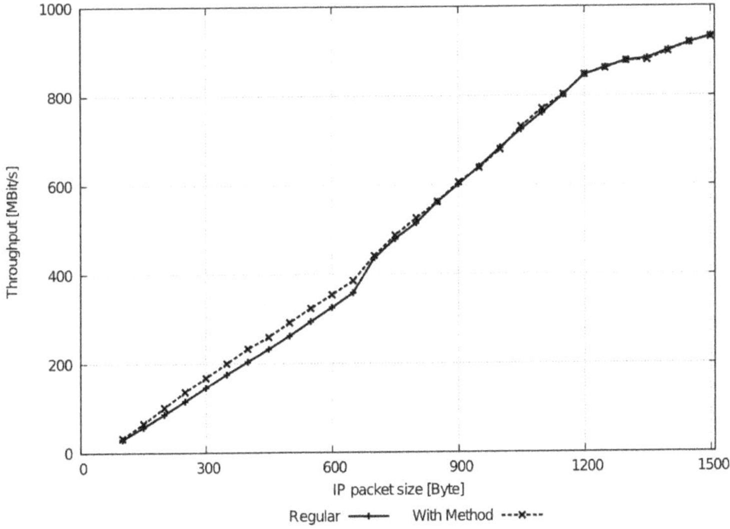

Figure 3: UDP Throughput Comparison

Second, we study the reliability of capturing and identifying "Wake-Up" packets. If individual packets are dropped or not analyzed, e.g., due to high load, the device might miss "Wake-Up" packets rendering the IP address assignment mechanism ineffective. In the worst case this could result in situations in which the device cannot be accessed at all. The reliability with which "Wake-Up" packets are captured and processed, depends on two different circumstances: first, the packets must actually reach the bridge and may not be discarded beforehand, for example due to high load in the attached network segments. Second, the packets must be successfully captured and processed independently from the device's network load; i.e., even when the maximum throughput is transferred across the device the packets must be received and processed correctly for the authentication mechanism to work reliably.

The first effect solely depends on the details of the network segments attached to our bridge and is independent from our IP-less operation and IP address assignment mechanism as discussed in this paper. Hence, we only assured that this aspect did not affect our results when examining the reliability of the receive and processing mechanism under full link load.

We tested the reliability with which "Wake-Up" packets are received by flooding the bridge with UDP traffic at full link speed. Within this traffic we sporadicly transmitted single "Wake-Up" packets. We performed this test repeatedly with and without flooding the bridge with UDP traffic. In both cases the detection rate of "Wake-Up" packets was 100%.

Finally, the impact of flooding the device with valid or invalid "Wake-Up" packets needs to be evaluated. Such a situation could occur either in the case of brute force attacks when an attacker repeatedly sends "Wake-Up" packets in order to guess the correct combination or when an attacker attempts to perform a denial-of-service attack against the device in order to impair the network functionality or the ability for others like the legit network administrators to authenticate with the device.

Technically there is no difference if an attacker is performing a denial of service attack or tries to break the authentication mechanism using brute force. In both cases an attacker will flood the device with "Wake-Up" packets which may affect the device negatively, e.g., by exhausting its resources. Such resources are: network bandwidth, CPU usage, or memory usage. In this context UDP is problematic as it can be used generally for denial-of-service attacks on networks by simply flooding datagrams. This is a known issue and solutions as well as their limitations are well researched (Cabrera, et al. 2001) (Mirkovic & Reiher 2004). Since this is a general issue that is not specifically connected to our proposed IP-less operation we do not assess this here but rather analyse the effects of flooding the prototype with invalid "Wake-Up" packets on the CPU and memory performance.We assessed the impact of flooding authentication tokens by comparing the effects of putting our test device under heavy UDP load and by flooding it with an authentication message as could be done in an attempted denial of service attack. The test setup was identical to the one used for the throughput and round trip time performance benchmarks above. Flooding UDP traffic and sending authentication messages was done from the same computer. During flooding with UDP traffic we could not observe any significant CPU and memory utilization. While flooding with "Wake-Up" packets, however, we noticed a change in the CPU usage: as shown in Figure 4 nearly 30% of the CPU time was used for executing kernel level code and another roughly 30% of the CPU time was used for executing user level code. However, we see very high potential for increasing the performance of our prototype. Primarily the explicitness of kernel-level filters could be improved. There are also more approaches to improve packet-filtering and packet-processing in general (Fusco et al. 2010)(Leogrande et al. 2011), which could be applied to further increase the performance.

Furthermore, the prototypical software implementation was primarily designed as a proof of concept and the critical code paths have not yet been optimized. Finally, there might be a chance to increase the performance even further by implementing the critical code paths in lower level languages like C or assembly.

5. Conclusion

In this paper, we evaluated the performance and practicability of a mechanism for IP-less operation and on demand IP address assignment for managed data link layer devices. Analogous to port knocking on firewalls, the IP-less operation and on demand IP address assignment allows a safer operation when IP connectivity is not needed while retaining the possibility to connect to the device over IP at any time.

We implemented a prototype on an embedded x86-based Linux system and assessed its performance during regular operation, the reliability of capturing and processing packets for triggering IP address assignment, and the impact of flooding attacks like brute force or denial of service attacks.

Our results show that the network performance in regular operation is not significantly affected. Moreover, the reliability of capturing and analyzing "Wake-

Up" packets was 100% even under high network load and flooding with other traffic. There was a noticeable increase in CPU-load during a DoS scenario, but bandwidth limitations will be reached long before serious CPU or memory issues arise. During regular operation, even when facing high traffic, there was no overly memory or CPU usage. Further optimizations of our implementation are possible and will be conducted in the future. In summary, our results show that our method for IP-less operation and on demand IP address assignment can be practically used.

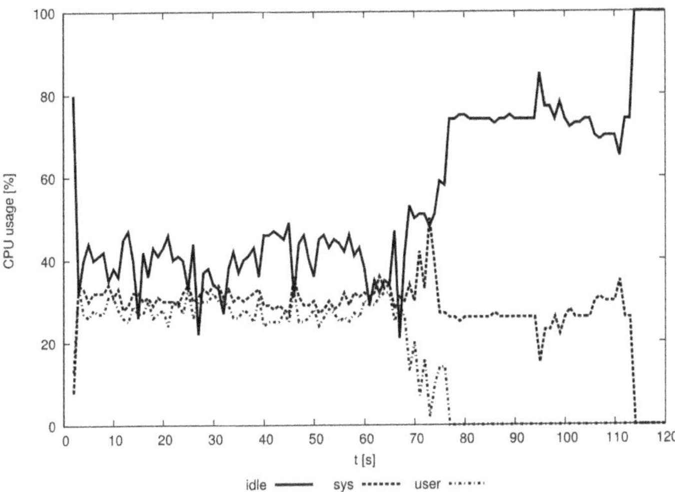

Figure 4: CPU Utilization while Flooding "Wake-Up" Packets

In the future, we are planning to research improved authentication mechanisms and protocols as well as means for further increasing the performance. Options for more sophisticated protocols include steganography techniques for hiding authentication data in other protocols like DHCP making it harder for an attacker to detect the presence of a concealed device, even during authentication. Furthermore, we will research options for applying our method to virtualized environments. While the network characteristics of virtualized environments may differ from physical networks (Gad et al. 2011a) (Gad et al. 2011b) we expect, based on the experience from our prior work on virtualization, that our results gained in this paper can be applied to virtualized network equipment as well. Moreover, we will also look into the possibility of having a separate, randomly chosen "hidden network" making it harder to find the concealed device even after it acquired an IP address. Finally, this technology could also be deployed by an attacker to secretly tap into a victims network. Hence, we are also going to research methods for detecting the presence of such concealed devices.

6. References

Al-Bahadili, H. & Hadi, A. H. (2010). Network security using hybird port knocking, International Journal of Computer Science and Network Security 10(8).

Cabrera, J. B. D., Lewis, L., Qin, X., Lee, W., Prasanth, R. K., Ravichandran,B. & Mehra, R. K. (2001). Proactive detection of distributed denial of service attacks using mib traffic variables-a feasibility study, Proceedings of the International Symposium on Integrated Network Management, pp. 609–622.

deGraaf, R., Aycock, J. & M. Jacobson, J. (2005). Improved port knocking with strong authentication, Proceedings of the 21st Annual Computer Security Applications Conference.

Eggendorfer, T. & Weber, D. (2007). Running a port forwarding firewall system on a bridge, Proceedings of the Fourth IASTED International Conference on Communication, Network and Information Security, pp. 122–126.

Fusco, F., Deri, L. & Gasparakis, J. (2010). Towards monitoring programmability in future internet: challenges and solutions, Proceedings of the 21st Tyrrhenian Workshop on Digital Communications: Trustworthy Internet (ITWDC).

Gad, R., Kappes, M., Mueller-Bady, R. & Ritter, I. (2011a). Is your virtualized network really what you think it is?, Fourth International Conference on Internet Technologies & Applications, Wrexham, UK, pp. 128–135.

Gad, R., Kappes, M., Mueller-Bady, R. & Ritter, I. (2011b). Network performance in virtualized environments, 17th IEEE International Conference on Networks, Singapore, pp. 275–280.

Haller, N. (1995). The s/key one-time password system, IETF RFC 1760.

IEEE (2004). Standard for Local and Metropolitan Area Networks – Media access control (MAC) Bridges – IEEE Standard 802.1D

Kappes, M. & Happel, F. (2009). Tackling network security in small to medium businesses, Proceedings of the 3rd International Conference on Internet Technologies and Applications, Wrexham, UK.

Krzywinski, M. (2003). Port knocking from the inside out, SysAdmin Magazine.

Leogrande, M., Ciminiera, L. & Risso, F. (2011). Modeling filtering predicates composition with finite state automata, Proceedings of the 19th International Conference on Software, Telecommunications and Computer Networks.

Liew, J., Lee, S., Ong, I., Lee, H. & Lim, H. (2010). One-time knocking framework using spa and ipsec, International Conference on Education Technology and Computer.

Mirkovic, J. & Reiher, P. (2004). A taxonomy of ddos attack and ddos defense mechnisms, ACM SIGCOMM Computer Communication Review 34(2): 39–53.

Rash, M. (2006). Single packet authorization with fwknop, ;login: USENIX Magazine 31(1).

Sly Technologies, Inc. (2012). jNetPcap, last accessed 02/10/2012. URL: http://jnetpcap.com

Tcpdump/Libpcap (2012). libpcap, last accessed 02/10/2012. URL: http://www.tcpdump.org

Worth, D. (2004). Ck: Cryptographic one-time knocking, Talk slides, Black Hat USA.

Establishing Discernible Flow Characteristics for Accurate, Real-Time Network Protocol Identification

R.G.Goss and R.A.Botha

Institute for ICT Advancement and School of ICT
Nelson Mandela Metropolitan University, Port Elizabeth, South Africa
e-mail: ryan@goss.co.za; reinhardta.botha@nmmu.ac.za

Abstract

As the number of business applications, games and other real-time applications adopting peer-to-peer communication approaches increase, so too does the requirement for accurate identification of these protocols on the network. This movement is attributed mostly to increased scalability in application deployment, reducing the overall cost of network resources. Without the identification of critical applications, networks run the risk of becoming overwhelmed by lower-priority, less important protocols, reducing resources available to higher priority applications. Deep packet inspection and statistical characteristic profiling have been used to identify various application flows, however there is an apparent disconnect between the two. Whilst both produce fairly accurate results, this paper aims to increase the accuracy of these systems by marrying the two into a single classifier using artificial neural networks.

Whilst many traffic profiling systems examine the full network flow post-termination, this paper proposes a methodology for utilizing the unique characteristics of network traffic flows which distinguish various applications at the beginning of the flow, in real-time, allowing early identification and thus effective control of a flow within the first few packet exchanges.

Keywords

Network Traffic Flows, Deep Packet Inspection, Traffic Classification, Statistical Profiling, Flow Discrimination, Artificial Neural Network, Sigmoidal Logistic Regression

1. Introduction

The growth of network communications has always been hampered by the finite resources available, restricted by a number of elements, the most prominent being bandwidth availability. These limitations are often imposed by the availability of physical wiring and/or the cost of provisioning the services through a 3rd party, such as the national telecommunications company. The available bandwidth, therefore, needs to be managed, providing optimal use of available resources to satisfy customer/user demand. Application protocols which comprise network traffic need to be identified in order to be effectively managed and prioritised. The identification and categorization of network traffic flows aids network administrators in quickly diagnosing problems, network capacity planning tasks and identifying misuse of the provisioned resources (Wright et al., 2006).

In times past, network administrators extracted Open System Interconnection (OSI) layer 4 port and protocol information from packet headers to identify and classify traffic. This method is not suitable in today's next generation networks as the ports and protocols used for a particular flow are chosen by the two communicating hosts. Hosts can therefore negotiate alternative layer 4 information, bypassing various filters and restrictions (Alshammari & Zincir-Heywood, 2008). The inefficiency of port-based classification methodologies in successfully matching these evasive protocols forced researchers to consider a number of alternatives.

Deep Packet Inspection (DPI) serves as one such alternative, aiming to solve these problems by tracking each flow's OSI layer 7 protocol information, applying predefined signatures and searching the packet's payload for string matches. This method of traffic identification can be extremely accurate, as long as the underlying payload is not encrypted or otherwise opaque (Alshammari & Zincir-Heywood, 2008). DPI is often applied to the first few packets of a connection, since the layer 7 protocol information is exchanged at the very beginning of the connection.

Whilst DPI has proven its worth as a flow classification methodology, it falls short when inspecting opaque application protocols such as encrypted traffic flows. It has been argued that much information can be inferred about a traffic flow by observing various statistical characteristics of each flow.

This paper is proposes a set of discriminators which, when used in conjunction with one another, provide enough granularity to accurately identify an application protocol in real-time, within the first few packet exchanges of newly established flows. The premise of this paper is that by the marriage of statistical and DPI discriminators, a suitable granularity of flow information can be inferred within the first 4 payload-carrying packets of host-to-host data exchange. This process is demonstrated through experimentation, discriminating a group of applications from one another.

2. Related Work

A significant amount of research has been conducted in the identification of the underlying application protocol at the early stage of a network flow's existence, through statistical analysis and DPI. For example, Bernaille et al. (2006) describes a statistical method of grouping Transport Control Protocol (TCP) flows which exhibit similar behaviour, using K-Means, Gaussian mixture model, and spectral on Hidden Markov Model techniques. According to Bernaille et al. (2006), packet size information obtained during the first few packet exchanges of a flow serve as a good metric for identifying the underlying application protocol. Gargiulo et al. (2009) asserts that significant accuracy can be achieved in identifying a flow's application protocol by examining the direction of the first four packets along with the payload sizes of each. Moore & Papagiannaki (2005) argue that in some cases, the accuracy achieved by observing the first payload-bearing packet is enough to identify the protocol, whilst in others up to 1Kbyte of payload is required before a decision is made. Various statistics including minimum, average and maximum packet lengths derived from a flow are described by Alshammari et al. (2007) as suitable discriminators for identifying a flow's underlying application protocol.

The ideas set forth by this paper are built on the observations of these works, verified through experimentation.

3. Methodology

The authors conducted a number of experiments in order to determine a base set of discriminators, which would be granular enough to distinguish application protocols from one another. Each experiment built on the discriminator set used by its predecessor, creating a more complex, granular classifier. The results of these experiments are presented at the end of this paper, providing a strong set of discriminators for use in the early identification process.

The objective of the experiments was to define a set of discriminators which, when applied to early packet data, would provide enough granularity to uniquely identify each application protocol, rather than simply group them by their operational characteristics as described by Zuev & Moore (2005).

4. Experimentation

A literature study was undertaken to determine popular discriminators for consideration in the final flow identification engine. The selected discriminators served as input vectors for use in training and testing a number of neural networks, each for a unique protocol.

Discriminators that rely on capturing the complete flow were stripped from the list of potentials as this hinders early, real-time detection. The list of literature reviewed and a summarized output of the common discriminators proposed are outlined in Table 1.

	Protocol	DST Port	SRC Port	Payload Stats	PKT Order Dir	PKT IAT	DPI
Li, Z. et al. (2007)	x	x	x	x			
Auld, T. (2007)				x			
Bernaille, L. et al. (2006)				x	x	x	
Este, A. et al. (2008)				x	x		
Gargiulo, F. et al (2009)		x		x	x		
Moore, A. W. et al (2005)		x	x	x	x	x	
Moore, A. et al (2005)						x	x
McGregor, A. et al (2004)				x		x	
Huang, K. et al (2008)							x
Alshammari, R. et al. (2007)				x		x	

Table 1: Popular Discriminators in Flow Detection

According to Table 1, certain flow attributes were more popular than others. These discriminators, including the Destination Port, Source Port, Payload Statistics, Packet

Order Direction, Packet Inter-Arrival Time and Deep Packet Inspection were considered for the experiments of this paper. Of these discriminators, those which bore reference to packet header information (DST and SRC ports) were removed, preventing the effect of client or server port manipulation. Packet Inter-Arrival Time (PKT IAT) was also removed from consideration, due to its dependence on the latency of the communications medium, traffic shaping mechanisms and congestion at any given time.

Experimental data was collected using a 60 minute snapshot of network traffic flows recorded on a Local Area Network (LAN) segment at a large corporate establishment.

At the end of the recording process, each flow was manually identified and marked by the authors for verification purposes. In accordance with Bernaille, L. et al (2006) and Gargiulo, F. (2009), only Transport Control Protocol (TCP) flows were recorded as part of the snapshot flow set. Furthermore, flows where the initial synchronize (SYN) packet was not observed were excluded as the discriminators rely on the first few packet exchanges of each flow. Table 2 provides a break down of the remaining, manually identified flows.

Protocol	Recorded Flows
HTTP	4452
HTTPS	3147
SSH	392
FTP	102
POP3	62
SMTP	17

Table 2: Observed Network Traffic Flows

Based on the direction of the initial SYN packet, both the client and the server host can be identified and thus the direction of packet flow. Packets with no payload were assumed to be normal TCP control packets, which provide the reliable transport platform for the encapsulated application protocol operations.

Artificial Neural Networks (ANN) were used as classifiers in the experiments, therefore the inputs needed to meet basic ANN requirements, falling within the bounds of 0.0 and 1.0. The authors accomplished this by the application of a sigmoidal logistic regression function, producing a probability value between 0 and 1.

The application flows captured were used to train a variety of Feed-forward, Back Propagation Artificial Neural Networks. A neural network was created and trained for each of the six application protocols identified in table 2. A subset of flow discriminators were chosen for each of the experiments, incorporating the discriminators used by their predecessor. For each experiment, the training set values were passed through each neural network and the accuracy of the results noted.

For consistency, each neural network consisted of a number of inputs which matched the number of discriminators for that experiment's particular feature subset. Directly connected to each of the input neurons was a second, hidden layer whose neuron count matched that of the input layer. Finally, a single neuron, connected to each of the neurons in the hidden layer, represented the output layer. The output neuron was responsible for producing a decimal value between 0 and 1, indicating the certainty that the inputs provided matched the protocol the neural network was trained to identify.

The extracted discriminators from the flow snapshot were fed to each neural network in turn over a period of 1000 iterations. The flows which the network should match were marked with a "1" as an expected output, whilst those the network should not match a "0". For example, the neural network created to match the Hypertext Transfer Protocol (HTTP) would have all HTTP flow inputs marked with a 1, whilst the remaining 5 input sets marked with a 0.

After a successful training session, the inputs and their respective outputs were once more passed through each neural network in order to determine accuracy. The actual output for each discriminator input set was compared to the expected output and the variance noted. A separate score was tallied for matching both the expected 0 (correctly identifying a protocol other than the one the network was trained to identify) and expected 1 (correctly identifying a protocol the network was trained to identify). A high degree of accuracy is required in order to demonstrate a clear discrimination between the various protocols across each of the 6 trained neural networks.

5. Experiment 1: Directional Discrimination

The first discriminator set tested included the directions for each of the first 4 payload-bearing packet exchanges. Client to server packets were marked with a 0, whilst server to client packets with a 1. The observed patterns for each protocol and the number of times each were detected are shown in Table 3.

	FTP	HTTP	HTTPS	SSH	POP3	SMTP
0100	4					
0101	98				62	17
0110				392		
1000		2105	1428			
1001		254	287			
1010		1856	1166			
1011		21	242			
1100		216	12			

Table 3: Payload-carrying Packet Directionality

Table 4 denotes the results observed, post training process, when passing each network's training set through it and comparing the actual result to the expected result. The probability for each expected case was determined and the average percentile achieved noted. A well trained classifier is expected to reach an average probability score in excess of 90%, indicating its level of understanding of the data within the training set.

	FTP	HTTP	HTTPS	SSH	POP3	SMTP
EXPECT 0	99.42%	99.34%	99.14%	99.97%	99.59%	99.86%
EXPECT 1	50.13%	0.93%	1.37%	98.73%	35.97%	7.29%

Table 4: Results of Experiment 1

Table 5 details the results observed when a single flow of each application protocol was passed through each of the neural networks, gauging their effectiveness in recognizing them.

Protocol	Ordered Classifier Probability Results
FTP	FTP (48.28%) POP3 (35.97%) SMTP (7.29%) SSH (1.23%) HTTPS (0.43%) HTTP (0.01%)
HTTP	HTTP (1.33%) HTTPS (0.70%) SMTP (0.01) POP3 (0.00%) FTP (0.00%) SSH (0.00%)
HTTPS	HTTP (1.33%) HTTPS (0.70%) SMTP (0.01%) POP3 (0.00%) FTP (0.00%) SSH (0.00%)
SSH	SSH (99.74%) HTTPS (0.20%) SMTP (0.12%) FTP (0.11%) POP3 (0.08%) HTTP (0.01%)
POP3	FTP (48.28%) POP3 (35.97%) SMTP (7.29%) SSH (1.23%) HTTPS (0.43%) HTTP (0.01%)
SMTP	FTP (48.28%) POP3 (35.97%) SMTP (7.29%) SSH (1.23%) HTTPS (0.43%) HTTP (0.01%)

Table 5: Experiment 1 - Classifier Accuracy in Identification

6. Discussion

Experiment 1 illustrates that using even a limited number of discriminators; a fair degree of certainty can be inferred upon the flow's underlying application protocol. FTP, SSH, POP3 and SMTP protocols exhibited similar characteristics in that the first packet originated from the server to the client, whilst the HTTP and HTTPS flows first payload-carrying packet was from the client to the server. Table 3 shows the similarities between HTTP and HTTPS in the direction of packet flows – something expected as HTTPS is essentially an encrypted HTTP stream. These similarities in directionality explain why the training process resulted in the HTTPS and HTTP neural networks providing low degrees of accuracy. POP3, SMTP and FTP also exhibit directionality similarities and thus suffer from inaccurate distinction at this level. Table 5 shows that the FTP classifier incorrectly scored higher than the SMTP and POP3 protocols for their own protocol test. Furthermore, in the case of SMTP, both the FTP and POP3 classifiers exhibited a higher probability than the SMTP protocol itself. SSH is the only protocol that does not share directionality discriminators, hence the high degree of accuracy in matching both SSH and "other" protocols (99.97% and 98.73% respectively) with so few discriminators. The grouping of multiple protocols into distinct classes using directional discriminators was also noted by Bernaille, L. et al (2006), Este et al. (2008) and Gargiulo, F. et al (2009).

7. Experiment 2: Direction and Packet size Statistics

The second experiment built on the first by adding the average, minimum and maximum payload sizes for the first 4 payload-carrying packets to the discriminator set. The inputs thus grew from 4 in the first experiment, to 7 in the second.

After the training process had completed, the following results were observed.

	FTP	HTTP	HTTPS	SSH	POP3	SMTP
EXPECT 0	99.52%	99.85%	99.87%	99.98%	99.89%	99.86%
EXPECT 1	60.61%	33.50%	18.21%	98.99%	10.02%	7.86%

Table 6: Results of Experiment 2

Table 7 details the results observed when a single flow of each application protocol was passed through each of the neural networks, gauging their effectiveness in recognizing them.

Protocol	Ordered Classifier Probability Results
FTP	FTP (46.12%) POP3 (10.71%) SMTP (7.64%) HTTP (0.55%) SSH (0.38%) HTTPS (0.10%)
HTTP	HTTP (42.47%) HTTPS (0.03%) SMTP (0.00%) POP3 (0.00%) FTP (0.00%) SSH (0.00%)
HTTPS	HTTPS (39.43%) SSH (0.00%) HTTP (0.00%) SMTP (0.00%) POP3 (0.00%) FTP (0.00%)
SSH	SSH (99.91%) SMTP (0.09%) HTTPS (0.06%) POP3 (0.01%) FTP (0.00%) HTTP (0.00%)
POP3	FTP (46.24%) POP3 (9.94%) SMTP (7.72%) SSH (0.43%) HTTP (0.30%) HTTPS (0.12%)
SMTP	FTP (46.09%) POP3 (8.85%) SMTP (7.86%) SSH (0.48%) HTTP (0.26%) HTTPS (0.12%)

Table 7: Experiment 2 - Classifier Accuracy in Identification

8. Discussion

Experiment 2 increased the granularity of the flow information by including additional discriminators. Flows which exhibit small payload exchanges, including real-time applications such as SSH, will over the course of the flow exhibit a much lower average payload size than that of a bulk transfer application such as HTTP. Experiment 2 tested if this was plausible within the first 4 packet exchanges. The results of experiment 2 clearly indicate an increase in accuracy for all but one protocol, POP3. Although HTTP and HTTPS bare resemblance in packet directionality patterns, packet size variances between the two protocols as early as the first 4 packets appeared evident. This increase in identification ability is indicative of strengthening pattern identification within the protocol as the packet size statistic discriminators are added to the discriminator set. Table 7 indicates that using packet size statistics, HTTP is now more discernable from HTTPS and thus the probability score for HTTPS correctly placed the HTTPS classifier as the identifier for the HTTPS protocol. No change was noted for the probability positioning for the SMTP and POP3 classifiers.

9. Experiment 3: Direction, Packet Size and Payload

The final experiment conducted was an attempt to combine the statistical classification process with that of DPI. DPI is most commonly implemented using regular expressions, attempting to match patterns within strings. The motivation for this 3rd experiment was the assumption that application protocols require a certain amount of initialization before any data exchange could take place and that this initialization will take place within the first few payload-carrying packets of a flow. For this reason, the first 3 bytes of payload from the first 2 payload-carrying packets were extracted and converted to their ASCII integer values. These 6 new values were then included in the discriminator set from experiment 2, bringing the total neural network inputs to 13.A set of 6 new neural networks were created and the new training sets applied.

The subsequent results were reported as follows:

	FTP	HTTP	HTTPS	SSH	POP3	SMTP
EXPECT 0	99.99%	99.94%	99.94%	99.99%	100.00%	99.99%
EXPECT 1	98.17%	99.88%	99.80%	99.88%	98.86%	96.79%

Table 8: Results of Experiment 3

The results observed when passing a single instance of each of the 6 application flows to each neural network are recorded in table 9.

Protocol	Ordered Classifier Probability Results
FTP	FTP (98.07%) SMTP (0.087%) SSH (0.50%) POP3 (0.10%) HTTP (0.00%) HTTPS (0.00%)
HTTP	HTTP (99.93%) HTTPS (0.06%) SMTP (0.00%) POP3 (0.00%) FTP (0.00%) SSH (0.00%)
HTTPS	HTTPS (99.95%) HTTP (0.14%) SSH (0.00%) SMTP (0.00%) POP3 (0.00%) FTP (0.00%)
SSH	SSH (99.92%) FTP (0.02%) HTTP (0.00%) SMTP (0.00%) HTTPS (0.00%) POP3 (0.00%)
POP3	POP3 (99.06%) SSH (0.84%) SMTP (0.41%) HTTP (0.07%) HTTPS (0.00%) FTP (0.00%)
SMTP	SMTP (96.92%) FTP (2.36%) POP3 (1.00%) SSH (0.53%) HTTP (0.00%) HTTPS (0.00%)

Table 9: Experiment 3 – Classifier Accuracy in Identification

10. Discussion

Experiment 3 provided the most promising results as DPI discriminators were added to the directional and payload size discriminator set. The results recorded indicate the best understanding by each network across the board for all protocols. The increased granularity and uniqueness in application protocol initialization exchanges in the first few bytes of communication between hosts is to thank for this. Although HTTP and HTTPS share similarities in directional and payload size discriminators, the underlying payload of HTTP is plain-text, whilst HTTPS is encrypted. HTTPS will therefore use SSL control bytes during the first few packets of the data exchange, whilst HTTP will begin with HTTP request arguments. Further, whilst POP3 and SMTP exhibited similarities in their directional and payload size statistics, the underlying payload was very different. SMTP servers respond to newly established sockets by sending a "220", followed by a server message. POP3 servers will respond to new clients with "+OK" followed by a short string. This difference in early application protocol exchange clearly distinguishes the one protocol from the other. Table 9 indicates exact matching for each of the selective flow tests, with the closest second matching classifier reporting a variance of 94.56% to the nearest rival in the case of SMTP. The authors believe this may be accredited to the lack of flows captured for the SMTP protocol when compared with the others.

11. Conclusion

The observed results conclude that the marriage of statistical and DPI discriminators form the best possible chance for accurately discerning one protocol from another at the early stages of a network traffic flow. Furthermore, increasing the number of discriminators to the neural networkincreased the granularity of the application protocol, creating a better possibility for pattern identification between protocols and thus higher degrees of accuracy in identification.

Increasing the granularity of flow information over the course of 3 experiments produced an increasing accuracy in identifying each protocol. Furthermore, similar protocols exhibited a decline in their probability scores, indicating increased understanding of the protocol each were trained to identify.

This paper therefore proves that it is possible to identify and classify application protocol flows in real-time, at the beginning of the flow, using discernible flow characteristics such as packet directionality, packet size statistics and DPI. This paper further concludes that it is possible to apply this technique to encrypted and plain-text flows alike and that due to the removal of dependence on packet header information, it is possible to detect these protocols on any port or protocol.

12. References

C.V. Wright, F. Monrose& G. M. Masson (2006), "On Inferring Application Protocol Behaviors in Encrypted Network Traffic", *Journal of Machine Learning Research 7,* 2006, pp. 2745-2769

Alshammari, R. & Zincir-Heywood, A. (2008), "Investigating Two Different Approaches for Encrypted Traffic Classification", *Sixth Annual Conference on Privacy, Security and Trust, The IEEE Computer Society*, 2008, pp. 156 - 166

Williams, N., Zander, S. &Armitage, G., (2006), "A Preliminary Performance Comparison of Five Machine Learning Algorithms for Practical IP Traffic Flow Classification", *ACM SIGCOMM Computer Communication Review 7*, Volume 36, Number 5, October 2006

Li, Z., Yuan, R. & Guan, X. (2007), "Traffic Classification – Towards Accurate Real Time Network Applications", *In HCI (4)*, pp. 67-76, 2007

Auld, T., Moore, A.W. & Gull, S.F. (2007), "Bayesian Neural Networks for Internet Traffic Classification", *IEEE Trans. On Neural Networks*, 18 (1) pp. 223-239, January 2007.

Bernaille, L., Teixeira, R. &Salamatian, K. (2006), "Early Application Identification", *Proceedings of the 2006 ACM CoNEXT conference*, 2006

Este, A., Gargiulo, F., Gringoli, F., Salgarelli, L. &Sansone, C. (2008), "Pattern Recognition Approaches for Classifying IP Flows", *Structural, Syntactic and Statistical Pattern Recognition – Lecture Notes in Computer Science*, Volume 5342, pp. 885 – 895, 2008

Gargiulo, F., Kuncheva, L.I., &Sansone, C. "Network Protocol Verification by a Classifier Selection Ensemble".*In Proceedings of MCS.*Pp314-323, 2009.

Moore, A. W. & Zuev, D., "Discriminators for use in flow-based classification", *Technical report, Intel Research*, Cambridge, 2005.

Moore, A. & Papagiannaki, K. (2005), "Toward the Accurate Identification of Network Applications", *Lecture Notes in Computer Science,* pp 41-54, vol 3431, 2005.

McGregor, A., Hall, M., Brunskill J., &Lorier P., "Flow Clustering Using Machine Learning Techniques", *Passive and Active Measurement Conference (PAM)*, Apr 2004.

Huang, K. & Zhang, D., "A Byte-Filtered String Matching Algorithm for Fast Deep Packet Inspection," *Young Computer Scientists, 2008. ICYCS 2008. The 9th International Conference for* , pp.2073-2078, 18-21 Nov. 2008

Alshammari, R. &Zincir-Heywood, A.N., "A flow based approach for SSH traffic detection," *Systems, Man and Cybernetics, 2007.ISIC. IEEE International Conference on* , pp.296-301, 7-10 Oct. 2007

Goss, R & Botha, R, "Traffic Flow Management in Next Generation Service Provider Networks - Are We There Yet?",*Information Security South Africa Conference,2011.*

Wright, C. V., Monrose, F. & Masson, G. M., "On Inferring Application Protocol Behaviors in Encrypted Network Traffic", *Journal of Machine Learning Research 7,* pp. 2745-2769, 2006

Zuev, D. & Moore, A. W., "Traffic Classification using a statistical approach", *Passive and Active Network Measurement, Lecture Notes in Computer Science*, 2005, Volume 3431/2005, pp 321-324, 2005

Chapter 2

Security and Privacy

Towards Efficient and Privacy-Preserving Network-Based Botnet Detection Using Netflow Data

S.Abt and H.Baier

Center for Advanced Security Research, Faculty of Computer Science, Hochschule Darmstadt, Germany
e-mail: {sebastian.abt|harald.baier}@cased.de

Abstract

Botnets pose a severe threat to the security of Internet-connected hosts and the availability of the Internet's infrastructure. In recent years, botnets have attracted many researchers. As a result, many achievements in studying different botnets' anatomies have been made and approaches to botnet detection have been developed. However, most of these approaches target at botnet detection using raw packet data. While this data provides the most complete view on botnet induced traffic, it usually cannot efficiently be collected at large network nodes transferring multi-Gigabits per second. Additionally, a deep inspection of network packets endangers the users' privacy. In order to solve these problems different detection methods based on Netflow data have been proposed. To contribute to advances in Netflow-based botnet detection research, we first give an overview of currently known approaches and compare their advantages and disadvantages. We then argue that Netflow-based detection requires the availability of a reference data set based on real data and present a modular data collection environment that is able, amongst others, to generate Netflow data at an ISP node. Finally, we present our vision of a future botnet detection framework based on Netflow data.

Keywords

Botnet detection, Netflow data, reference data set, large network operator, privacy.

1. Introduction

Together with this growth of the Internet a sub-culture constituting the *Internet underground economy* has evolved, aiming at doing business by abusing the Internet's open architecture and structure as well as ingenuous Internet users. The means this underground economy uses for their infamous purposes are manifold. For instance, *phishing* is used to steal user credentials. *Spam e-mails* are used to distribute phishing URLs or *malware* (e.g. worms, trojans, key loggers, scareware) in order to infiltrate a user's computer. Infiltrated computers are used to further distribute phishing URLs or malware or to launch *denial of service (DoS) attacks* (Mirkovic and Reiher, 2004), (Freiling et al., 2005), (Thing et al. 2007), causing severe financial damage (Patterson, 2002). Often, these infiltrated computers are remotely controlled by a miscreant and are usually referred to as *bots*. Many bots grouped together and equally controlled by an attacker are called *botnet*. Botnets have evolved to become one of the biggest annoyances large network operators have to cope with (Arbor Netwokrs, 2005-2011).

Since some years, the question on how to detect botnets has attracted various researchers and different approaches have been published (Freiling et al., 2005), (Gu et al., 2007), (Gu et al., 2008), (Gu et al., 2008), (Racine, 2004), (Karasaridis et al., 2007), (The Honeynet Project, 2005), (Livadas et al., 2006), (Strayer et al., 2006), (Binkley and Singh, 2006), (Ramachandran et al., 2006), (Goebel and Holz, 2007). However, almost all of this work targeted at host-based detection or utilized full packet data for network-based approaches. Approaches utilizing full packet data are commonly referred to as performing deep packet inspection (DPI). Unfortunately, DPI by definition only inadequately takes privacy aspects and efficiency considerations into account. With DPI, recording and analysis of full network traffic is required, which efficiency-wise is not feasible on network links transferring multiple Gigabit/s. Additionally, illegitimate access to DPI-based systems or data recorded by them effectively uncovers possibly private communication (e.g. personal email, HTTP sessions) and thus seriously endagers the communicating parties' privacy. Therefore, the applicability of DPI in high-traffic environments is restricted. We believe that this classical proceeding does not succeed very well in defending against botnets: Host-based detection alone obviously seems to be ineffective as malware and virus detection systems have been released for years, yet the botnet threat is growing, and clearly both efficiency and privacy are essential requirements for network-based detection systems.

In order to comply with these requirements, network-based botnet detection not only has to be based on efficient detection algorithms, but also has to make use of data sets that can efficiently be gathered and protect users' privacy. Data that fulfill both demands are *Netflow data.*

The contributions of the paper at hand are as follows:

1. We aim at reviewing the state of the art in botnet detection with a focus on its applicability to large networks (e.g. an Internet Service Provider). We come up with a comparison of currently proposed approaches.

2. Based on this discussion, we conclude that in order to advance research in this area, an openly available Netflow reference data set satisfying both data efficiency and user privacy has to be created. Up to now such public data set is missing (we speculate about the reasons for this in Section 4). We contribute to this area of research by presenting an extended, network operator centric and easy to manage honeynet environment suitable for collecting botnet induced Netflow data.

3. Furthermore, we develop a roadmap to get a Netflow-based detection appliance, which may easily be integrated in network operators' infrastructures and which may lead to a global botnet early warning system.

The outline of the remainder of this paper is as follows: Section 2 gives an overview on the fundamentals of botnets and introduces Netflow data. Section 3 reviews existing approaches in botnet detection and discusses their issues. After that, Section 4 describes our proposal for a data collection environment of Netflow data and our experiences after its deployment. In Section 5 we propose our roadmap to come to a Netflow-based botnet detection appliance. Finally, Section 6 concludes this paper.

2. Botnets and Netflow Data

This section introduces the basic facts on botnets and on Netflow data that are necessary to present our approach on Netflow-based botnet detection and our collection center of Netflow data.

2.1. Botnets

Botnets are based on a herd of compromised computers that are called bots and are under control of a *botmaster*. To create a botnet, a botmaster has *(1)* to *infect* remote hosts, *(2)* to decide on the *command and control* structure and protocol used within the botnet, and *(3)* to launch further *malicious activities*. These three aspects characterize a botnet and will be described next.

Host infection is the process of compromising a victim's computer. Common attack vectors to infect a device are *remote exploitation*, infection through *mail attachments*, *drive-by downloads* (Li et al., 2009), (Feily et al., 2009) and *direct infection*. Remote exploitation shares commonalities with worm propagation (Adeel et al., 2009). Attackers scan possible targets for known vulnerabilities that can be used to compromise a particular victim's computer by injecting malicious code. Mail attachments are distributed via spam mails. By launching the binary attached to a mail, the bot installs itself on the client device. With drive-by downloads, a user's device is infected by simply browsing websites containing malicious content that targets at the web browser or its plugins (Provos et al., 2007). Direct infection usually happens by exchanging infected storage devices like USB devices, compact flash cards, CD-Roms, etc.

After infection, a host can participate in a botnet. For coordination of a bot's activity, the bot has to receive commands from its botmaster via a *command and control (C&C) channel*. The C&C topology can either be *centralized*, i.e. a hub and spoke topology with one or more fixed rendezvous points bots can connect to, be a *peer-to-peer* architecture where each bot can act equally as client as well as server to forward messages, or be *randomly* structured showing no fixed topology, i.e. no single bot knows about the presence of more than one single infected other machine (Bailey et al., 2009).

Finally, compromised hosts that are connected to a botnet can be abused for various *malicious activities* upon the request of the botmaster. These activities include, but are not limited to, *DoS attacks*, *host infections*, *distributing spam e-mails*, *spying*, *hosting or sharing (illegal) data*, *data stealing*, *bandwidth trading*, *proxying*, and *click fraud* (Govil, 2007), (Liu et al., 2009), (Thing et al., 2007).

2.2. Netflow Data

In a computer network, a *Netflow record* or, in short, *flow* is a statistic derived from an unidirectional data stream between two communication systems that shares common attributes at the network layer (L3) and the transport layer (L4). A flow comprises packets offering the same source and destination IP addresses, source and destination port numbers, and layer 4 protocol type number at a specific period of time. More formally, we write a flow occuring at a specific point in time t as a 5-tuple, which we denote by f_t, i.e. we have f_t = *(srcIP, dstIP, srcPort, dstPort, L4Proto)*. The attributes constituting a flow f_t are called *flow keys* and serve as unique identifiers during flow creation. By filling a *flow cache* with flow keys as well as non-key attributes and statistics, Netflow records are created on intermediate network nodes (e.g. routers or switches) during packet forwarding (Cisco Systems, 2007). After creation, Netflow records are exported to a *flow collector* either after expiration of a pre-defined timer or if a communication channel represented by a flow is closed (e.g. after having seen a TCP FIN or TCP RST packet). Alongside with the flow keys, further non-key attributes are exported. The most interesting ones being the amount of bytes and packets transferred and, in case of a TCP channel, TCP flags set. Netflow records can be collected and exported in different format versions. The currently most commonly used version is Cisco System's proprietary Netflow version 5 (Cisco Systems, 2007). More recently, the Internet Engineering Task Force (IETF) standardized an extended, more flexible and freely avaible version called IPFIX (Claise, 2008).

The definition given above stresses our point about Netflow data fulfilling both, efficiency and privacy requirements predominant in large networks. First, Netflow records can be efficiently created in high-traffic environments as creation is inline with packet forwarding. This effectively transforms an ISPs packet forwarding network into a sensor network without the need for additional capital investment. Second, neither additional header information, nor any payload information is inspected during creation or exported to a flow collector. Hence, Netflow records contain very limited amount of potentially sensitive information, if any[1]. Thus, utilizing Netflow data by definition protects the user's privacy much better than any content-inspecting approach could do as no payload is touched. Additionally, due to not capturing the packets' headers or payloads, using Netflow significantly (see Sect. 4.2) reduces the amount of data that has to be analyzed as well as the processing power required for analysis. Hence, using Netflow data for botnet detection seems to be an interesting and promising approach, both, privacy- and efficiency-wise.

3. Botnet Detection

Detection of botnets has been of interest to various researchers and companies around the world and still is. Common techniques to counter this threat can be classified according to detection methodology, locality, and data source used. *Detection methodology* can either be *signature-based* or *anomaly-based* (Liu et al., 2009), (Feily et al., 2009), (Scarfone and Mell, 2007), (Bailey et al., 2009). The *locality* of botnet detection can either be *host-based* or *network-based* (Scarfone and Mell, 2007). Finally, the *data source* available for botnet detection or detection of malicious activity stemming from botnets can be *raw packet data*, *Netflow data*, *application traces* (e.g. command executions), *system log files*, or *bot binaries* (Bailey et al., 2009). We will next classify current approaches that specifically

[1] IP address data could be regarded as sensitive information.

address origin botnet detection and represent current state of the art according to these criteria. Afterwards we discuss their eligibility for use in high-traffic environments.

Approach	Methodology	Locality	Data source
(Freiling et al., 2005)	sign.-based	host-based	bot binaries
(Racine, 2004)	sign.-based	netw.-based	Netflow data
(Gu et al., 2007), (Gu et al. 2008a), (Livadas et al., 2006), (Strayer et al., 2006), (Binkley and Singh, 2006)	anom.-based	netw.-based	raw packet data
(Ramachandran et al., 2006)	anom.-based	host-based	log files
(Goebel and Holz, 2007)	sign.-based	netw.-based	raw packet data
(Gu et al., 2008b), (Karasaridis et al., 2007)	anom.-based	netw.-based	Netflow data + add. information

Table 1: Summary of classification of current botnet detection approaches

3.1. Classification of Current Approaches

(Freiling et al., 2005) introduced a root-cause methodology to detect DDoS attacks launching botnets by collecting bot binaries using a honeypot (The Honeynet Project, 2005) and infiltrating the botnet by connecting to the botnet's IRC C&C channel using a "silent drone". We classify this as host- and signature-based approach utilizing bot binaries.

Racine proposed making use of behavioral characteristics of bots (Racine, 2004). He found that IRC-based bots were mostly idle, only responding to commands from their botmaster. To characterize IRC behavior, Racine made use of Netflow data. Thus, this is a network- and signature-based detection approach utilizing Netflow data.

(Strayer et al., 2006), (Livadas et al., 2006) proposed a multi-step network-based approach using machine learning techniques and temporal clustering, i.e. anomaly-based, on raw packet data. This approach does not make use of any packets' payloads, however, due to its use of packet inter-arrival times during temporal clustering, this approach will not work with Netflow data.

(Binkley and Singh, 2006) proposed a network- and anomaly-based algorithm combining IRC message statistics and TCP work weight. By examining IRC messages, this approach relies on packets' payloads and thus utilizes raw packet data. Furthermore, it will not work with encrypted communication.

(Ramachandran et al., 2006) proposed using DNS blacklist counter-intelligence to find spam-generating botnet members. Their approach is based on the insight that botmasters have to determine their bots' blacklist status. This is a host- and anomaly-based approach utilizing system log files (i.e. a DNS server's log files).

(Goebel and Holz, 2006) proposed a network- and signature-based approach, Rishi, to detecting IRC-based botnets. Rishi uses n-gram analysis to identify patterns of nicknames commonly used by botnets. This approach is limited to IRC-based C&C and cannot detect encrypted communication. As it analyzes IRC messages, this approach makes use of raw packet data.

In (Gu et al., 2007), Gu et al. proposed a system called BotHunter. BotHunter is a botnet detection system that uses IDS-driven dialog correlation. BotHunter is a network- and anomaly-based approach utilizing raw packet data. In (Gu et al., 2008a), Gu et al. proposed a more advanced detection system called BotSniffer. BotSniffer aims at detecting spatial-temporal correlation and similarity patterns, i.e. crowd-like behaviour, in network traffic. As BotHunter, BotSniffer is a network-based anomaly-based detection system utilizing raw packet data. Further, Gu et al. propose a system called BotMiner (Gu et al., 2008b) that extends BotSniffer by clustering similar communication plane (C-plane) traffic and activity plane (A-plane, i.e. malicious) traffic. After that, cross-cluster correlation is performed to identify suspicious hosts. BotMiner is protocol and structure independent and makes use of Netflow data in the C-plane. However, A-plane clustering is conducted using raw packet data. BotMiner is a network- and anomaly-based system.

An approach utilizing Netflow data and external triggers is proposed by (Karasaridis et al., 2007). Karasaridis et al. studied the detectability of IRC botnet controllers on backbone networks by calculating distances between monitored flow data and a pre-defined IRC traffic profile. Their system utilizes external triggers (e.g. IDS alerts, scans, spam e-mails, system logs) to identify malicious hosts. After that, these hosts' Netflow data is analyzed to find candidate control conversations (CCC) with C&C hosts. Due to not depending on packets' payloads during analysis, this system is capable of detecting encrypted communication as well.

3.2. Issues in high-traffic environments

As this classification and discussion of current botnet detection approaches shows, besides (Racine, 2004) all approaches make either (additional) use of raw packet data or are host-based systems. This reflects current state of the art in botnet detection research.

These methods, however, are not feasibly applicable to large networks and high-traffic environments for the following reasons:

1. Host-based systems require the network operator to have access to the end users' devices, which is usually not the case, or force the end user to run specific detection software on all of its devices in order to gain access to the Internet. However, due to anti-discrimination regulations, in most countries the latter is not possible.

2. Capturing and analyzing raw packet data at transfer rates of multi-Gigabits per second in real-time is technically infeasible and additionally puts high financial burden on the network operators. Further, such systems are

restricted to the traffic as seen on a single network node and hence can't benefit from a network operator's spatially large footprint.

3. Categorically inspecting raw packets puts the end user's privacy at risk and contradicts current jurisdiction in many countries.

A promising alternative to raw packet data that has attracted the broader field of network attack detection and high-speed intrusion detection research (cf. (Abt, 2009)) is the use of Netflow data, which satisfies the following requirements:

1. As no information on a packet's payload is revealed, Netflow data do contain only a limited amount of sensitive information, if any. Hence, categorically inspecting Netflow data does not conflict with the end users' privacy.

2. Due to early data reduction at the collection point, flow data can efficiently be processed in near real-time and thus increases detection efficiency.

3. Netflow-based botnet detection comes almost free of additional capital investment as network operators can utilize their existing network devices as distributed sensor nodes.

4. Concurrently using network devices as sensor nodes provides a wide view on current network activity, leveraging the detection of malicious events caused by botnets.

Interestingly, besides (Racine, 2004), a botnet detection system heavily utilizing Netflow data has been proposed by researches at AT&T Labs (Karasaridis et al., 2007), which we believe emphasizes our view on the feasibility of systems based on Netflow data in large networks. Additionally, (Coskun et al., 2010) utilizes Netflow data for identifying “mutual contacts” of bot infected hosts that have originally been detected using different detection strategies.

4. A Reference Data Collection Environment

As discussed before, efficiency and privacy requirements have to be met by botnet detection approaches feasible for use in high-traffic environments. Netflow data honour these requirements. However, only few approaches (Gu et al., 2008b), (Racine, 2004), (Karasaridis, 2007) utilize these data. We believe that the reason for this is twofold: first, no publicly available data set of these data sources exists that can be used to develop, train and test algorithms. Second, such data can best be won in a target environment and therefore cooperation of high-traffic network operators is essential. Unfortunately, however, cooperating with such organizations in this context is usually difficult as collecting Netflow data possibly requires re-configuration of an organization's infrastructure, which binds (human) resources and possibly puts its infrastructure at additional risk. To counter these issues, we've developed a modular data collection environment that aims at reducing a network operator's workload in participating and generates data that can be used for algorithm development and evaluation. We will describe this system in Section 4.1 and present first experiences in Section 4.2.

4.1. Architecture

The system we developed is depicted in **Error! Reference source not found.**. It is currently hosted with an Internet Service Provider supporting this work and consists of several components that will be explained next. It can easily be used to integrate other Internet Service Providers as well as gateways of large institutional networks (e.g. of companies or universities) in the data collection process.

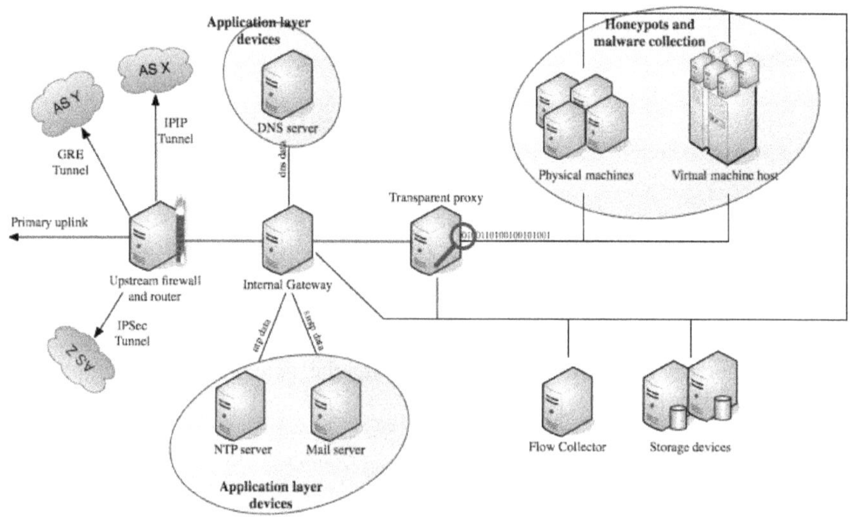

Figure 1: Scheme of the data collection environment. Different autonomous systems (AS) can easily be added by using IP tunneling mechanisms

Upstream firewall and router The upstream firewall and router is used as the network termination point of this setup that connects the data collection system to the rest of the world. The primarily functionality of this component is as follows: first, it protects the Internet from getting attacked by bot-infected hosts from within the system and limits the intense of attacks that are launched from the inner by filtering and rate-limiting all outgoing traffic. Second, this component terminates virtual upstream connections to other network operators by using standardized tunneling protocols like IP security (IPSec), generic routing encapsulation protocol (GRE) or IP-in-IP tunneling, facilitating the virtual integration of this data collection environment into other networks.

Internal Gateway The internal gateway acts as gateway between different subnets the honeypots reside in and can provide dynamic IP address assignment by use of DHCP. Additionally, the internal gateway is used to re-route specific protocols to special application layer devices to capture side-effects caused by botnet activity and to simulate host infections in a controlled, clean-slate environment (cf. (Gorecki, 2007)).

Transparent proxy The transparent proxy device creates and collects netflow data as well as raw packet traces (as used for DPI) for the traffic observed.

Application layer devices Application layer devices are used to handle specific suspicious application layer protocols (e.g. SMTP, NTP, DNS) found in the infiltrated hosts' network traffic and thus can produce system log files typically found in such environments.

Honeypots The honeypots are used to expose itself as potential victims and mostly run on virtual or physical machines as we aim at capturing network traces of bot infection processes and not only at capturing malware samples, as is the focus of mwcollect (Freiling et al., 2005) or nepenthes (Baecher et al., 2006)). In general, basically any operating system can be setup on these nodes either physically or virtualized with varying network configurations simulating both, higher-speed systems with static IP addresses as well as lower-speed dial-up connections with changing IP addresses.

Storage devices The storage devices provide redundant network attached storage for virtual machine images and are used to safely store the collected data.

Our data collection framework, as described above, has the following advantages and novelties in contrast to similar data collection approaches (Freiling et al., 2005), (The Honeynet Project, 2005), (Rajab et al., 2006):

- The system has been carefully designed in cooperation with an Internet Service Provider and hence integrates very well in large networks.

- The system can be easily integrated in other than the hosting ISP's environments. This potentially raises the footprint of the detection system as IP address ranges from various network operators from geographically distant regions, and hence different time zones, can be used to collect data (Dagon et al., 2006).

- The system does not interfere with legitimate users' data and thus does not raise any privacy concerns during data collection.

- The system is capable of capturing Netflow data as well as raw packet data, system log files and application layer data.

4.2. Data Collection and First Experiences

As noted above, development of this system has been supported by an Internet Service Provider and a first installation has been deployed with this ISP for a period of 19 days (without any virtual connection to any other ISP). During this time, we ran a darknet consisting of three subnets spanning three different /8 prefixes (85/8,

95/8, and 62/8). Each subnet consisted of 32 IP addresses, i.e. a /27 subnet. We run 18 honeypot instances at a time during this time frame. The operating systems used varied between Microsoft Windows XP, Windows Vista, Windows 7, and Debian GNU Linux 5.0. Using this configuration, we collected approximately 30 GB of raw packet data and 4 GB of Netflow data. These network traces are completely comprised of suspicious and/or malicious traffic as the devices run within the subnets were not expected to cause any network activity. By comparing the volume of raw packet data with Netflow data collected in this time frame, one can clearly see the massive data reduction capabilities achievable by prefering Netflow data over raw packet data. In our case, the reduction was almost 81%, which clearly emphasizes the gain in both, efficiency and privacy that can be achieved using Netflow data for botnet detection.

The analysis of the collected data is still ongoing work. However, to gain a first insight in the data we used the Snort signature-based intrusion detection system to analyze the captured raw packets. The results of this analysis revealed that the captured traffic mostly consisted of network- and port-scans, worm distribution traffic as well as botnet traces with Microsoft Windows XP and Microsoft Windows Vista being the only infected systems. This is particular interesting as all operating systems were installed without any further modifications. For the Debian GNU Linux 5.0 installation we additionally added 10 credentials commonly found in SSH-scan attempts to facilitate the exploitation of these instances and the establishment of an centralized command and control rendezvous point. In contrast, the fastest exploitation of a Windows XP machine did not last longer than 1:34 minutes.

5. Advancing Netflow-based Botnet Detection

We believe that using Netflow data is both an efficient and privacy-preserving approach to botnet detection feasible for large networks and high-traffic environments. In order to advance research in this direction, the compilation of a labeled reference data set is essential. Using our data collection environment, we will next proceed at compiling such a labeled reference data set by clustering and correlating the traces we collected thus far (and will collect in future). To automate this work, we're looking forward to enhance our data collection environment by means to automatically cluster, correlate and classify network traces. Additionally, we plan to mix the won and classified malicious traces with representative traffic traces belonging to well-known benign network traffic. We will collect this benign traffic at various network demarcation points (e.g. university campus traffic, ISP data center traffic, residential dial-up customer traffic) of different network operators and behind commercial firewall systems (i.e. pre-filtered traffic traces).

Further to that, we believe that for large-scale botnet command and control detection and in order to defeat the threat emerging from botnets, the existence of an open source Netflow-based detection appliance is essential. Such an appliance and its algorithms should

1. be easy to integrate into existing service provider networks,
2. be able to effectively and efficiently detect botnet C&C traffic,

3. be self-adapting to changing conditions, such as the emergence of new bot families or C&C topologies,

4. and should provide interfaces for human-appliance interaction as well as inter-appliance interaction, i.e. the exchange of information belonging to possibly malicious activities between different network operators.

While the latter requirement seems to be especially important to obtain a Netflow-based early warning system, care has to be taken to exchange the necessary information in a privacy-preserving way and according to national jurisdiction.

Given these requirements, additional to the compilation of a state of the art reference data set, we propose studying the following topics in order to advance the area of privacy-preserving Netflow-based botnet detection and to develop a detection appliance suitable as global botnet early warning system. *Flow anonymization*: in order to exchange information between network operators it is essential to anonymize Netflow-traces and related information in a way that *(i)* no sensitive information on the end user or its habits can be won and *(ii)* the correlation of different events is still possible. *Entropy of Netflow data*: we believe it is worth studying the entropy of Netflow data in contrast to raw packet data's entropy in order to gain further insight on what can be detected using network flow data and what cannot. *Netflow-based detection metrics*: in order to detect botnet activity from Netflow data, reliable detection metrics are essential. Systematically studying this field of research should ultimately advance botnet detection research. *Detection algorithms*: for Netflow-based detection of botnet command and control traffic, the development and assessment of specially tailored detection algorithms is necessary to satisfy detection accuracy, efficiency and effectivity. *Combined Netflow-based botnet detection*: combining network flow data with system log files that can equally easy be collected by network operators as flow-traces (e.g. DNS queries, mail traffic, NTP queries) should increase detection accuracy while not affecting detection

6. Conclusion

In this paper, we discussed several approaches to botnet detection that currently exist and reflect current state of the art. Amongst these, we found only one purely Netflow-based approach. We believe, that Netflow-based approaches are promising in high-traffic environments as they contribute to efficiency and protect a user's privacy. We further believe, however, that in order to advance research in Netflow-based botnet detection, the compilation of a labeled reference data set is essential.

In order to compile such a reference data set, we propose a modular data collection environment that can easily be integrated in different network infrastructures and that has been used to collect a total of 34 GB suspicious Netflow and raw packet traces. Further, we highlighted possible future work and open questions that should be studied next and sketched a roadmap to the development of a Netflow-based detection appliance suitable for application in large network provider environments.

The data set collected using the above sketched platform as well as specific configuration details and management scripts will be made availably to researchers by mail to the authors.

7. Acknowledgments

This work has been partially supported by the German Federal Ministry of Education and Research under grant number 01BY1201F and by CASED.

8. References

Abt, S., (2009), "A statistical approach to flow-based network attack detection", Bachelor's thesis, Darmstadt University of Applied Sciences, Faculty of Computer Science, Darmstadt.

Adeel, M., Tokarchuk, L., Cuthbert, L., Feng, C.S., and Qin, Z.G., (2009), "A distributed framework for passive worm detection and throttling in p2p networks", in *Proceedings of the 6th IEEE Consumer Communications and Networking Conference,* pp. 1-5.

Arbor Networks, (2005-2011), *Worldwide Infrastructure Security Report,* Arbor Networks, Inc., http://www.arbornetworks.com/report (last accessed: January 2012).

Baecher, P., Koetter, M., Holz, T., and Dornseif, M., (2006), "The nepenthes platform: An efficient approach to collect malware", in *Proceedings of the 9th International Symposium on Recent Advances in Intrusion Detection (RAID 2006).*

Bailey, M., Cooke, E., Jahanian, F., Xu, Y., and Karir, M., (2009), "A survey of botnet technology and defenses", in *Proceedings of the 2009 Cybersecurity Applications & Technology Conference for Homeland Security,* pp. 299-304.

Binkley, J., and Singh, S., (2006), "An algorithm for anomaly-based botnet detection", in *Proceedings of the 2nd Conference on Steps to Reducing Unwanted Traffic on the Internet.*

Cisco Systems, (2007), "Netflow Services Solutions Guide", http://www.cisco.com/en/US/docs/ios/solutions docs/netflow/nfwhite.html (last accessed: January 2012).

Claise, B. (Editor), (2008), "Specification of the IP Flow Information Export (IPFIX) Protocol for the Exchange of IP Traffic Flow Information", RFC 5101, http://tools.ietf.org/html/rfc5101.

Coskun B., Dietrich, S., Memon, N., (2010), "Friends of an enemy: Identifying local members of peer-to-peer botnets using mutual contacts", in *Proceedings of the 26th Annual Computer Security Applications Conference*, pp. 131-140.

Dagon, D., Zou, C., and Lee, W., (2006), "Modeling botnet propagation using time zones", in *Proceedings of the 13 th Network and Distributed System Security Symposium.*

Feily, M., Shahrestani, A., and Ramadass, S., (2009), "A survey of botnet and botnet detection", in *Proceedings of the 2009 Third International Conference on Emerging Security Information, Systems and Technologies*, pp. 268–273.

Freiling, F., Holz, T. and Wicherski, G., (2005), "Botnet tracking: Exploring a root-cause methodology to prevent distributed denial-of-service attacks" in *Proceedings of 10 th European Symposium on Research in Computer Security,* pp. 319-335.

Goebel, J., and Holz, T., (2007), "Rishi: Identify bot contaminated hosts by irc nickname evaluation", in *Proceedings of the first conference on First Workshop on Hot Topics in Understanding Botnets.*

Gorecki, C., (2007), "Trumanbox – improving malware analysis by simulating the internet", Diploma thesis, RWTH Aachen University, Department of Computer Science, Aachen.

Govil, J., (2007), "Examining the criminology of bot zoo", in *Proceedings of the 6th International Conference on Information, Communications Signal Processing*, pp. 1-6.

Gu, G., Porras, P., Yegneswaran, V., Fong, M., and Lee, W., (2007), "Bothunter: Detecting malware infection through ids-driven dialog correlation", in *Proceedings of the 16th USENIX Security Symposium,* pp. 167-182.

Gu, G., Zhang, J., and Lee, W., (2008a), "Botsniffer: Detecting botnet command and control channels in network traffic", in *Proceedings of the 15th Annual Network and Distributed System Security Symposium (NDSS'08).*

Gu, G., Perdisci, R., Zhang, J., and Lee, W., (2008b), "Botminer: Clustering analysis of network traffic for protocol-and structure-independent botnet detection", *Usenix Security Symposium.*

Karasaridis, A., Rexroad, B., and Hoeflin, D., (2007), "Wide-scale botnet detection and characterization", in *Proceedings of the first conference on First Workshop on Hot Topics in Understanding Botnets.*

Li, C., Jiang, W., and Zou, X., (2009), "Botnet: Survey and case study", in *Proceedings of the International Conference on Innovative Computing, Information and Control,* pp. 1184-1187.

Liu, J., Xiao, Y., Ghaboosi, K., Deng, H., and Zhang, J., (2009), "Botnet: Classification, attacks, detection, tracing, and preventive measures", in *EURASIP Journal on Wireless Communications and Networking,* Vol. 2009.

Livadas, C., Walsh, R., Lapsley, D., and Strayer, W., (2006), "Using machine learning techniques to identify botnet traffic", in *Proceedings of the 2nd IEEE LCN Workshop on Network Security (WoNS'2006).*

Mirkovic, J. and Reiher, P., (2004), "A taxonomy of ddos attack and ddos defense mechanisms," *ACM SIGCOMM Computer Comunications Review.*

Patterson, D., (2002), "A simple way to estimate the cost of downtime," in *Proceedings of the 16th USENIX conference on System administration,* pp. 185-188.

Provos, N., McNamee, D., Mavrommatis, P., Wang, K., and Modadugu, N., (2007), "The ghost in the browser analysis of web-based malware", in *Proceedings of the first conference on First Workshop on Hot Topics in Understanding Botnets,* pp. 4-4.

Racine, S., (2004), "Analysis of internet relay chat usage by ddos zombies", Master's thesis, Swiss Federal Institute of Technology, Zurich.

Rajab, M., Zarfoss, J., Monrose, F., and Terzis, A., (2006), "A multifaceted approach to understanding the botnet phenomenon" in *Proceedings of the 6th ACM SIGCOMM conference on Internet measurement.*

Ramachandran, A., Feamster, N., and Dagon, D., (2006), "Revealing botnet membership using dnsbl counter-intelligence", in *Proceedings of the 2nd conference on Steps to Reducing Unwanted Traffic on the Internet.*

Scarfone, K., and Mell, P., (2007), "Guide *to Intrusion Detection and Prevention Systems (IDPS)", Recommendation of the National Institute of Standards and Technology,* Special Publication 800-94.

Strayer, W., Walsh, R., Livadas, C., and Lapsley, D., (2006), "Detecting botnets with tight command and control", in *Proceedings of the 31st IEEE Conference on Local Computer Networks.*

The Honeynet Project, (2005), "Know your enemy: Tracking botnets", http: //www.honeynet.org/ (last accessed: January 2012).

Thing, V., Sloman, M., Dulay, N., Venter, H., Eloff, M., Labuschagne, L., Eloff, J., and VonSolms, R., (2007), "A survey of bots used for distributed denial of service attacks," *IFIP International Federation for Information Processing,* vol. 232, pp. 229.

The Insider Threat Prediction and Specification Language

G.Magklaras[1] and S.M.Furnell[1,2]

[1]Center for Security, Communications and Network Research,
Plymouth University, Plymouth, UK
[2]School of Computer & Security Science, Edith Cowan University, Australia
e-mail: info@cscan.org

Abstract

Various information security surveys and case studies indicate the importance and manifestation of the insider threat problem. One of the most important tools to address insider threats is to enable the researchers to build case studies and express/replay threat scenarios. The Insider Threat Prediction and Specification Language (ITPSL) is a Domain Specific Language (DSL) created to provide a systemic way to describe insider threats and misuse incidents. This paper presents the scope of creation as well as the design philosophy of the language. An early language compiler prototype and its underlying insider threat monitoring framework are presented followed by an evaluation of the language against real world insider threat scenarios. The paper concludes with a brief discussion of the future trends in insider threat monitoring and specification.

Keywords

Insider misuse, insider threat specification, logging engine, Domain Specific Languages, insider threat signature

1. Insider Threat and its specification

Information Technology (IT) security threats concern every component of the modern computing infrastructure world. Pfleeger et al., (2003) defines the term threat in an IT infrastructure context as "a set of circumstances that has the potential to cause loss or harm". These circumstances might involve human-initiated actions (intentional IT intrusions), flaws in the design of the computer system and environment factors (natural disasters). In the Information Security literature, the term "insider" has been defined by means of highlighting different parts of the problem. However, it always refers to legitimate users, people that are trusted to access the IT infrastructure. Trust is a key issue and a good general definition of an "insider" that emphasizes this is the following Probst et al., (2009): "An insider is a person that has been legitimately empowered with the right to access, represent, or decide about one or more assets of the organization's structure". This definition gives a wide perspective.

Insider IT misuse threats have been documented in recent information security surveys. The ISBS 2010 (PwC, 2010) and the CSI 2010 (Richardson, 2010) are two examples that shed light in different parts of the insider misuse threat problems.

Neither the information security surveys nor the stories in the press can provide a clear picture of the mechanism with which the problem manifests itself in IT infrastructures. This clear picture should ideally display a mechanism that shows how a threat is realized into a misuse act. This is the field of Insider Threat Specification, the process of using a standardized vocabulary to describe in an abstract way how the aspects and behavior of an insider relate to a security policy (Caelli et al., 1991) based misuse scenario.

Personality, organizational role, financial status and access credentials are some examples of insider aspects. In contrast, the insider behavior refers to the actions of an individual for accessing, representing or deciding about organizational assets.

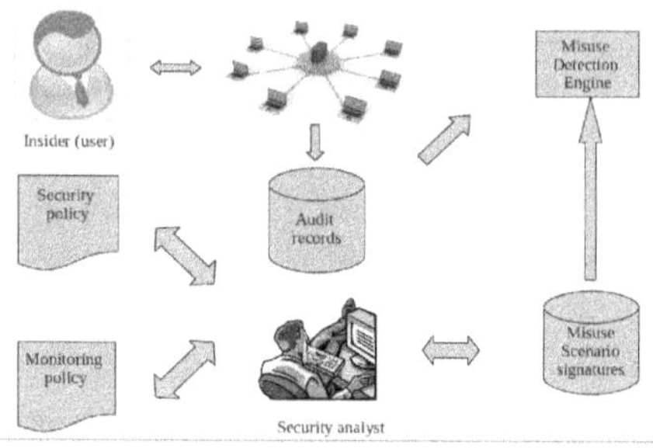

Figure 1: Misuse detection information flow

A security policy defined misuse scenario implies the existence of a monitoring policy. The security policy (Caelli et al., 1991) defines in plain language the borders between acceptable and unacceptable usage of IT resources. However, this plain language description must then be converted into suitable monitoring statements. Bace, (2001) discusses the difference between a security and a monitoring policy. Figure 1 illustrates the misuse detection information flow. The actions of an insider are monitored using a tailored logging engine (Magklaras et al., 2011) and generate audit records. The security analyst will consult the security policy and generate a suitable monitoring policy. The next step is to construct Misuse Scenario signatures expressing various insider threats. The misuse signatures are constructed so they describe certain monitored events and on the basis of the collected audit records, certain misuse incidents or insider threats (series of events that are likely to generate misuse incidents) can be detected.

2. The scope of ITPSL

The previous section defined the term threat and how it should be specified. Understanding the relationship between a threat specification language and a threat model, a common technique to study threats is vital for setting the scope of our proposed language. Figure 2 illustrates such the relationship between the Insider Threat Prediction and Specification Language (ITPSL) and an insider threat model (Magklaras et al., 2005).

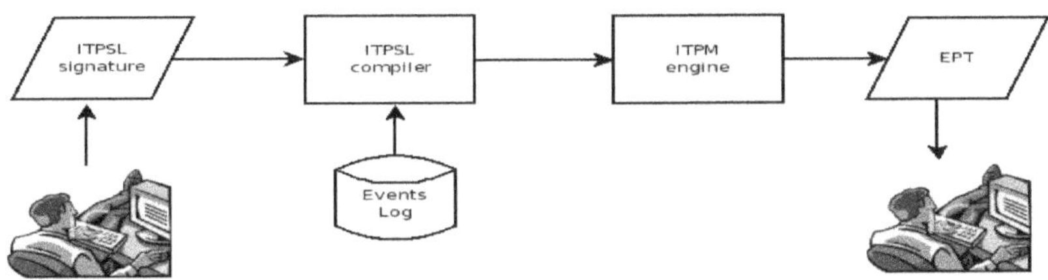

Figure 2: The relationship between ITPSL and a threat model

The flow of information starts with a security analyst writing a description of the particular insider misuse scenario, using the ITPSL semantics. The signature is validated by a compiler that translates the signature directives to query commands and makes use of the logging infrastructure, in order to examine whether the criteria and metrics the signature mentions exist in the system. The Evaluated Potential Threat (EPT) is a score indicating the likelihood of a threat occurring given the detected conditions.

The emphasis is on the ability to make insider case repositories. An early report outlining aspects of the insider threat to the US government information systems published by NSTISSAM, (1999) considers the absence of case repositories as one of the limiting factors in the field of insider IT misuse mitigation research. In addition, Capelli et al., (2006) state clearly the need to keep detailed records of employee actions in relation to file access, application usage and network connection matters. Brancik (2008) mentions the importance of suitable tools to produce Key Fraud Signatures (KFS) to aid insider threat mitigation and thus signifies the overlap between insider misuse and the field of digital forensics.

As a result, ITPSL should be viewed as a specialized language that is able to encode system level data that concern legitimate user actions, in order to aid the process of misuse threat prediction and assist computer forensic officers in the process of examining insider misuse incidents. As such, ITPSL's target audience is the security analyst/expert, as well as the seasoned IT administrator in charge of system operation and security issues. Both of these types of domain experts should be able to express insider misuse scenarios by using the language semantics to construct signatures of threat scenarios.

3. The design philosophy of ITPSL

The ITPSL scope defines clearly a specific task of expressing insider threat metrics. This paves the way for the selection of a mechanism that allows the language designer to focus on the problem in question. A Domain Specific Language (DSL) is a semantic mechanism tailored specifically for describing the details of a particular task. The main goal is the usage of appropriate semantics to reduce the effort required to reference and manipulate elements of that particular domain.

Spinellis (2001) defines a Domain Specific Language as "programming language tailored specifically to an application domain: rather than being for a general purpose, it captures precisely the domain's semantics". DSL schemata have been employed successfully in a number of different areas. Consel (2004) discusses the range of applications that have employed a DSL that includes device driver construction, active networking and operating system process scheduling.

DSLs are categorized as external and internal ones. An internal DSL is implemented as an extension of the semantics of a generic programming language. ITPSL follows the external DSL approach allowing for freedom to create the semantics from scratch with commonly changed parameters to be altered without recompilation issues and no dependence on host language idiosyncrasies. This approach has been followed by a number of security related research DSLs such as CISL by Feirtag et al., (1999) and Panoptis by Spinellis et al., (2002).

The ITPSL semantics is the second important aspect of the design philosophy. Software language engineers relate semantics to the term language by using the following definition: "A description of the semantics of a language L is a means to communicate a subjective understanding of the linguistic utterances of L to another person or persons." (Kleppe, 2009).

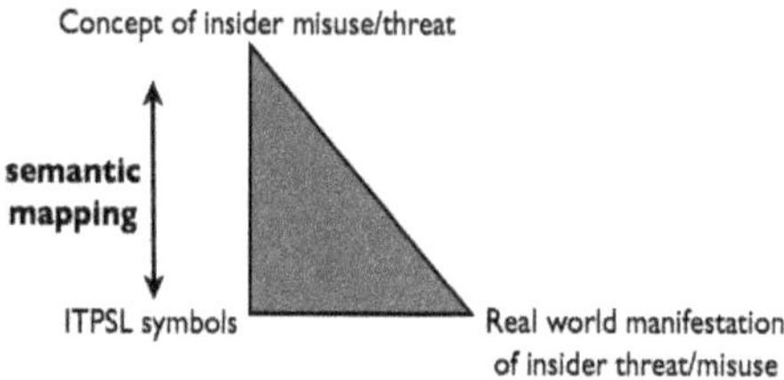

Figure 3: Semantic mapping in ITPSL

Figure 3 illustrates the role of semantics in ITPSL. The semantic triangle mapping (Kleppe, 2009) is all about connecting the symbols of ITPSL to the human expert's view of how insider misuse incidents or threats occur in a computer system. On the right hand side of the triangle resides the real world system view. Thus, the hypotenuse of the triangle symbolizes the differences between the concept and the real world manifestations of threats and misuse incidents. Finally, ITSPSL is an XML DSL markup. XML is a universal data exchange language. All ITPSL signature sections conform to the XML well formed rules (Goldberg, 2009) and a specific XML schema against which are validated.

4. The ITPSL markup

At the heart of the semantic framework lies the form of the ITPSL signature, a semantic structure that represents the encoding of an insider threat. Figure 4 shows the general structure of an ITPSL signature. It consists of a header section followed by the main body of the signature where sub-blocks of file, exec, network and hardware statements are encapsulated, in accordance to the different types of the LUARM audit log data in (Magklaras et al. (2011).

```
<itpslsig>
<itpslheader>
        <signid> <md5sum of date and second, type of OS, current number of processes>
        </signid>
        <signdate>
                <year> dddd </year>
                <month> dd </month>
                <day> dd </day>
        </signdate>
        <ontology>
                <reason> "intentional" | "accidental" </reason>
                <revision> d.d </revision>
                <user_role> "admins" | "advanced_users" | "ordinary_users" </user_role>
                <detectby> "file" | "exec" | "network" | "hardware" | "multi" </detectby>
                <multihost> yes | no </multihost>
                <hostlist> host1,hostgroup1,...hostn,hostgroupn </hostlist>
                <weightmatrix>n_events, W_event1, W_event2,...,W_eventn </weightmatrix>
                <os> "linux" | "windows" | "macosx" | "unix" </os>
                <osver> "2.4" | "2.6" | "2000" | "Vista" | "7" </osver>
                <threatkeywords> keyword1 keyword2 ... keyword5
                 </threatkeywords>
                [ <synopsis> "text that describes the signature's purpose and function"</synopsis>]
        </ontology>
</itpslheader>
<itpslbody>
        <mainblock>
                <mainop> "AND"|"OR"|"XOR"|"as_a_result_of" | "justone"</mainop>
                <subblock>
                        ....|
                </subblock>
        </mainblock>
</itpslbody>
</itpslsig>
```

Figure 4: The ITPSL signature structure

The ontology header subsection is of particular importance for the creation of signature repositories. An ontology is a data model that represents a set of concepts within a domain (or formally known as domain of discourse in linguistic terms and the relationships between those concepts. A variation of the threat model published by (Magklaras et al., 2005) and the audit engine data (Magklaras et al., 2011) constitute the data model and the domain that the proposed markup language addresses.

As discussed in previous sections, ITPSL is trying to address the lack of insider threat scenario repositories. When such a repository is constructed, facilities to search and relate signatures (descriptions of threat scenarios) will be important and thus the language must have both semantic and data identifiers to allow security specialists to locate a class of signatures. For example, one could select all signatures that use network detection criteria, or all signatures that target p2p client installation and detect their presence at multiple levels ('multi' refers to a combination of employing 'file', 'exec', 'network' and 'hardware' detection statements). A third example could be the last two revisions of a particular set of signatures or a set of signatures whose weight matrix places more emphasis on network detection criteria.

The <reason> tag specifies whether we are searching for a threat that is a result of deliberate actions (intentional) or accidental mistakes (accidental). The <revision> tag makes possible to trace signatures whose detection criteria are modified to improve the accuracy or to examine slightly different aspects of the target problem. In that case, the 'signid' identifier remains the same amongst the related signatures.

```
<itpslbody>
        <mainblock>
                <mainop>OR</mainop>
                <subblock>
                        <subop>single</subop>
                                <usercanaccessdir>
                                        <userid>NOT (mikes,ridh)</userid>
                                        <dirname>OR (Contracts,Salary)</dirname>
                                        <location>/storage/cn1/Payroll</location>
                                        <singledir>yes</singledir>
                                        <ability>just-read</ability>
                                </usercanaccessdir>
                </subblock>
                <subblock>
                        <subop>single</subop>
                                <groupcanaccessdir>
                                        <groupid>NOT (hrpersons,accounts)</groupid>
                                        <dirname>OR (Overtime)</dirname>
                                        <location>/storage/cn1/Payroll</location>
                                        <singledir>yes</singledir>
                                        <ability>just-read</ability>
                                </groupcanaccessdir>
                </subblock>
        </mainblock>
</itpslbody>
```

Figure 5: An example ITPSL signature body

Figure 5 illustrates an example of an ITPSL signature in an information leakage detection scenario. In particular, we are interested to check the accessibility of the Payroll directory folder (/storage/cn1/Payroll). The main-block consists of two sub-blocks. The first one contains a 'usercanaccessdir' directive as the access control policy mentions that only certain user names (mikes,ridh) should access the 'Salary' and 'Contracts' sub-folders. The <userid>NOT (mikes,ridh)</userid> tag is expanded to all other userids of the host and the directory access check is performed for each one of them.

In contrast, the second sub-block contains a 'groupcanaccessdir' because the other part of the policy defines two distinct groups (hrpersons, accounts) that should access the 'Overtime' folder. The <groupid>NOT(hrpersons,accounts)</groupid> tag is expanded to all non system groups (root, wheel) and then to all resulting usernames that belong to these groups, in order for the check to be performed for each user account member.

5. Implementing and evaluating ITPSL

Figure 6 illustrates the components of the ITPSL compiler prototype system. The prototype system consists of a number of relational tables and Perl scripts, as well as an XML Schema file (validate.xsd). This file describes the syntax of the ITPSL signature and helps the various tools ensure that the processed signature is consistent with the syntax and format of the language. On the left hand side of Figure 5, the 'submitsig.pl' script helps the user submit a syntactically correct signature to the

ITPSL signature repository ('signatures_repository.sql'). This repository implements the ITPSL signature ontology (ITPSL signature header). In contrast, the 'searchsig.pl' and 'getsig.pl' are used to search and retrieve one or more signatures from the ITPSL signature repository.

The fetched signatures are then fed to the main ITPSL compiler module ('itpslc.pl'). This module has the vital job of interpreting LUARM data by turning the ITPSL signature semantics into misuse detection and prediction output, informing the analyst on whether something is happening (misuse detection) or is about to happen (threat prediction).

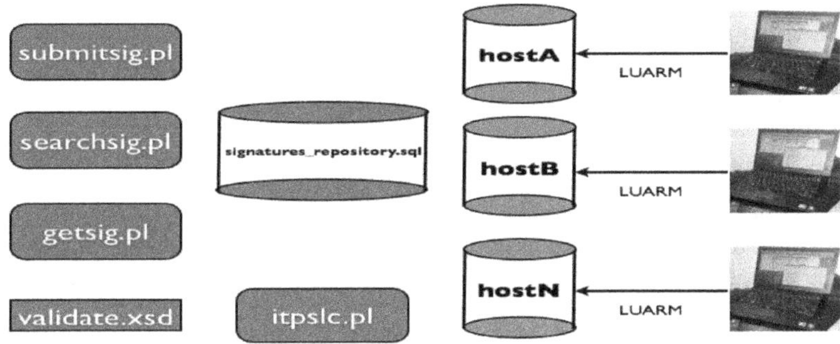

Figure 6: The ITPSL prototype system

Evaluating a DSL language like ITPSL requires a carefully designed process. DSLs like general purpose programming languages can be evaluated empirically. While this empirical process is still valuable, today the tasks of building and evaluating DSLs have become part of the Software Language Engineering (SLE) discipline (White et al., 2009). SLE improves dramatically the quality of DSL evaluation. However, it still leaves important gaps in the process of measuring vital language attributes such as expressiveness, effectiveness, usability and maintainability.

For these reasons, a controlled experiment (Magklaras, 2011) on insider IT misuse detection and prediction scenarios was chosen to evaluate the language. The scenarios were derived from real world incident data collected by testers of the LUARM audit engine (Magklaras et al., 2011) and the misuse game had three important entities:

1. **The users**: The people that are associated to a particular scenario and have unique user-id and authentication credentials.
2. **The analyst**: The person who was responsible for examining the logs and using ITPSL to detect/predict the threats and the associated users (security officer or a third party security auditor).
3. **The IT infrastructure**: A number of Linux workstations with shared filesystems that simulated an IT infrastructure.

There were four scenarios that represented a range of common IT misuse incidents. Scenario 1 was a typical Intellectual Property theft scenario with the added complexity of a masquerade attack. Scenario 2 re-enacted the detection of accessing pornographic material. Scenario 3 is an example of an insider IT misuse prediction task. In essence, it aims to demonstrate the decision theoretic information features of ITPSL and help the analyst predict the installation of a dangerous DoS attack tool by an ordinary user. The fourth and last scenario of the game is also demonstrating a predictive operation of file access control settings that could produce accidental (non intentional) information leak. The scenarios were discussed during an initial briefing amongst the analyst and three IT specialists that would re-enact these incidents by playing the role of the misuser for each scenario. After the initial briefing, the users met amongst them to discuss a role allocation for each scenario without the knowledge of the analyst. At that point, LUARM was activated and logging commenced for a period of 4 weeks. After this audit period, results were collected and verified with the users by the analyst.

6. Evaluation of results and conclusions

The game scenario (Magklaras, 2011) results revealed that ITPSL is a useful framework that can help researchers and practitioners profile a large range of common misuse incidents, expressing both threat detection and prediction. The language and underlying audit engine provided useful clues for all four scenarios.

The submitsig.pl and searchsig.pl (Figure 6) ITPSL utilities can create insider misuse incident signature repositories, combining the description of static and live forensic data under one common semantic framework. ITPSL is the first misuse detection language to support decision theoretic information. The association of weights and events facilitates insider threat prediction based on the analyst's view of how the threat precursors occur at file, network, process execution and hardware device level. Despite the fact that none of the scenarios provided a true opportunity to test event correlation across multiple hosts, ITPSL is equipped with operators such as the <onhost> tag, which could bind certain events to specific hosts and permit cross-host event correlation.

However, there are certain areas where ITPSL has weaknesses. One important issue to consider is the expressive granularity of the events. ITPSL (and its underlying audit record) capture file, network endpoint and process creation data. All applications generate these types of events in an operating system. However, not all of these events are meaningful to insider misuse detection and prediction at that level. There is a category of applications whose file, network and process execution operations are not easy to interpret. A great example is that of database applications where the observation of file access patterns do not reveal any clues about what kind of information is accessed and in what manner. In order to address that problem, the Intrusion Detection System (IDS)/Intrusion Prevention System (IPS) community suggests application-integrated monitoring (Phyo et al., 2003), a technique where audit records are generated by monitoring routines internal to the application itself. These routines know which internal events are of interest and can export relevant activities in specific audit log formats.

ITPSL (and its underlying logging mechanism) clearly needs certain semantic extensions to monitor applications such as databases, social networking sites and other applications that organize information using internal mechanisms. Everything else can be described by the proposed file, network, process and hardware semantics.

A last but equally important issue to consider is that of the monitoring framework scalability. The LUARM audit engine enforces a relational model (Codd, 1990) and the SQL interface (ISO/IEC 9075, 2008). This was a core design choice aiming to enhance the correlation versatility of the audit log structure. This goal was achieved, however, it imposes certain scalability limitations.

Relational databases have been at the forefront of massive data storage and organization for several decades. A number of different approaches enable relational databases to scale well, so that they can handle concurrently a large number of operations. Despite the success of employing relational database scalability measures, every practitioner agrees that the measures can become a cumbersome process and they have limits (Strandell, 2010). As the Relational Database scales horizontally (spread in various nodes), the complexity of managing software and hardware aspects in relation to interprocess communication increases.

The previous complexity and transaction volume requirements created a new generation of database products that are collectively referred to as 'NoSQL databases' (Zawodny, 2009). The 'NoSQL' term emphasizes the departure of these products from the traditional relational model, in an attempt to balance the need to scale and the need to preserve some of the properties of relational consistency . These products deviate from traditional RDBMS requirements such as data normalization and create simpler but faster key lookup mechanisms, in order to achieve massive concurrency and scalability. LUARM's SQL table schema is simple and does not require data normalization or embody any relational key constraints amongst the various client tables (audit levels). Consequently, it should be possible to port the audit log structure into a 'NoSQL' product and take advantage of its speed and scalability.

7. References

Bace R. (2000), "Intrusion Detection", First Edition, Macmillan Technical Publishing, Indianapolis, USA: 25. Page 227 discusses the distinction between the security and monitoring policies.

Brancik K.C. (2008), "Insider Computer Fraud An in-depth Framework for Detecting and Defending Against Insider IT Attacks", Auerbach Publications, Taylor & Francis Group, ISBN 1-4200-4659-4.

Caelli W., Longley D. and Shain M. (1991), Information Security Handbook, Stockton Press.

Cappelli D., Moore A., Shimeall T.J., Trzeciak R. (2006). "Common Sense Guide to Prevention and Detection of Insider Threats", 2nd Edition Version 2.1, Carnegie Mellon University Cylab,http://www.cert.org/archive/pdf/CommonSenseInsiderThreatsV2.1-1-070118.pdf

Consel C. (2004), "From A Program Family To A Domain-Specific Language", in Lengauer, C.; Batory, D.; Consel, C.; Odersky, M. (Eds.), Domain-Specific Program Generation, LNCS 3016, Springer-Verlag, pp. 19-29.

Codd E. (1990), "The Relational Model for Database Management", Addison-Wesley Publishing Company, 1990, ISBN 0-201-14192-2.

Feiertag R., Kahn C., Porras P., Schnackenberg D., Staniford-Chen S., Tung B. (1999), "A Common Intrusion Specification Language (CISL)", June 1999 revision, URL: http://gost.isi.edu/cidf/drafts/language.txt

Goldberg K. (2009), "XML: Learn XML the Quick and Easy Way", Second Edition, Peachpit Press, ISBN-13:978-0-321-55967-88, pp. 5-6 explain the rules of well formed XML.

ISO/IEC 9075(1-4,9-11,13,14) (2008) Information Technology-- Database Languages – SQL:, http://www.iso.org/iso/iso_catalogue/catalogue_tc/catalogue_detail.htm?csnumber=45498

Kleppe A. (2009), "Software Language Engineering – Creating Domain Specific Languages Using Metamodels", Addison-Wesley/Pearson Education, ISBN: 978-0321553454.

Magklaras G. (2011), "An Insider Misuse Threat Detection and Prediction Language", PhD Thesis, School of Computing and Mathematics, University of Plymouth, UK: Chapter 6 (pp. 113- 201) describes the ITPSL Language in detail. Chapters 7 and 8 (pp. 202-265) discuss the implementation of the language http://folk.uio.no/georgios/MagklarasPhDThesisv3.pdf

Magklaras G., Furnell S. (2005), "A Preliminary Model of End User Sophistication for Insider Threat Prediction in IT Systems", Computers & Security, Volume 24, Issue 5, August 2005, pp. 371-380.

Magklaras G., Furnell S., and Papadaki M. (2011), "LUARM: An Audit Engine for Insider Misuse Detection", International Journal of Digital Crime and Forensics, (IJDCF), pp. 37-49.

NSTISSAM. (1999), "The Insider Threat To US Government Information Systems", NSTISSAM INFOSEC /1-99, U.S. National Security Telecommunications And Information Systems Security Committee, http://www.cnss.gov/Assets/pdf/nstissam_infosec_1-99.pdf

Pfleeger C., Pfleeger S. (2003), "Security in Computing", 3rd edition, Prentice Hall, Englewood Cliffs, NJ, 1. ISBN:0130355488: Page 6 contains the definition of the term "threat" in an information security context.

Phyo A., Furnell S. (2003), "Data Gathering for Insider Misuse Monitoring", Proceedings of the 2nd European Conference on Information Warfare and Security, Reading, UK, 30 June - 1 July, pp247-254.

Probst C., Hunker J., Bishop M., Gollman D. (2009), "Countering Insider Threats", ENISA Quarterly Review Vol. 5, No. 2, June 2009, pp. 13-14.

PwC (2010), "INFORMATION SECURITY BREACHES SURVEY 2010 | technical report", http://www.pwc.co.uk/eng/publications/isbs_survey_2010.html

Richardson R. (2010), "15th Annual 2010/2011 Computer Crime And Security Survey", http://gocsi.com/2010_survey_purchase

Spinellis D. (2001), "Notable design patterns for domain-specific languages", The Journal of Systems and Software Volume 56, Issue 1 (2001), pp. 91-99.

Strandell T. (2010), "Open Source Database Systems: Systems Study, Performance and Scalability", VDM Verlag Dr. Müller, ISBN: 978-3639093506.

White J., Hill J.H., Tambe S., Gokhale A., Schmidt D.C. (2009), "Improving domain- specific language reuse with software product line techniques", IEEE Software Vol. 26, No. 4, pp.47–53.

Zawodny J. (2009), "NoSQL: Distributed and Scalable Non-Relational Database Systems", Linux Magazine web portal, http://www.linux-mag.com/id/7579/

How the Certified Information Systems Security Professional Certification Supports Digital Forensic Processes

S.Rule, A.Stander and J.Ophoff

Department of Information Systems, University of Cape Town
e-mail: Samantha.Rule@uct.ac.za

Abstract

This paper explores whether a relationship exists between the Certified Information Systems Security Professional (CISSP) certification and digital forensics. The key findings show that the CISSP Common Body of Knowledge (CBK) covers a wide spectrum of information security practices, processes, and procedures and that the CISSP certification can provide a basic introduction to digital forensic processes and concepts from an incident response perspective. However, the CISSP certification does not bestow an in depth knowledge of digital forensic processes upon those who attain this certification. The CISSP CBK therefore does not support digital forensic processes beyond providing a basic understanding of what digital forensics is and the general concepts found within the digital forensic realm.

Keywords

Digital Forensics, Certified Information Systems Security Professional

1. Introduction

It is often thought that an individual with Certified Information Systems Security Professional (CISSP) Information Security certification does not need additional specialised skills to handle digital forensic incidents. Very little research exist to show if this viewpoint is correct and with the increase of cybercrime in recent years, it is important to know if organisations are adequately equipped to handle incidents of this nature.

This paper shows how the Certified Information Systems Security Professional (CISSP) Information Security certification supports digital forensic processes, with a particular interest in incident response from both an information security perspective as well as from a digital forensic readiness perspective.

The following sections provide some background on the CISSP certification, as well as the digital forensic concepts under investigation.

2. The CISSP Common Body of Knowledge

According to Tittel and Stewart (2003) the very essence of the CISSP is contained in the Common Body of Knowledge (CBK) which divides the field of information security into ten distinct domains. The CBK forms the basis for the (ISC)² education and certification programs and is regularly updated to ensure that it stays abreast of the fast pace of changing technologies and the ever growing number of creative ways that alleged criminals find to circumvent security controls (Harris, 2008).

The CISSP focuses on generally accepted concepts, techniques and approaches to designing, implementing and maintaining strong effective information security. Less focus is given to the details involved in creating security policies, practices, and procedures. This means that although the CISSP certification can equip an information security specialist to understand digital forensic concepts and processes, it does not necessarily make the information security specialist a digital forensic expert.

The following subsections review the CBK domains relevant to digital forensic processes.

2.1. Legal regulations, compliance, and investigations

This domain (formally known as law, investigations and ethics) covers general computer crime legislation, regulations and investigative measures and techniques used to determine if an incident has occurred as well as the gathering, analysis and management of evidence if it exists. Tittel and Stewart (2003) assert that individuals wishing to obtain the CISSP credential should ensure that they are familiar with relevant cybercrime laws and regulations as well as the proper investigative techniques to gather evidence and incident handling.

2.2. Telecommunications and network security

In this domain the transmission methods, transport format and security measures used to provide confidentiality, integrity, availability and authentication for transmission over private and public networks and media is discussed. According to Tittel and Stewart (2003) CISSP candidates should understand and be able to perform security reviews of email systems, telephony communications, as well as network attacks and counter measures.

2.3. Information security and risk management

Information security management establishes the foundation for a broad and all-inclusive security program to ensure the protection of an organisation's information assets. Information security management communicates the risks accepted by the organisation due to the currently implemented security controls and continually works to cost effectively enhance the controls to minimise the risk to the organisation. Risk management involves being able to perform data classification and risk assessments which will classify the organisation's assets, identity the threats and rate the vulnerabilities so that the necessary controls can be implemented (Bell, 2010).

2.4. Access control

It is important to be able to identify, authenticate, authorise, and monitor who or what is accessing the assets of the organisation, as this is vital information required to protect the assets from vulnerabilities and threats. According to Tittel and Stewart (2003) CISSP candidates need to understand how to plan, design and implement numerous authentication and access control systems. They also need to be able to monitor and audit the efficiency of the controls implemented.

2.5. Physical security

Physical security incorporates the security from the outside perimeter of a facility to the inside office space, including all information security systems (Bell, 2010). CISSP candidates need to understand and be familiar with the concepts affecting physical security as well as the possible security threats. This includes threat prevention and detection and being able to respond to these alerts or alarms (Tittel and Stewart, 2003).

2.6. Operations security

The security principal of availability is the core goal for operations security. Operations security is used to identify the controls placed on hardware, media, and the people who administer and have privilege access to any of the resources. Monitoring and auditing are the mechanisms used to identify any security events and report the information to the appropriate individual, group of individuals or system (Bell, 2010).

3. Incident Response

It is important for organisations to be prepared for security incidents that could take place due to the sharp rise in cybercrime. According to Tipton and Henry (2007) incident response or incident handling has become a primary function of today's information security professionals. Mandia (2003) describes incident response as a multifaceted discipline as it requires resources from various operational units found within an organisation such as human resources, technical experts, security professionals, business managers, legal advisors and end users. Any of these individuals could find themselves involved with responding to a security incident.

Many organisations establish a team of individuals who have special expertise, referred to as a Computer Security Incident Response Team (CSIRT). The CSIRT steps into action and immediately responds when a security incident occurs. A security incident can be defined as any negative event that takes place, during which some aspect of computer security has been threatened or compromised, where there is a loss of data confidentiality, a disruption of data or system integrity, or a disruption to (or denial of) data or system availability (Grance et al., 2008).

CISSP candidates must be familiar with the following set of procedures for incident response.

3.1. Triage

The term triage refers to the sorting, categorising and prioritising when an incident occurs. Triage encompasses the detection, identification and notification sub-phases. In triage incident handlers need to take in all the information available, investigate its severity and then set priorities on how to deal with the incident.

3.2. Reaction

According to Harris (2008) this includes the following phases of incident response. In the containment phase the damage must be mitigated and once the incident has been contained, an analysis of what took place during the incident must be conducted. Next, in the analysis phase, more data is gathered to understand how the incident took place. Finally, in the tracking phase, the source of the incident is identified, if the incident was internal or external, and how the source of the incident was accessed.

3.3. Follow-up

Once the incident is understood, the next stage is the follow up stage which is where the necessary fix is implemented to prevent this type of incident from occurring again in the future (Harris, 2008).

4. Digital Forensic Readiness

A digital forensic investigation is a process to determine and relate extracted information and digital evidence to produce accurate information for review by a court of law. The digital forensic investigation procedures developed by traditional forensic scientists focused on the procedures in handling evidence, while the procedures developed by the technologists focused on the technical details in capturing evidence. Many digital forensic investigators have chosen to follow the technical procedures and forget about the purpose and core concept of a digital forensic investigation. For this reason, legal practitioners sometimes have difficulty in understanding the processes and tasks involved in digital investigations (Ieong, 2006).

An important concept following on from forensic investigation is digital forensic readiness. This is defined as the ability of an organisation to maximise the use and collection of digital evidence while minimising the costs of a forensic incident investigation (Rowlingson, 2004). Digital forensic readiness equips an organisation with processes and procedures to follow when a digital forensic incident has occurred. The goal of these steps is to ensure that the operations and infrastructure are able to fully support an investigation (Carrier and Spafford, 2003).

According to Rowlingson (2004) a framework for digital forensic readiness should contain the following ten steps:

1. Identify the various business scenarios and processes where there is digital evidence, and reduce the impact of any digital crime.

2. Identify the types of digital evidence and their sources, and to know and understand what evidence is available across all the systems and applications used by the organisation.
3. Produce an evidence requirement statement so that those responsible for managing the business risk can communicate with those running and monitoring the information systems through an agreed requirement for evidence.
4. Ensure that any evidence collected is preserved as an authentic record.
5. Secure evidence for a longer period; off-line storage of data may be required for evidence at a later date. Digital evidence must at all times, be secure and tamper-proof.
6. Understand and document what processes or events must be monitored and audited in order to detect incidents before they take place.
7. Know how and when to react to a formal investigation.
8. Ensure that forensic awareness training is developed and provided for the organisation's employees.
9. Produce a policy that describes how an evidence case should be assembled.
10. Have legal advisors review the case file from a legal standpoint.

The following section will examine the research results of how the CISSP certification supports digital forensic processes.

5. Research Data

The sample group selected for the research comprised members of the Information Security Group Africa and members of the Special Interest Groups for Forensics and eCrime. This particular sample was selected as information security, and in particular digital forensics, is a highly specialised field. All of the respondents were individually contacted about participation in the research. An Likert-style electronic survey questionnaire was sent to 25 respondents, from which 16 completed responses were received.

The 16 respondents hold various professional certifications: 11 respondents currently hold the CISSP credential from (ISC)², while 10 respondents hold certifications that were not listed. Two of the respondents hold digital forensic specific qualifications, the GIAC Certified Forensic Analyst, the Certified Forensic Examiner and the vendor specific certification, the AccessData certified Examiner.

The research was aimed at information security professionals and digital forensic investigators in order to establish whether CISSP certified information security professionals are able to assist digital forensic practitioners. As of 2009 (ISC)² had certified 66,000 individuals globally and it could be of great value to the digital forensic discipline to be able to leverage and make use of these individuals.

The main limitation that was observed was the small number of information security professionals who either work in digital forensics or are CISSP certified. With only 16 responses and the limitation of focusing on a small geographical location (South Africa) the findings may be insignificant as there are a much smaller group of CISSPs and digital forensic investigators located in South Africa versus globally.

Despite these limitations it is believed that the overall research findings are still relevant.

The following subsections analyse the data collected by the research. The analysis is grouped according to the research questions.

5.1. Research question 1: Does the CISSP support digital forensics?

Respondents had to rate how relevant each domain of the CISSP was to digital forensics. The following domains were rated most relevant, in descending order: Legal regulations, compliance and investigations (87.5%); Telecommunications and network security (81%); Access controls (75%).

Legal Regulations compliance and Investigations was rated as either relevant or very relevant by 87.5% (14 out of 16) of respondents. A further 64% of these respondents currently hold the CISSP certification. Comments provided by respondents in support of their answer showed that the reasons for selecting relevant or very relevant included, "The legal/law domain is just as important an area of the forensic environment. The content is however not purposefully supportive of digital forensics; but does interact with various sections as mentioned above".

The domain "telecommunications and network security" was rated either relevant or very relevant by 81% (13 out of 16) of the respondents, a further 70% of these respondents currently hold the CISSP credential. 75% (12 out of 16) of the respondents rated "Access controls" as either relevant or very relevant, a further 75% of these respondents hold the CISSP credential.

The following domains were rated least relevant, in descending order: Business Continuity, compliance and investigations (56%); Security Architecture and design (31%).

Business continuity compliance and investigations was rated as the least relevant to digital forensics by 56% (9 out of 16) of the respondents. 75% of these respondents currently hold the CISSP certification. 31% (5 out of 16) of the respondents rated security architecture and design as having some relevance, for how it relates to digital forensics. All of these respondents are CISSP certified.

Does being CISSP certified enable an individual to be able to conduct a digital forensic investigation? 62% (10 out of 16) of respondents disagreed or disagreed strongly that the CISSP certification enabled an individual to conduct a digital forensic Investigation. 60% of the 10 respondents who either disagreed or strongly disagreed currently hold the CISSP certification. Some comments provided by respondents in support of their answer included: "There is very little forensic information in the CBK"; "CISSP CBK covers a wide range of topics with very little depth"; "With a CISSP being a more theoretical accreditation, it would in my eyes not provide much benefit to digital forensic investigations on all levels".

Does the CISSP CBK give an individual sufficient knowledge on incident response? 50% (8 out of 16) respondents were undecided whether the CISSP CBK gave an individual sufficient knowledge on incident response. 62.5% of these 8 respondents currently hold the CISSP certification. One of the comments provided by a respondent to explain the reason for being undecided stated that "the mile wide aspect allows an individual to know a little about most aspects but specialists are required to assist and provide the depth of understanding needed to complete a forensic plan." This echoed the sentiments of most of the respondents who were undecided, citing that the CISSP allowed for a general overview rather than for in depth knowledge.

Does the CISSP certification enable individuals to draft information security policies? 50% (8 out of 16) respondents were undecided about whether or not the CISSP certification enabled individuals to draft security policies. 71% of 7 respondents who currently hold the CISSP credential agreed that the CISSP certification enabled individuals to draft information security policies. Comments provided by the respondents in support of their answer showed the following reasons for agreeing; "it's an excellent management level IS security certification and "the CISSP definitely provides one with a good basic understanding of the underlying principles of security fundamentals, processes, risk assessments".

If you hold a CISSP certification, how do you rate the content covered in the CBK for digital forensics? Taking into account that 50% of the respondents currently hold the CISSP certification, 25% of the respondents indicated that it was covered while 75% of the respondents indicated that there was some coverage of digital forensics in the CISSP CBK. Some comments provided by the respondents include: "The material covers that focus too lightly"; "There is very little forensic information in the CBK"; "Although I do not have a CISSP, I am very familiar with the CBK for it, as while it is an excellent management level IS security certification; it does not address Digital Forensics at anything other than a superficial level in the investigation and legal domain".

Reviewing these comments, it is possible to deduce that these respondents believe that the CISSP CBK does not contain enough information about digital forensics for an individual to be able to conduct a digital investigation.

5.2. Research question 2: To what extent does the CISSP support digital forensic readiness?

The following three questions relating to forensic readiness were asked in the electronic questionnaire.

Is incident response and forensic readiness the same? 56% (9 out of 16) respondents disagree that incident response and forensic readiness is the same. A further 78% of the 9 respondents that disagreed currently hold the CISSP certification. One respondent commented that, "I do believe that it (the CISSP) may be useful in devising a response plan for forensic readiness."

Should organisations include forensic readiness in their information security policies? 81% (13 out of 16) of the respondents agreed or agreed strongly that organisations should include forensic readiness in their information security policies.

62% of the 8 respondents who agreed and agreed strongly currently hold the CISSP credential. One of the respondent's comments stated that, "the CISSP holder will have a thorough understanding of security architectures and where evidence might reside within a particular network."

Does having an incident response plan enable an organisation to be forensic ready? 50% (8 out of 16) of the respondents disagreed or disagreed strongly that having an incident response plan enabled an organisation to be forensic ready. 62% of the 8 respondents that disagreed or disagreed strongly currently hold CISSP credentials.

Analysing the responses from the questionnaire, it can be noted that the CISSP does support digital forensic readiness, but not to the full extent that is required for an organisation to be forensic ready.

5.3. Research question 3: Is there a relationship between security incident response, which a CISSP would investigate, and digital forensic readiness?

The following three questions relating to incident response were asked in the electronic questionnaire.

Should the CSIRT be able to conduct a digital forensic investigation? 50% (8 out of 16) of the respondents agreed or agreed strongly that it is important for the CSIRT to be able to conduct a digital forensic investigation and 87.5% of the 8 of the respondents currently hold the CISSP credential. Comments provided by respondents in support of their answers showed that the reasons for agreeing or agreeing strongly included; "CISSP provides the basic knowledge to conduct an investigation but depending on the nature of the incident and the responder's knowledge and qualifications, a certified Forensic Investigator could be required."

Should law enforcement be contacted when a security incident takes place? 44% (7 out of 16) respondents were undecided whether to contact law enforcement when a security incident takes place. 62.5% of these 7 respondents currently hold the CISSP certification. 44% (7 out of 16) respondents agreed and agreed strongly that law enforcement should be contacted when a security incident takes place. 71% of the 7 respondents that agreed and strongly agreed currently hold the CISSP certification.

Should forensic investigations only be conducted by specialists and trained individuals? 94% (15 out of 16) of the respondents agreed or agreed strongly that forensic investigations should only be conducted by specialists and trained individuals. 67% of the 15 respondents that agreed or agreed strongly currently hold the CISSP credential.

Comments provided by respondents in support of their answers included, "having a certification (CISSP) does assist an individual with being able to do an investigation but at the end of the day real experience and other related courses/certifications specific to Digital Forensics are much more important". This echoed the sentiments of most of the respondents who agreed or strongly agreed, mentioning that the

CISSP allowed for a general overview rather than for in depth knowledge of performing forensic investigations.

5.4. Research question 4: Are there information security principles or processes that support digital forensic readiness?

The following three questions relating to the importance of incident response and forensic readiness for an organisation were asked in the electronic questionnaire.

Is it important to conduct user awareness for incident response and forensic readiness? 81% (13 out of 16) of the respondents answered that it was important or extremely important to conduct user awareness training for incident response and forensic readiness. 69% of the 13 respondents believing it is important or extremely important currently hold the CISSP credential.

How do you rate the importance of a Computer Security Incident Response Team for an organisation? 87.5% (14 out of 16) of the respondents believe that it is important or extremely important that an organisation has a CSIRT. 78.5% of the 14 respondents agreeing that it was important or extremely important to an organisation to have a CSIRT currently hold the CISSP certification.

How important is it for an organisation to have an incident response plan? 100% of the respondents answered that it is extremely important or important that an organisation has an incident response plan. 62.5% 10 of the respondents answered that it is extremely important with 90% of the 10 respondents holding a CISSP certification. The remaining 37.5% (6 out of 16) respondents answered that it was important for an organisation to have an incident response plan. 33% of 6 respondents hold a CISSP certification.

Reviewing the analysis of the data and the respondents' comments, it can be deduced that there are information security principals or processes that support digital forensic readiness.

By its very nature, digital forensics is a reactive process as it responds to an event that has already occurred. Information security on the other hand is a proactive process, placing controls and preventative measures in a bid to prevent security incidents from occurring in the first place.

The main research question attempted to determine how the CISSP certification supports digital forensics. It emerged from the literature and the data analysis that the CISSP CBK broadly covers information security at a high level and is more theoretical than practical. The CBK also gives the information security professional a general introduction to digital forensic investigations especially in the areas of evidence collection and the chain of custody. However, the CISSP CBK does not equip an information security professional with the skills required to be able to perform a digital forensic investigation that will stand up to legal scrutiny. The following quote from one of the respondents succinctly states the current situation: "It will help, but is not necessarily enough knowledge".

6. References

Bell, L., (2010), CISSP Fast Track Certified Information Systems Security Professional, http://www.alctraining.com.au/pdf/cip.pdf (Accessed 22 September 2010)

Carrier, B. and Spafford, E. (2003), Getting physical with the digital investigation process, http://citeseerx.ist.psu.edu/viewdoc/download?doi=10.1.1.76.757&rep=rep1&type=pdf (Accessed 28 August 2010)

Grance, T., Kent, K. and Kim, B., (2008), Computer security incident handling guide. Retrieved August 24, 2010 from http://csrc.nist.gov/publications/nistpubs/800-61-rev1/SP800-61rev1.pdf

Hancock, B. (2000), Truly certified: Security certifications update, *Computers & Security*, 19(6), pp. 479-480

Harris,S. (2008), *CISSP All-In-One Exam Guide (4e)*, McGraw-Hill, New York

Ieong, R. (2006), FORZA – Digital Forensics investigation framework that incorporate legal issues, *Digital Investigation*, 3(1), pp. 29-36.

Mandia, K., Prosise, C. and Pepe, M. (2003), *Incident response and computer forensics (2e)*, McGraw-Hill/Osborne, California

Rowlingson, R. (2004), A Ten Step Process for Forensic Readiness, *International Journal of Digital Evidence*, 2, pp. 1-28

Tipton, H.F., Henry, K. (2007). *Official (ISC)² Guide to the CISSP CBK* Boca Raton, Florida: Auerbach Publications

Tittel, E., & Stewart, J. M. (2003). Dissecting the CISSP exam. *Certification Magazine*, 5(2), SG11-SG13.

An Access Control Framework for Protecting Mobile Health Records: The Case Study of Developing Countries

R.Ssembatya

Department of Computer Science, University of Cape Town, South Africa
e-mail: richard.ssembatya@uct.ac.za

Abstract

Mobile health records are a good way of providing users with on-demand access to health care data. Standard approaches of securing health records include role-based access control (RBAC) because this is a flexible approach to assign permissions to a wide variety of users. However, traditional RBAC models are not designed to enforce fine-grained access control. For instance, in mobile health record systems, it is difficult to configure a policy that permits a patient to selectively share his/her personal records with healthcare workers. Therefore, defining policies that express application-level security requirements with respect to mobile records is challenging. In this paper, we present an RBAC inspired framework that provides fine-grained encryption for mobile health records where patient records have different access control policies. Our proposed framework ensures that the data can be made available securely offline. This approach can leverage systems where information needs to be shared securely under constraints of energy and/or Internet coverage.

Keywords

Role Based Access Control, Attribute-Based Encryption, Mobile Health Records

1. Introduction

Electronic health records (EHRs) are basically medical records in electronic format (Markle Foundation, 2004; department of health and human services, 2006). EHRs can exist on a variety of computing devices and can be accessed online via Internet technologies. The popularity of the Internet as a vehicle for communication has resulted in an increased drive to cut the costs of healthcare services by encouraging the use of EHRs. The new healthcare scenario has led to the provision of web services that support the distribution of healthcare information. The process by which healthcare information is shared can be depicted as shown in figure 1 below. The hospital server runs an access control program that verifies that the parties (health workers, insurance companies and other healthcare organization) accessing patient's records have appropriate permissions. When a user makes a request to access the records, access control authorities verify the request and determine the access rights. A user with appropriate permission(s) will be able to access the records.

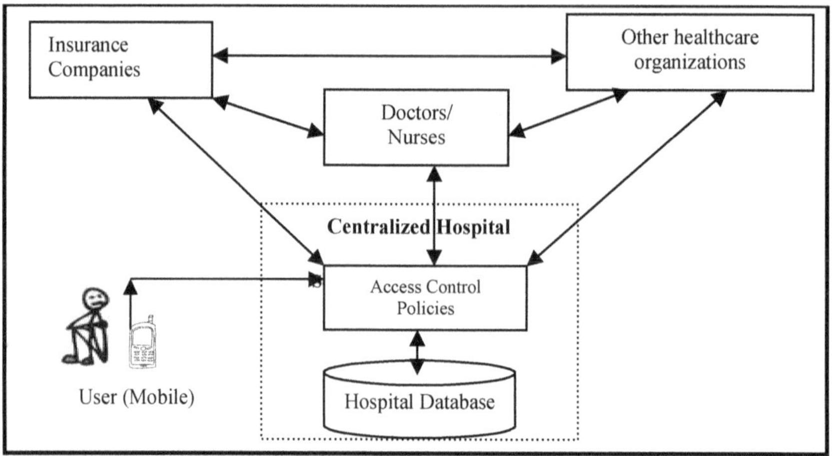

Figure 1: E-Health Scenario

Although a lot of work has been done in the design of Internet-based health care systems, little has been done on tailoring these systems to mobile devices yet, to date, mobile phones are one of the most widely used computing devices in the world.

Furthermore, mobile phones are increasingly becoming cheaper and affordable especially to the population in developing countries particularly in Africa. Given the fact that most parts of Africa are characterized by general poor infrastructure such as bad roads, poor transport systems, non-existent electricity in rural areas, lack of centralized services and frequent power outages in urban areas, mobile phones could provide a better alternative way to access EHRs. However, as in conventional Internet-based systems, mobile health records raise questions pertaining to security and privacy (Fisher and Madge, 1996). Users want the convenience of data access and availability but are also concerned about cases of unauthorized access (Annas, 2003; Li et al, 2005).

Securing and guaranteeing availability of mobile health records is a complex and difficult task to accomplish. One of the methods of guaranteeing privacy in E-health systems is via access control (Benaloh et al, 2009). Access control mechanisms are designed to secure data at the server to verify that patients' records are accessed by authorized users. In many cases, this has been a fairly effective approach. However, when the server fails or becomes unavailable for example due to power outages that is common in developing countries, access control decisions cannot be made, making EHRs unreachable. In addition, access control approaches such as traditional RBAC model are not designed to provide fine-grained access control. For instance, in mobile health record systems, it is difficult to configure a policy that permits a patient to selectively share personal records to healthcare workers. In addition, although there several XML-based standards such as Clinical Document Architecture (CDA) that calls for protecting EHRs, none of the standards provide enough guidelines for protecting and transporting EHRs (HL7 web site, 2011). Therefore, a mobile access control framework that protects and selectively shares EHRs using a mobile phone is a good way of ensuring secure and on-demand access to EHRs. The aim of the framework is to empower patients to grant access to specific potions of their data without the need for a single centralized server. As well, the proposed framework supports the availability of EHRs even when hospital servers are offline. This reduces the need to rely on server based access control authorizations for the provision of EHRs.

The rest of the paper is structured as follows. In Section 2, the background work on role-based access control schemes for enforcing security and privacy of mobile health data is presented. In Section 3, the proposed access control framework that is inspired by the concept of attribute-based encryption is introduced, followed by an example scenario in healthcare environment in section 4. Finally, in Section 5, conclusions are given and future work is discussed.

2. Related Work

In this section, a survey of related work that motivates this paper is discussed, first by providing an overview of the existing access control architecture for patient centered health record systems and then examine some of the techniques that investigate the problem of enforcing access control policies for selective sharing of EHRs.

Szolovits et al (1994) introduced the concept of patient centered health information systems that integrate personal health information across institutions. Szolovits's concept was extended by Simons et al, (2005) to build the PING architecture which enables a patient to maintain electronic copies of his/her records that are encrypted at a storage site of the patient's choice. The PING server handles encryption and performs the authentication as well as authorization of users. Similar to PING is Indivo (Mandl et al, 2007). Indivo is an online system that keeps patient's health data encrypted at the Indivo server. Access control decisions are mediated by the Indivo server according to institutional defined security policies. This approach violates the design goal described above, since the trusted Indivo server must be kept online in order to mediate access control decisions.

Gupta et al (2006) developed a criticality-aware access control model which regulates access control for pervasive applications. However, their model did not provide a fine grain control on when and who can exercise the extra privileges needed for an emergency situation. Ardagna et al (2010) extended the criticality-aware access control model (Gupta et al (2006)) to provide a break-the-glass model where policies are separated into different categories starting with access control policies, emergency policies and a break-the-glass policy. When a user requests an access, the system checks regular access control policies and if the request is denied, the system overrides the decision by break-the-glass policy. The drawback of this approach is that the override depends on a fixed decision procedure that does not consider reasons for denial. Literature also reveals other access control models based on purposes (Byun et al (2005) and Yang et al (2007)). However, according to Jin et al (2009), purpose based access control alone cannot meet all the patient's privacy protection requirements.

The Role based access control (RBAC) model is commonly used in E-health systems for securing access to EHRs (Sandhu et al, 2002; Eyers et al 2006). Solutions proposed by Becker and Sewell (2004), Bhatti et al (2006), Georgakakis et al (2011) and Eyers et al (2006) use RBAC mechanism to address organizational security management and provide meaningful access control decisions for EHR systems. However, none of them support selective sharing of EHRs and thus cannot support a more fine-grained access control.

Benaloh et al (2009) explored the challenges of preserving patient's privacy and advocated that security in EHR systems be enforced via encryption in addition to access control policies. They proposed hierarchical identity based encryption (HIBE) and searchable encryption to construct a privacy preserving EHR system. The system allows a patient to selectively share the records among doctors and healthcare providers without the need to rely on an online server for access control decisions. Selective sharing is based on hierarchical encryption. Patient's records are partitioned into hierarchical structure and each portion is encrypted with a corresponding key. Private sub keys are derived from root private key by the patient. The drawback of hierarchical based encryption is the limitation of flexibility in the access structure that is, it does not allow more expressiveness in the access structure.

3. Access Control Framework

The framework utilizes the recent development of dual-policy attribute based encryption which combines ciphertext-policy attribute based encryption and Key-policy attribute based encryption to support more expressiveness in the access structure (Attrapadung and Imani 2009). Dual-policy attribute based encryption was built on the concept of attribute based encryption (ABE) introduced by Sahai and Waters (2005). In an ABE system, user's keys and ciphertexts are labeled with a set of descriptive attributes. A particular key can be used to decrypt a particular ciphertext only if there is a match between the attributes of the ciphertext and the user's key (Goyal et al, 2006; Bethencourt et al, 2007; Waters, 2008). ABE system enables an access control mechanism over encrypted data by specifying access policies among private keys and ciphertexts. ABE is typically described in two flavors; ciphertext-policy ABE and key-policy ABE. In ciphertext-policy ABE, each ciphertext is bound together with a policy describing who is entitled to decrypt it (Bethencourt et al, 2007). The user's private key will be associated with an arbitrary number of attributes expressed as strings. In the proposed framework, when the hospital data clerk enters records for encryption, he also specifies an associated access structure over attributes. A user will only be able to decrypt a ciphertext if that user's attributes pass through the ciphertext's access structure. The roles of the users in the healthcare organization are defined by the user attributes, which in turn specify the permissions that the user can be assigned. Users with a given role can access the records using role key.

The second flavor of ABE is key-policy ABE (Goyal et al, 2006; Sahai and Waters, 2005). With key-policy ABE, individual patient records are tagged with XML specific attributes and access to these records are granted by generating private keys that are embedded with access policies determining which records may be accessed. In the proposed framework, key-policy system provides keys to temporary users such as researchers that have limited access to EHRs database. Individual keys then specify a particular policy defining which records the key can access.

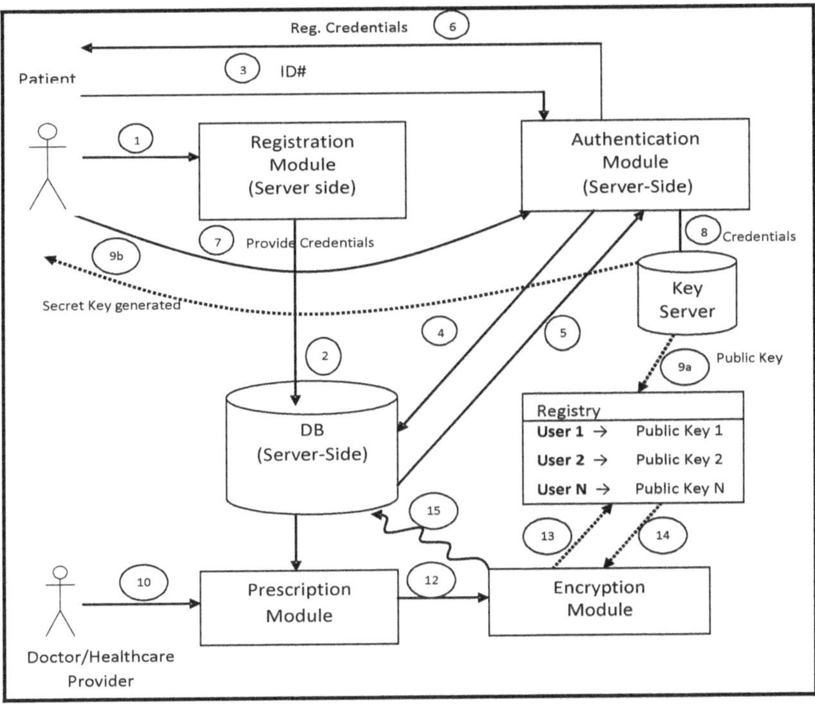

Figure 2: An Access Control Framework

Figure 2 above provides an overview of the components of the framework. When the record is created, the prescription module parses the record into an XML hierarchical structure where sensitive parts are selected for encryption under a policy that is appropriate for the record. The marked parts can then be encrypted using ciphertext-policy ABE (where the role of the parties is taken by the attributes and the access structure contains authorized sets of attributes) or key-policy ABE scheme under a set of attributes such as patient age, date of birth or any other non sensitive attributes that are related to the record. Once the records have been encrypted, it can be stored at the hospital server (Figure 2 (2)) and can also be exported to a patient's mobile phone.

The provider can continue accessing the locally stored records using the existing access control of the records. However, anyone without an appropriate ABE private key that satisfies the policy will not be able to decrypt the records.

A trusted master controller (key server Figure 2 (8)) manages ABE decryption keys and RSA public and private keys. The RSA public and private key pair enables patients to securely download and receive key updates. The keys are manually delivered onto patient's mobile phones (e.g. through the use of a USB) in order to prevent the most likely online attacks. This narrows the attack model of the key server to attackers who have only physical access. Both individual hospital employees and the patients obtain their ABE decryption keys from an offline key server. The patients can view their records by using a mobile health application browser to access the records. The application should access appropriate hospital server storage to download the ciphertext-policy ABE encrypted records. The encrypted records can then be stored on the patient's mobile phone for portability.

To prevent malicious users from accessing the key on the mobile phone, a random passphrase provided by the user will be used to encrypt the key on the patient's mobile phone using SQL Cipher encryption scheme (Android web site, 2011). The scheme is an SQLite extension in Android that provides transparent 256-bit AES encryption on a mobile phone (Android web site, 2011). "The data protected by this type of encryption and stored by Android apps is less vulnerable to access by malicious apps, protected in case of device loss or theft, and highly resistant to mobile data forensics tools that are increasingly used to mass copy a mobile device during routine traffic stops" (Android web site, 2011).

3.1. Key Revocation

User revocation is an important yet difficult issue in E-health systems. One major limitation in dealing with revocation of users in any system is that access to data that users have already seen cannot be revoked. Luan et al (2009) proposed an architecture that deploys an online mediator for every decryption such that revoked users cannot be authenticated. The drawback of this architecture is that the mediator must be kept online in order for users to decrypt thus violates the main design goal of this study. The proposed framework enforce revocation by associating user's secret key with an expiration date say Y. Records are encrypted on some date Z such that users can decrypt only if Y>=Z. The access privilege of users will be automatically revoked after the expiration date. To enable earlier revocation of users, we adopt (Yu et al (2008)) architecture that supports revocation by broadcasting an update message to update CP-ABE public and private keys. The hospital administrator simply encrypt the patient's new ABE key with the patient's RSA public key and make them available in a key chain for downloads.

3.2. Granting Access

Authorized hospital employees and patients obtain their keys from the hospital's ABE master controller (key server). In the proposed framework, two types of keys can be generated; a ciphertext-policy key or role key; each key corresponds to user roles and is embedded with fixed attributes that are related to the user. For example, patient age/name, user type (doctor, Lab technologist, patient, counselor), department and key expiration date.

3.3. Access Policy

The access policy of the framework consist of monotone Boolean formula that use only logical 'and' and logical 'or' gates referencing a list of attributes that are embedded into user's private key. For instance, given the attributes Doctor, Nurse, and health centre 3 (HC3), the hospital may specify a policy to allow a record to be read by a Doctor or Nurse or a consultant with ID = CID005, all attached to HC3.

$$((\text{Doctor} \vee \text{Nurse}) \wedge \text{HC3}) \vee \text{ID: CID005})$$

The ciphertext-policy and the key-policy ABE approaches can be combined into a single scheme referred to as dual-policy ABE scheme (Attrapadung and Imani, 2009). The scheme enables multiple users to access similar/the same medical record provided the users satisfy the authorization constraints. Our framework combines the two approaches. The encryptor (hospital administrator/data clerk) associate the record simultaneously with both a set of attributes that annotate the record itself and an access policy that states the type of users that will be able to decrypt the record. Similarly, a user is given a private key assigned simultaneously for both a set of attributes that annotate user's credentials and an access policy that states the type of record the user can decrypt.

4. Example Scenario

Consider the case of a hospital where Grace is a data clerk and John a patient. When Grace submits a new or modified record for storage at the hospital server, the record is parsed into an XML structure where sensitive parts are selected for encryption by encryption module under an appropriate role based access policy. Users (Patients and healthcare workers) whose attributes satisfy the access policy are able to decrypt the records with their secret attribute keys. The policies are initially specified by the hospital in order for the system administrator to make meaningful access control decisions. The encrypted records are then transferred to the hospital's own server for storage and can also be exported to a patient's mobile phone to facilitate offline access.

John (patient) presents the appropriate credentials to the hospital. Since some nations in developing countries do not have national IDs, John's credentials may be *(e.g. Passport, driving permit, National social security card (NSSF) e.t.c.)* for proper authentication. After John has been authenticated, the hospital ABE master controller (key server) generates John's ABE private key and subsequently send it to John's mobile phone. John then uses the mobile health application browser to interface with the hospital server and download the ciphertext-policy ABE encrypted records as shown in Figure 3.

The hospital server supports only read access to the encrypted individual health records and the encrypted records can be exported on John's mobile phone for portability. In order to enable offline access, John uses ABE private keys stored on the mobile phone to decrypt the records. John may decide to share encrypted records using Bluetooth technologies or decrypt the records and share them with a physician through the exchange of mobile devices. We recognize this as a limitation and an open problem for future research.

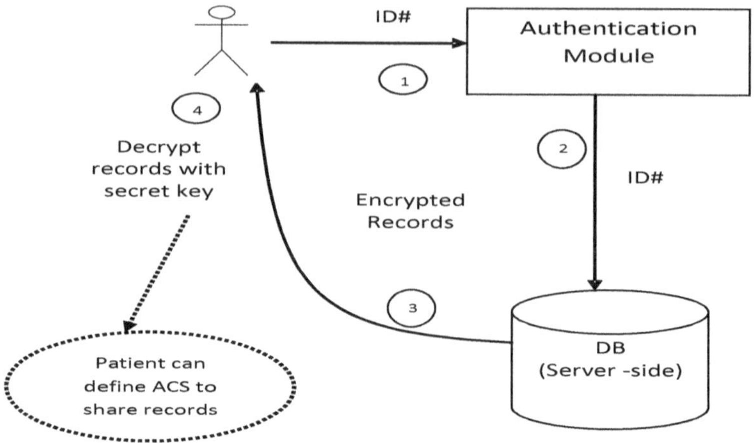

Figure 3: Patient Downloads the Records

5. Conclusion and Future Work

Controlling access to EHRs is a key requirement of mobile health systems. Access control models such as RBAC can be used to authorize access to various healthcare resources. However, RBAC is not equipped to support selective sharing of composite EHRs and so cannot support fine-grained access control. Additionally, when hospital servers are unavailable, access control decisions cannot be made, making EHRs unreachable. In this paper, an access control framework that makes use of Attribute Based Encryption (ABE) is proposed. ABE is used to provide fine-grained based encryption restricting access of EHRs. Furthermore, it provides an access control mechanism over encrypted data by specifying access policies among private keys and ciphertexts.

In order to assess the usability and practical importance of our framework, a system implementation appears an interesting future work.

6. References

Android Web Site (2011). http://giv.to/cP9Lnu. (Accesses 4th June 2011).

Annas, G. J. (2003), "HIPAA Regulation - A New Era of Medical Record Privacy", *The New England Journal of Medicine* 348:1486-1490.

Ardagna, C., Vimercati, S., Foresti, S., Grandison, T., Jajodia, S. and Samarati, P. (2010), "Access control for smarter healthcare using policy spaces", *Computers & Security* Vol. 29, pp. 848-858, 2010.

Attrapadung, N. and Imani, H. (2009), "Dual-Policy Attribute Based Encryption", *in Proc. ACNS,* 2009, pp.168-185.

Becker, M. Y. and Sewell, P. (2004), "Cassandra: Flexible trust management applied to electronic health records", *In Proc. of IEEE 17th Computer Security Foundations Workshop*, pages 139–154.

Benaloh, J., Chase, M., Horvitz, E. and Lauter, K. (2009), "Patient controlled encryption: Ensuring privacy in medical health records", *In ACM CCSW* 2009.

Bethencourt, J., Sahai, A. and Waters, B. (2007), "Ciphertext-policy attribute-based encryption", *In Proceedings of the 2007 IEEE Symposium on Security and Privacy*, pages 321-334. IEEE Computer Society.

Bhatti, R., Moidu, K. and Ghafoor, A. (2006), "Policy based security management for federated healthcare databases (or RHIOs)", *In Proc. of the international workshop on Healthcare information and knowledge management*, pages 41–48.

Byun, J. W., Bertino, E. and Li, N. (2005), "Purpose based access control of complex data for privacy protection", *In Proc. of 10th ACM symposium on Access control models and technologies (SACMAT)*, pages 102–110.

Eyers, D. M., Bacon, J. and Moody, K. (2006), "OASIS role-based access control for electronic health records", *In IEEE Proceedings*, pages 16–23.

Fisher, F. and Madge, B. (1996), "Data Security and Patient Confidentiality: The Manager's Role", *The International Journal of Bio-Medical Computing*.

Georgakakis, E., Nikolidakis, S. A., Vergados, D. D. and Douligeris, C. (2011) "Spatio temporal emergency role based access control (STEM-RBAC): A time and location aware role based access control model with a break the glass mechanism" *ISCC* 2011, pp. 764-770

Goyal, V., Pandey, O., Sahai, A. and Waters, B. (2006), "Attribute-based encryption for fine-grained access control of encrypted data", *In Proceedings of the 13th ACM conference on Computer and communications security*, pages 89-98.

Gupta, S., Mukherjee, T. and Venkatasubramanian, K. (2006) "Criticality aware access control model for pervasive applications, *In Proceedings of 4th Annual IEEE International Conference on Pervasive Computing and Communications*, Pisa, Italy, 2006.

HL7 Web Site (2011). http://www.hl7.org/. (Accesses 24th March 2012).

Hu, J., Chen, H. and Hou, T. (2009), "A hybrid public key infrastructure solution (HPKI) for HIPAA privacy/security regulations", Computer Standards and Interfaces, 32 (5-6): 274–280.

Jin, J., Ahn, G. J., Hu, H., Covington, M. J. and Zhang, X. (2009), "Patient centric authorization framework for sharing electronic health records", *SACMAT'09*, June 3–5, 2009, Stresa, Italy

Li, M., Poovendran, R. and Narayanan, S. (2005), "Protecting Patient Privacy against Unauthorized Release of Medical Images in a Group Communication Environment", *Computerized Medical Imaging and Graphics*, 2005.

Luan, I., Milan, P., Svetla, N., Pieter, H. and Willem, J. (2009) "Mediated ciphertext-policy attribute-based encryption and its application", *In WISA*, 2009.

Mandl, K., Simons, W., Crawford, W and Abbett, J. (2007), "Indivo: a personally controlled health record for health information exchange and communication", BMC Medical Informatics and Decision Making, 7(1): 25.

Markle Foundation (2004), "Connecting for Health. Connecting Americans to their healthcare. Final report of the working group on policies for electronic information sharing between doctors and patients", New York: www.connectingforhealth.org/resources/final_phwg_report1.pdf. (Accessed 5th Nov 2011)

National Committee on Vital and Health Statistics Web site (2006). Personal health records and personal health record systems: A report and recommendations. Washington: Department of Health and Human Services. http://www.ncvhs.hhs.gov/0602nhiirpt.pdf. (Accessed 6th November 2011)

Sahai, A. and Waters, B. (2005), "Fuzzy identity-based encryption", *In Advances in Cryptology, EUROCRYPT*, pages 457-473, 2005.

Sandhu, R., Coyne, E., Feinstein, H. and Youman, C. (1996), "Role-based access control models", *IEEE Computer*, 29 (2):38-47, 1996.

Simons, W.W., Mandl, K. D. and Kohane, I. S. (2005), "The PING Personally Controlled Medical Record System", Technical architecture. *Journal of the American Medical Informatics Association.* 12(1):263-268.

Szolovits, P., Doyle, J., Long, W. J., Kohane, I. and Pauker, S. G. (1994), "Guardian angel: Patient-centered health information systems", Technical report, 1994.

Waters, B. (2008), "Ciphertext-policy attribute based encryption: An expressive, efficient, and provably secure realization", *Cryptology ePrint Archive*, Report 2008/290.

Yang, N., Barringer, H. and Zhang, N. (2007), "A purpose based access control model", *In Proc. of 3rd International Symposium on Information Assurance and Security (IAS)*, pages 143–148.

Yu, S., Ren, K. and Lou, W. (2008), "Attribute-Based Content Distribution with Hidden Policy", *In Proc. Of NPSEC'08*, Orlando, Florida, USA, 2008.

Chapter 3

Mobile and Wireless Networking

A Feasibility Study into Tracking Wi-Fi Enabled Mobile Devices

M.Dagnall[1] and N.L.Clarke[1,2]

[1]Centre for Security, Communications and Network Research, Plymouth University, Plymouth, UK
[2]School of Computer & Security Science, Edith Cowan University, Australia
e-mail: info@cscan.org

Abstract

Modern mobile and portable devices such as laptops and smart phones are expensive technologies that are often the target of theft. In the event that they are lost or stolen, it is desirable to recover them and their contents if possible. Whilst existing tracker technologies can often provide a rough geo-location, they lack in providing resolution in the last few hundred meters. This research focuses on the development of a mobile system for locating WiFi enabled portable devices via the WiFi signal emanating from them. A mobile localisation system utilising a combination of a directional Yagi antenna and the received signal strength was developed and shown to be effective at locating WiFi sources at ranges from 45m to 500m away depending on the environment.

Keywords

Mobile, WiFi, Tracking, Localisation, Yagi Antenna, 802.11g, Directional, WLAN

1. Introduction and Background

WiFi enabled portable devices such as smart phones and laptops are regularly targeted by thieves or misplaced by their users with 850,000 mobile phones stolen across the UK in 2007 (Flatley, et al, 2009). In the event of theft of loss, recovery is desirable either to recover the device or its contents. The physical value can be in the region of hundreds or thousands of pounds but its contents such as confidential, commercial or classified information in some cases could far exceed the physical value of the device. During a recent study of major European organisations, the financial loss resulting from a missing laptop averaged €35,000, with the total impact totalling €1.29 billion (Ponemon Institute, 2011). Due to the items portable nature, once it has been stolen in could conceivably be secreted in numerous environments. There is therefore a justifiable need to track and locate WiFi enabled portable devices in the event that they are stolen.

Current solutions employed in the tracking location of lost or stolen devices typically employ a combination of some of the following technologies:

- GSM – The mobile cell can be used to locate the portable device
- GPS – The GPS coordinates can be broadcast by a GSM module
- RF 173Mhz – Localisation via traditional wildlife tracking

GSM cell location cannot always be relied upon to provide sufficient resolution to recover the device on its own. Typically, GPS does not perform well inside buildings (Bakhru, 2005; Bajaj et al, 2002) and in the event that the GPS signal is lost an alternative method of locating the device is required. Even when these technologies do work, they frequently only provide an approximation of the location, rather than a specific location. Traditional RF tracking solutions (i.e. those used for tracking wildlife) can be employed, but this is with a cost penalty as this is additional functionality to be incorporated into the device. Therefore, alternative options need to be researched that are capable of providing a finer granularity of tracking capability for the last few hundred meters. Given the widespread adoption of 802.11 WiFi modules, this research seeks to establish whether this signal can be repurposed in order to locate the box instead of traditional RF methods.

There are existing applications of WiFi for localisation but these are principally focused on some form of triangulation which requires multiple receivers in order to do so. Generally the location of the receiver is known and so are the expected path losses. RADAR is an established tracking system based on RF for locating individuals or object in buildings. It relies on multiple access points with overlapping coverage in order to function. The combination of received signal strength measurement and signal propagation modelling facilitates location (Bahl & Padmanabhan, 2000). Due to the varied environments that mobile devices operate in signal propagation modelling is not viable. The tracking unit should be capable of being used for tracking in isolation so more established triangulation methods are not suitable.

In this paper, we focus on localising 802.11g signal sources using a directional antenna. Section 2 of this paper illustrates how the tracker was developed. The 3rd section summarises the results from a series of experiments with section 4 discussing the implications of the findings. The final section presents the conclusions.

2. Development of the WiFi Tracker

In order to facilitate tracking the WiFi signals back to their source the tracker required 3 basic components:

1. A directional antenna for obtaining a vector to the target
2. A method of obtaining WiFi signal metrics that are suitable for tracking
3. A method of displaying the metrics in a manner usable for tracking

These components were developed and employed as follows:

1. The Pheenet ANT-120YN 2.4 GHz Yagi antenna was used as Yagi antennas typically provide high gain with a narrow focus (Rosham & Leary, 2004). This narrow focus facilitated the directional nature of the antenna.
2. The RSSI (Received Signal Strength Indicator) and the MAC address can be obtained from a WiFi adapter connected to a directional antenna. This allows the strength of the received signal to be captured along with its identity. The output from the Linux command *iwlist scan* provides a list of WiFi sources and their RSSIs available to the WiFi adapter. This output was

programmatically captured and filtered in order to obtain the RSSI for a specified MAC address (i.e. the target's MAC address). The sample rate achieved was 0.3Hz, that is the RSSI and list of WiFi sources to be filtered was updated every 3 seconds. A GUI was developed in Java and a signal strength bar was used to display the signal strength associated with the target's MAC address. This provided a simple hot and cold measure of RSSI VS. Direction.

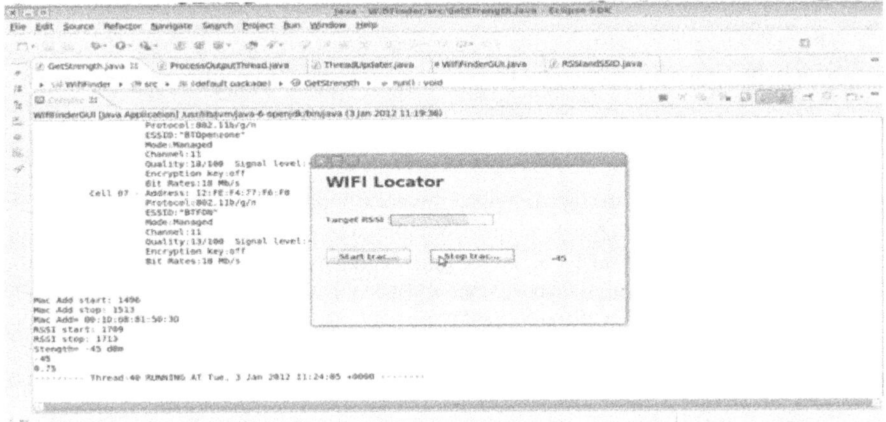

Figure 1: Screen shot of GUI displaying high RSSI

The antenna was connected to a USB WiFi adapter with an external antenna connected. This was connected to a Linux Ubuntu OS laptop which was used to host the RSSI capture and GUI functionality.

Figure 2: System architecture

3. WiFi Tracker Methodology & Results

A range of environments were chosen for experimentation and testing of the WiFi tracker, those discussed in this paper are:

1. Clear countryside
2. Urban terraced
3. Urban City Centre
4. Large building, analogous in layout to a shopping centre

In order to simulate a WiFi enabled target, a simple 802.11g domestic access point (AP) was used.

The RSSI was captured as a power and the units are measured in dBm accordingly. A note on the difference between 0 signal strength (no signal) and 0dBm (1mW power): Where a signal was lost in its entirety, that value has been changed from 0 to -100dBm (effectively no signal). This is because a strength of 0dBm (1mW) was not measured, being high signal strength/power and would have misrepresented the results.

1. ***Clear countryside***

   The AP was placed at the edge of an open space and the maximum distance at which the target's signal could be recorded with direct line of sight was 560m

2. ***Urban Terraced***

   For this experiment the AP was placed centrally on the ground floor of a double glazed, terraced property with the windows closed. Scanning was initiated and RSSI readings were taken at increasing distances after turning left out of the property until the signal was lost at 45M. Turning right out of the property resulted in a maximum distance of 112M being reached prior to the signal being lost. The experiment was repeated with the windows open but it had no significant impact on the range with identical distances being recorded at which the signal was lost.

3. ***Urban City Centre***

   The access point was placed on the 4th floor of an office block in a large city centre. The total area of the 4th floor was 1438 $m^{2.}$ The maximum distance at which the target's signal could be recorded with direct line of sight was 200m away. The front of the building was surveyed by sweeping the antenna from side to side on each floor. The signal was significantly stronger on the right hand side of the 4th floor, which cut down the most likely search area to 448m^2. Upon entering the building, no further signals could be detected on the preceding floors until entering the 4th floor. Once it was confirmed that the 4th floor contained the target, it was located by sweeping the antenna and following the strongest signal within 3 minutes. In figure 3, the signal strength can be seen increasing as the tracker gets closer to the target.

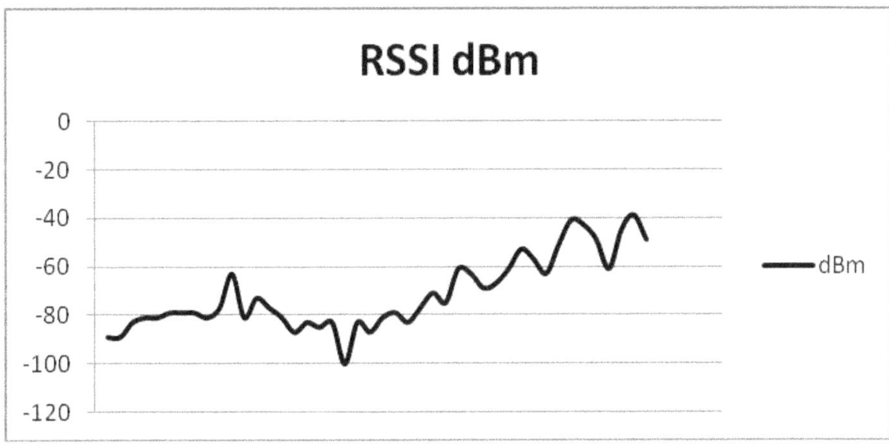

Figure 3: 4th floor RSSI over Time during search

There were 15 windows of the 4th floor and they were coated in a heat reflective film. Two of the windows were open, 20 signal strength readings were taken from the front of the building with the windows open and then closed in order to determine if the open windows were significant. The RSSIs measured are shown in Figure 4.

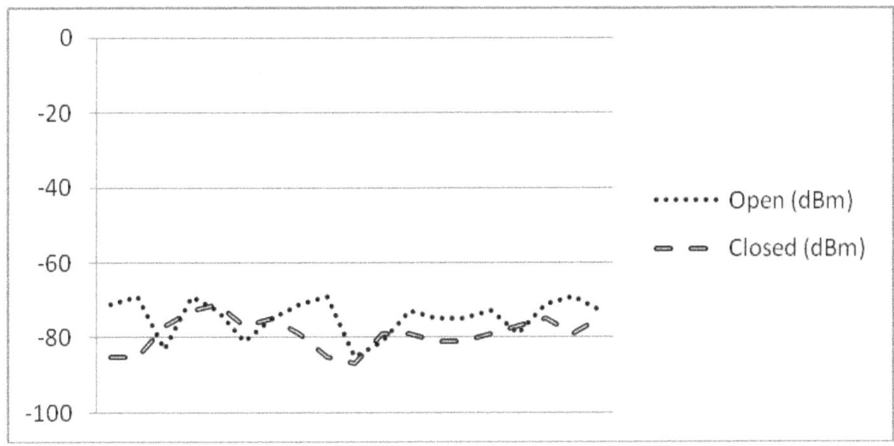

Figure 4: RSSI(dBm) Open heat reflective windows VS Closed

4. Large Building

This site is a large office building with accommodation for 2000 employees and a total floor space of 35,000m^2. It contains a large central atrium with stairs and lifts giving access to floor plates on each side of the atrium, a lay out common to many shopping centres. The AP was hidden by an assistant in an unknown location and locating the target was attempted from outside the building. It took 12 minutes to find the target. After surveying the exterior of the building, the location of the target was approximated to be on the second floor in the west quadrant of the building. Upon entering the building the signal was lost but following the building layout and ascending the stairs resulted in the signal being required and traced back to its source. The AP was found located in a room with an area of 990m^2. The signal was subject to reflections and in places ghosting was encountered. However, this was easily eliminated, by taking readings in other directions and following the strongest RSSI.

4. Experimental Discussion

The objectives of the experimentation were as follows:

1. How far away from a target can the tracking solution start reading the RSSI?
2. Is it possible to locate a target using the tracking solution?
3. Is it possible to locate a target using the tracking solution in a variety of environments?

The maximum range in clear line of sight possible with the equipment used for the research in the environments available was 0.5km. Clear line of sight may be useful in a situation where the target is not in an urban environment. The maximum effective distance achieved was 200m from an elevated position and from between 45m and 112m from at ground level. It is therefore possible to cover a larger area without obstructions to line of sight to the 802.11 scanner than in an urban environment where there are obstructions. However this does not necessarily lessen the effectiveness of the tracker. A range of a 100m or so within a built up area is acutally quite effective. Streets and building layouts can be used as visual guides for the tracker to follow in combination with the RSSI and vector prodivded by the directional antenna.

If the WiFi source is placed in an elevated position, then this range can be at least doubled. Ideally, an environment with a building surrounded by clear line of sight for up to a kilometer would be used for ascertaining the exact range but such a bulding was not available at the time of research. Also from an ideal perspective a range of building types would be used and a range of elevations but there has to come a point where the practical benefits would be outweighed by the logistics of this approach to the research.

During experiment 2, the maximum range was less than expected. The signal propagation was approximately 50% on the west side of the property than the east side. Although such a marked delta is initially surprising, further investigation of the construction of the building may explain the results. The walls on the north and west side of the property are unusual in being in excess of 450mm thick and solid. The wall on the east side is double skinned brick and significantly thinner.

According to (Ohrtman & Roeder, 2003) a window in a brick wall will reduce signal strength by 2dB and the brick wall by 3dB. However the attenuation caused by windows did not prove to be significant when testing the tracker in operation during experiments 2 and 3. The distances maximum tracker range was unaffected by opening of closing the properties windows and doors.

For line–of-sight (LOS) propagation the transmitting and receiving antennas must be in effective line of sight of one another. The qualifier *effective* is used as the atmosphere can refract signals and objects in the signals path may reflect, refract or scatter them (Stallings, 2005). Although reflections may result in false positive readings and could in theory make it very difficult to localise the target, testing has shown that reflection, refraction and scattering actually help the singal propogate. This means it is possible to follow the signal to its strongest source such as in a building where without this propogation, it may not have been picked up at all.

Being in a bulding, with lots of potential for ghosting, was not the issue it was orginally thought to be. This is because by applying a little common sense, the tracker can follow the building layout. By using the building corridors and doorways to guide the tracker, it is possible to locate targets even in larget buildings. This was demonstrated in experiments 3 and 4 when upon entering the building, it was sufficiently large that the signal found outside was lost. However because the signal was strongest when pointing up at a specific part of the bulding from the outside, the tracker can use the layout of the building to guide them to likely places to pick up the signal again.

The environment and its sensitivity/gain, affects the maximum range of the tracker. The environmental factors are not possible to control as the intended target when in use (a mobile device) is by design portable. In order to increase the effective range, the gain could be improved by using a more sensitive WiFi adapter or an antenna with higher gain. However this would need to be balanced against the impact of cost on the tracker and its portability.

5. Conclusions & Future Work

The WiFi tracker developed for this research can be used in order to locate a WiFi enabled targets such as a smart phone or laptop and provides a finer granularity of location tracking in the final few hundred meters.

The effective range of the tracker developed for this research is between 45m and 200m when the target is place in a building. The effective range is affected by environmental considerations such as the thickness of walls. Elevation has a significant impact on range, the range increases with elevation. With uninterrupted line of sight of the target, the range increases to approximately 500m.

Refraction and multipath interference was more of a help than a hindrance. The refraction of the signal around buildings allowed the signal to be followed back to the source by following the path of corridors and stairs.

Due to the limited range of the WiFi tracker, it is highly unlikely that it could be effectively deployed on its own in the field without the help of alternative tracking technologies such as GPS to guide operator to an effective start point.

Future work needs to focus upon the physical constructed for use commercially. It would ideally be as compact as possible. The tracker developed for this research required two hands to operate, which made opening doors and operating lift controls difficult. Weather proofing of the tracker would also be desirable as would some resistance to impact as it is likely that the tracker will be subject to both at some point during day-to-day use.

6. References

Bahl, P., & Padmanabhan, V. M. (2000). RADAR: an in-building RF-based user location and tracking system. *NFOCOM 2000. Nineteenth Annual Joint Conference of the IEEE Computer and Communications Societies. Proceedings. IEEE , 2 .*

Bajaj, R., Ranaweera, S. L., & Agrawal, D. (2002). GPS: Location-Tracking Technology. *Computer , 4*, 92-94.

Bakhru, K. (2005). A Seamless Tracking Solution for Indoor and Outdoor Position Location. *International Symposium on Personal, Indoor and Mobile Radio Communications , 3.*

Britsh Retail Consortium. (2011). Cash and Valuables in Transit: Best Practise Guidlines for Retailers. 2, 14. British Retail Consortium.

Flatley, J., Moon, D., Roe, S., Hall, P., & Moley, S. (2009). *Home security, mobile phone theft and stolen goods: Supplementary volume 3 2007/08 - British Crime Survey.* Home Office.

Ohrtman, F., & Roeder, K. (2003). *Wi-Fi handbook: building 802.11b wireless networks.* NY, US.

Ponemon Institute. (2011). *The Billion Euro Lost Laptop Problem: Benchmark study of European organisations.* Ponemon Institute.

Rosham, P., & Leary, J. (2004). *802.11 Wireless LAN fundamentals.* Indianapolis, US: Cisco Press.

Stallings, W. (2005). *Wireless Communications and Networks* (2nd Edition ed.). Upper Saddle e River, NJ, USA: Pearson Education.

Communications System for a Solar Car

J.N.Davies[1], M.Payne[1], P.Evans[1], G.Sparey-Taylor[1], N.Rvachova[2], O.Korkh[2] and V.Grout[1]

[1]Creative and Applied Research for the Digital Society (CARDS), Glyndŵr University, Wrexham, UK
[2]Poltava National Technical University, Poltava, Ukraine
e-mail: j.n.davies@glyndwr.ac.uk; s10001992@mail.glyndwr.ac.uk; s0101418@mail.glyndwr.ac.uk; spareytaylorg@glyndwr.ac.uk; rvacheva_n@mail.ru; korkholeh@gmail.com; v.grout@glyndwr.ac.uk

Abstract

This paper is intended to outline a project that will take place in order to produce a working interface and communications system for a solar car and its support vehicles. The system will be required to gather data from the cars sensors whilst displaying it to the driver in real time and transmitting the data to additional vehicles. Additionally voice contact is required between the vehicles. Progress information that has been collected must be stored and the appropriate web site updated when conditions permit. The specialized requirements of the computer software and hardware for the Team Gwawr solar car will also be considered.

Keywords

Solar car; Solar Car Monitoring; VoIP; Wifi; IEEE802.11g/n; Propagation models.

1. Introduction

Glyndwr University have designed and built a Solar Car that it enters into Solar Challenges (Team Gwawr Web Site 2012). These run at different times of the year in different countries and a typical challenge is the one run in October 2011 across Australia from Darwen to Adelaide Figure 1a show the route (World Solar Challenge Web Site, 2012). In 2012 there is a similar challenge proposed in South Africa Figure 1c shows the route (South Africa Solar Challenge Web Site (2012). The normal configuration for the event is that the Solar Cars run with 2 support vehicles Figure 2, one running in front and the other following. This convoy can stretch over a distance of 1.5km. Clearly the support vehicles require information on the performance of the solar car. Usually the route is over an inhospitable environment so the solution to this requirement is not a simple "off the shelf" task.

Monitoring the operation of a solar car is a complex task since there is a requirement to keep the driver informed about the important parameters of the car whilst in operation.

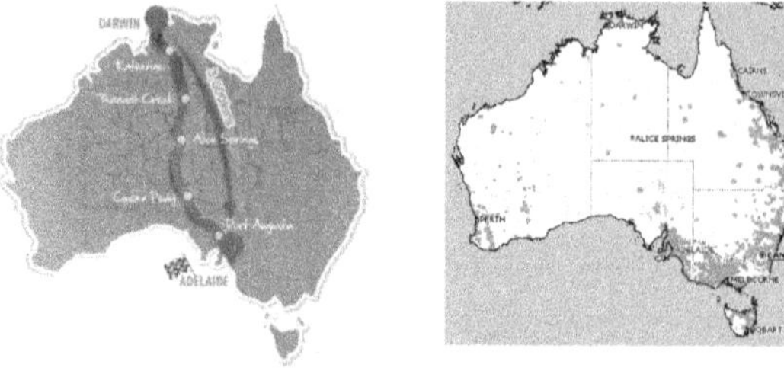

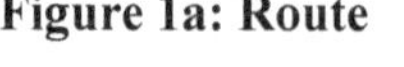

Figure 1a: Route

Figure 1b: Cellular coverage

Figure 1c: South Africa 2012

This paper considers the display and communication of the parameters associated with the health of the car, analyses the requirements of providing this communication link and proposes possible solutions.

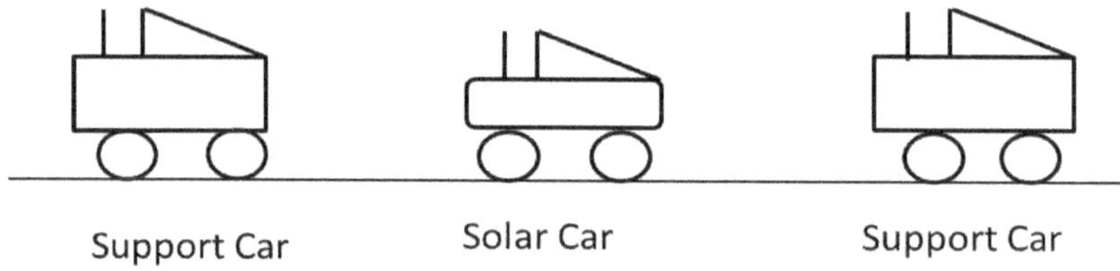

Figure 2: Typical support scheme used during challenges

2. Requirements of computer system

The project team associated with building and running the solar car are Engineers that do not have a Computer Science background. It was necessary to undertake an analysis stage to understand the interface between the car and the computer system but since the solar car is in a continual development environment the computer system requirements cannot be easily specified.

2.1. Physical Requirements

It is necessary to install much of the equipment within the solar car to prevent problems associated with support vehicles being out of communications range with the solar car. The external environment may be quite hostile due to the routes across deserts and the type of weather encountered, high and low temperature, varying levels of humidity. This will have a restriction on anything mounted outside the car e.g. wireless antenna. However the internal conditions are similar to a standard car since it is an enclosed space. There are some concerns which include heat, light, humidity, power and size. Additionally a great deal of thought needs to be given to both weight and power usage. The challenge usually involves driving in these hostile environments for up to10hrs / day.

2.2. Hardware Requirements

Clearly a low powered computer is required to run the software which should be reliable and run off the battery to reduce power taken from the solar car. It can be recharged every evening during the rest periods. Devices are needed to receive, store and display sensor information, provide feedback for the support cars so that they can update a website on the internet. From the visibility point of view the computer screens in the car is of great importance. Standard PCs devices could be used inside a sealed unit with appropriate vibration dampening. Similar PCs can be used in the support cars which would help with any maintenance problems. Techniques allowing peripheral visibility will enable the driver to assimilate complex information without looking away from the road. Displays in the dashboard may need hooding or can be inset into the dashboard in order to minimise direct sunlight exposure.

2.3. Data Collection and Display Software Requirements

There are numerous areas where sensor data can be taken to monitor the car's performance. Typical parameters that need to be monitored by both the driver and the support cars include the voltage, current and temperature of the batteries and the solar arrays. Other parameters include voltage, current temperature and frequency of the motor, the road speed and the surrounding environmental conditions e.g. temperature, wind speed etc. The data collected must be formatted and presented in a usable and intuitive way, accounting for the specific user interface and hardware limitations of operating the car. The driver should be able to select and view different parameters and be warned of any parameters that exceed or drop below predefined thresholds.

2.4. Communications requirement

A common feature of this type of application is associated with the type of area that is selected for the challenges. There is always a limitation on the route used which seems to have a lack of mobile networks both in terms of voice and data network. The sparse coverage necessitates the team to provide a private network so that reliable communication can be achieved (Telstra Com Web Site 2012).

The network will be required to provide the team with a reliable stream of data from the solar car along with additional voice communications. This will ensure that the support vehicles know the state of the solar car as well as the driver. A website will be updated to record the progress of the team whenever possible due to the limited and varying internet access this will include historic data of the route.

3. Possible Solutions

3.1. Data Collection & display Software

WPF and C# were used to communicate between applications by sending updates via TCP using the C# socket class. This can be used to synchronise applications across the three vehicles. Custom software was developed to meet the specific requirements of this project. To account for network instability, a robust system using Microsoft message queuing (MSMQ) was implemented in order to ensure data is not lost and prevent application crashes.

3.2. Communications Options

Any possible solution for the project must take into account the cost of the equipment and its availability since the team are in rural areas it must be reliable whilst still performing the necessary functions.

Where available mobile phone networks could be used to communicate with the internet, however due to the lack of availability this would not be suitable for the car data transmissions refer to figure 1b for typical network. WiMAX is a wireless standard that provides large area coverage at high speed which seems to be an obvious choice however due to the slow uptake of the technology the equipment is cost prohibitive for this project (IEEE Std 802.16h-2010). Wifi networks have been available for a number of years and have many consumer units available. This has driven down the cost of installing such a network however this technology does have limited range and was not designed for moving vehicles (IEEE Std 802.11-2007). Bluetooth specialises in low power short range communications which is suitable for in-car use but is unsuitable for the communications between the cars (IEEE Std 802.15.5-2009). Satellite communication was considered however the use of the dishes required to provide the communications link would provide a great problem when installed on the solar car due to the drag caused by wind resistance.

IEEE 802.11 will be focused upon for this paper because it is both easily obtainable and low cost however the range needs to be investigated further. In addition an IEEE 802.11 connection will be used from the support cars to upload the information to the internet. This upload will be carried out when and where appropriate, e.g. when passing through towns and in the evenings.

4. Investigation and Testing of Communications system

Standard wifi interfaces found in commercially available laptops was tested to find a value for the maximum distance that a signal could be detected as described in previous work (Davies J. N., Grout V., Picking R., 2008).

Measurements of the signal strength were taking at varying distance using Inssider (Inssider Web Site 2012), and the graph shown in figure 3 was drawn with dBs on the y axis (which is a log scale) and log distance on the x axis. Using a linear fit to the measured values the equation ($y = -23.293x - 45.695$) is obtained. Calculating the cut off distance using -85 dBs as the minimum strength then a distance of 46.8 metres is arrived at. Clearly this is not going to be suitable for this application therefore investigate into the gain of antenna was undertaken.

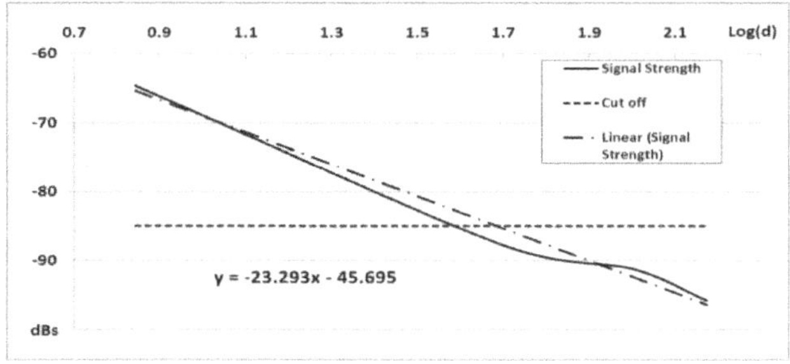

Figure 3: Standard laptop to laptop signal strength

4.1. Test Conditions

Much of the area that is going to be covered as part of the challenge is in free open space however there will be built up that will be passed through. As part of the tests it will be necessary to take into account urban as well as open areas. Most of the theory that has been put forward considers open free space so it is worthwhile recapping on this.

5. Theory of Transmission Signal Losses

As a receiver moves further from the signal source it receives less power because the signal is spread over a greater area, this is known as free space loss. Maxwell equations are a basis for this technology but there are many simplified models that have been used to enable calculations for the power received by an antenna under idealised conditions to be found. Friis Transmission Equation (Friis H.T. 1946) is one such model that has been used extensively for a number of years. The equation can be derived as such:

5.1. Friis Transmission Equation & Calculations

For an isotropic antenna for transmission and receiving in an open environment the power at the receiving antenna can be given by: $P_r = \frac{P_t}{4\pi d^2}$ where: P_r = Received power, P_t = Transmit power, d = Distance between antenna.

For an antenna with gain in the transmit direction this becomes: $P_r = \frac{P_t}{4\pi d^2} G_t$

Where: G_t = Transmit antenna gain. As the receiving antenna will have a limited effective area the equation becomes: $P_r = \frac{P_t}{4\pi d^2} G_t A_{er}$ Where A_{er} = Effective area of receiving antenna. The effective area for an antenna can also be expressed as: $A_e = \frac{\lambda^2}{4\pi} G$ Where: λ = wavelength. Therefore the received power is :

$$P_r = \frac{P_t G_t G_r \lambda^2}{(4\pi d)^2} \quad (1)$$

Usually the power and gain of an antenna is specified in db which is a log scale and so equation (1) becomes

$$Pr = Pt + Gt + Gr + 20\ Log_{10}\left(\frac{\lambda}{4\pi d}\right) \qquad (2)$$

Typical values for laptops used in this application discussed in this paper are:- Pt = 15dbm, Gt = 2db = Gr since it is symmetrical, λ the wavelength = c/f where f = 2.4 Ghz and c the speed of light. Putting these values in equation (2) for a distance of50m gives a receive power level of -85.03dbm. Figure 4 shows the graph created from the calculation and compares it with the measurements shown in figure 3.

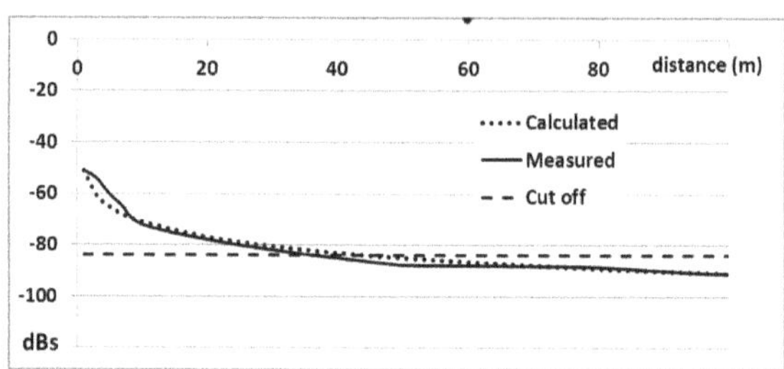

Figure 4 Calculated v Measured

From these graphs it can be seen that there is a close correlation between the calculated and measured values and the cut off distance of around 50m is confirmed.

Equation (2) can be re-arranged so that the gain require of the antenna for a given distance can be calculated - $2G = Pr - Pt - 20\ Log_{10}\left(\frac{\lambda}{4\pi d}\right)$

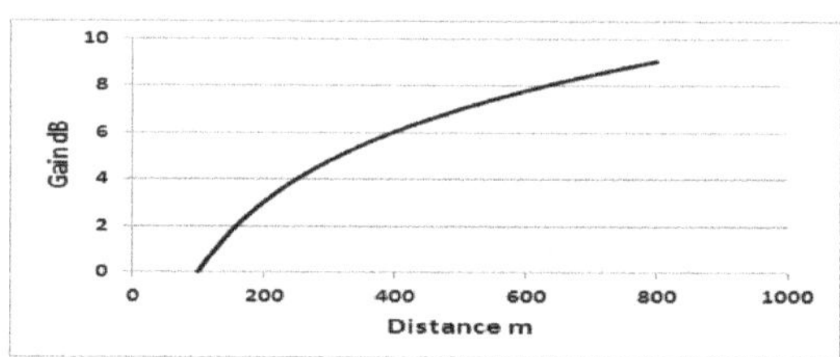

Figure 5 Gain require of antenna to achieve distance

5.2. Terrain

Normally for wifi networks operating at 2.4 Ghz the issue of operating in a mobile environment is not considered since the distance cover is usually within a radius of 50m. However in this application there needs to be an investigation into the effect of motion and environment.

There are a number of wireless propagation models but they are all empirical in nature. They have been produced to help understand the cell phones applications unfortunately most of the models developed do not apply 2.4GHz. Empirical models do not describe the exact behaviour due mainly to the problem of specifying accurately the environment under which it is being used. To this end there are a number of different models intended for use in different environments. One of the authoritative works in this area was carried out by Okamura in Tokyo city (Okamura, Y. et al. 1968). This was improved by Hata who added components for predicting the behaviour in city outskirts and other rural areas (Hata, M. 1980). There are numerous other models but they are based on this initial work. The Hata model for Suburban Areas is given by: $Lsu = Lu - 2\left(Log\,\frac{f}{28}\right)^2 - 5.4$. Where, LSU = Path loss in suburban areas. Unit: decibel (dB), LU = Average Path loss in urban areas. Unit: decibel (dB), f = Frequency of Transmission. Unit: megahertz (MHz) and for open areas is given by: $Lo = Lu - 4.78(Logf)^2 + 18.33\,Log\,f - 40.94$. Where, LO = Path loss in open area. Unit: decibel (dB), LU = Path loss in urban area. Unit: decibel (dB), f = Frequency of transmission. Unit: megahertz (MHz).

6. Measurements

So by using antenna with a higher gain at the receiver and transmitter it is possible the required distances will be obtainable. A series of measurements were undertaken to see how the manufactures antenna agree with the theory. USB 802.11n adapters that have an N type plug can be used to test out antenna of differing gains. Antenna to be tested will be the 3 dBi antenna that is supplied with the adapters. The following three antennas will also be used: Sitecom 5 dBi WL-030, Sitecom 7 dBi WL-032, Sitecom 10 dBi WL-031 (Sitecom Web Site 2012),

The first test that was undertaken was to see if there was a difference in the attenuation at each channel that is available to wifi. Results showed that channel 8 should be avoided.

6.1. Isotropic antenna

An isotropic antenna is one that radiates equally in all directions which is ideal for this application.

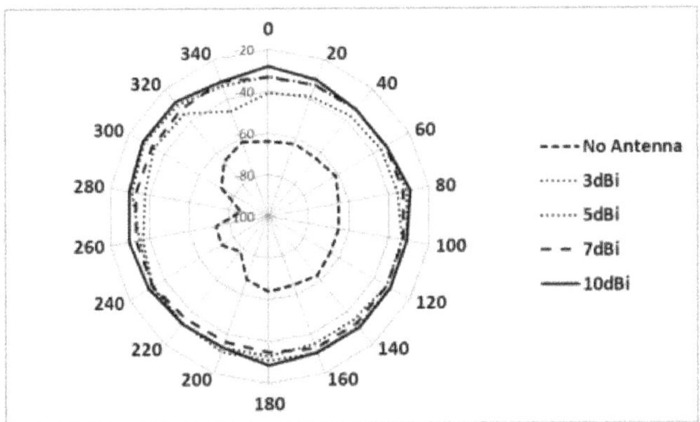

Figure 6: Polar plot of signal strength for antenna with different gains

However in reality this is not possible to build so careful measurements were taken at differing angles to enable a judgment to be made about the suitability of the antenna to be used. Figure 6 shows the results and it can be seen that any of the added antenna perform much better than the standard laptop. All these measurements were taken using the same equipment changing just the pole of the antenna and a distance 10 metres was used.

6.2. Signal strength versus distance

Test when then undertaken on a quiet, straight road to obtain the relationship of the signal strength at various distance from the transmitter. The laptop containg the usb IEEE802.11n interface was placed on a tripod and with the use of Insider the signal stength in dbs for was recorded. This was then repeated using anteanna with differing gains. The results can be seen in figure 7. It can be clearly seen that distances of 800 metres can be easily achieved. Its not possible to fit a straight line to these graphs since the plot is actual distance not on a logarithmic scale

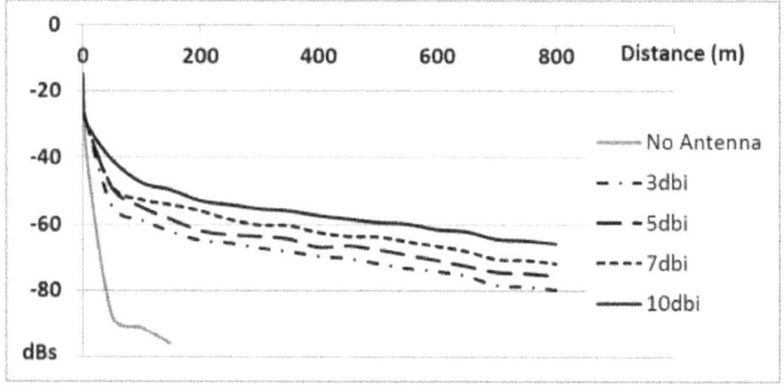

Figure 7: Signal strength for antenna varying with distance

6.3. Effect of speed of movement on signal strength

Due to the nature of the application an investigation into the effect if the signal strength whilst attached to a car travelling at speed. The intention is to mount the antenna to the external of the car to avoid problems associated with signal absorption by the carbon body. This antenna will then screw into the receiver which is mounted in the bodywork of the car immediately below.

An extended usb cable will then be used to attach the receiver to the laptop. By doing this it reduces the attenuation since the analogue signal is converted at the entry point. A series of tests were undertaken the maximum speed attempted was 70mph which was slightly beyond that expected for the solar car. These tests showed that there is little difference in the signal strength over the range 20 to 70 mph.

7. Voip Considerations

One of the major requirements of the system is to have the ability of voice communications between the cars. By referring to figure 1b it is clear that this can not be reliably provided by any of the standard cellular phone networks. The communications network setup between the cars is based on the IP protocol and therefore voice over IP (VoIP) is an obvious choice. By restricting the voice network to just the cars it means that a very small system can be used. There would be no need for a PBX and so one of the VoIP systems used frequently by the Games fraternity could be adopted. A number were investigated but Teamspeak (Teamspeak Web site 2012), and Mumble (Mumble Web Site 2011), were chosen as having the most appropriate features. The tests where done by using a standard laptop fitted with a combined headphone and speaker. A MP3 player was strapped to the microphone at one end and the recorded speech was judged by listening through the headset at the other end. This is a bit subjective since it relied on the person's objectivity but it ensured consistency of the transmission. An analysis of the results showed that low quality setting on Mumble is going to give the best performance.

8. Conclusions

The solar car application is quite unique in its requirements due to the challenges that are defined however there are likely to be a number of other applications with similar problems where vehicles travelling in convoy need to communicate. One of the major problems associated with this project was the un-availability of standard network services and therefore a novel approach had to be sought.

8.1. Results obtained

The analysis of geographical and testing conditions showed that the wireless technologies are the best solution for doing the monitoring of solar car characteristics. Custom built network structures were dismissed due to reliability and the ease of replacement of faulty equipment. Since WiMax technology is still being developed the availability of equipment is low and the cost is high so it was decided that the best choice is an IEEE 802.11n. Clearly IEEE 802.11n does not cover the distances required so it was necessary to do further investigations. Theoretical calculations showed that an antenna with a gain of 10db a distance of up to 800 metre could be achieved.

Another requirement of the project was to enable the cars to travel at speeds up to around 50mph in convoy. Further experiments showed that the effect of speed is very little and so the speed of cars is not a critical factor for the wireless network.

Due to the lack of network services it was also necessary to provide a VoIP system. to enable the drivers to communicate in remote areas. A number of VoIP systems were investigated the basis of the decision was that it needs to be small, compact and can be run on a low power processor. Experiments were carried out with Teamspeak and Mumble which showed that Mumble in low-quality settings was the best match to the requirements.

8.2. Future work

For the future it would be useful to do further work on the models associated with the surrounding environment. Clearly the vehicles will travel not only through desert like conditions but also through towns, small villages, forest areas and mountainous regions. The models would help confirm the operation in these environments. A justification for the use of a simplified VoIP application will be the subject of a future paper.

9. References

Davies J. N., Grout V., Picking R. (2008), "Prediction of Wireless Network Signal Strength within a Building", INC 2008, University of Plymouth.

Friis H.T.,(1946) Proc. IRE, vol. 34, p.254. 1946

Hata, M. (1980), "Empirical Formula for Propagation Loss in Land Mobile Radio Services", IEEE Trans. Vehicular Technology, VT-29, pp. 317 - 325, 1980

IEEE Std 802.11-2007, IEEE Standard for Information technology-Telecommunications and information exchange between systems-Local and metropolitan area networks-Specific requirements - Part 11: Wireless LAN Medium Access Control (MAC) and Physical Layer (PHY) Specifications

IEEE Std 802.15.5-2009, IEEE Standard for Information technology - Part 15.3: Wireless Medium Access Control (MAC) and Physical Layer (PHY) Specifications for High Rate Wireless Personal Area Networks (WPANs)

IEEE Std 802.16h-2010, IEEE Standard for Local and metropolitan area networks Part 16: Air Interface for Broadband Wireless Access Systems Amendment 3: Advanced Air Interface

Inssider Web Site (2012), "inSSIDer", http://www.metageek.net/support/downloads/, (Accessed 2 February 2012)

Mumble Web Site (2011), "Get Mumble", http://mumble.sourceforge.net/, (Accessed 8 February 2012)

Okamura, Y., et al., (1968), "Field Strength and its Variability in VHF and UHF Land-Mobile Radio Service", Rev. Elec. Comm. Lab. No.9-10pp. 825 - 873, 1968.

Sitecom Web Site (2012), "Range extenders & Access points", http://www.sitecom.com/range-extenders-and-access-points, (Accessed 8 February 2012)

South Africa Solar Challenge Web Site (2012), http://www.solarchallenge.org.za/ (Accessed 2 April 2012)

Teamspeak Web site (2012), http://www.teamspeak.com/?page=faq&cat= general&rate, (Accessed 8 February 2012)

Team Gwawr Web Site (2012), http://solarcarwales.co.uk/gwawrhomeeng.htm, (Accessed 2 February 2012)

Telstra Com Web Site (2012), "3G and GSM", http://www.telstra.com.au/mobile/networks/coverage/state.html, (Accessed 2 February 2012)

World Solar Challenge Web Site (2012), "Event Route", http://www.worldsolarchallenge.org/about_the_event/event_route, (Accessed 2 February 2012).

Extending Cognitive Fit Theory Towards Understanding Wireless Network Security Management in Small Organisations

K.Njenga and N.Manganyi

University of Johannesburg, Johannesburg, South Africa
e-mail: knjenga@uj.ac.za

Abstract

While large organisations effectively manage wireless network security through implementation of proper control procedures, anecdotal evidence suggest that smaller organisations lack such capacity (cognitive fit). The paper extends Cognitive Fit Theory as a theoretical lens towards understanding smaller organisations perceptions. In this paper we argue that the incapacity for small businesses to adequately deal with emergent wireless network security threats is as a result of a lack of match between understanding threats (problem representation) and how to mitigate against these threats (problem solving performance). The outcome of the paper is the development of a theoretical model that presents the perception of wireless network security threats from small organisations. The research takes specific focus on wireless network threats posed through war-driving under environments such as the 802.11x. From qualitative data analysis, empirical work confirms that smaller organisations *exhibited lack of cognitive fit,* in wireless network security management.

Keywords

Cognitive Fit, Wireless Network Security, Small Organisations

1. Introduction

Wireless computing technology is increasingly playing a major role in organisations (Varshney, 2003a). Many smaller organisations are becoming entirely dependent on the use of wireless network technologies for process level operations, while underestimating the consequences of security breaches (Loo, 2010). Empirical research suggests that it has been standard practice for large organisations to effectively manage and control the risk of wireless networks through implementing of proper control procedures. According to Bin, Yi-xian, Dong, Qi and Yang (2010), there are four main categories of research into wireless network security applicable to large organisations. These four categories of research depicted in Table 1, have provided large organisations with a framework for understanding and planning for best practice wireless network security (Bin *et al.*, 2010).

Category and Field	Classification
1. Research on standards for encryption key management	*Pre-distribution schemes, cryptography schemes, hash schemes, key infection schemes, and key management in hierarchy networks.*
2. Research on attacks and intrusion detection	*Managing awareness on external attacks and internal attacks on corporate networks.*
3. Research on standards for secure transmission of data across wireless networks	*Multi-path routing, reputation based schemes, secure routing for cluster or hierarchical sensor networks, broadcast authentication, secure routing defence against attacks.*
4. Research on identification of secure locations to place wireless access points	*Secure location scheme with beacons and secure location scheme without beacons.*

Table 1: Categories of Research for Wireless Network Security (Source: Bin *et al.*, 2010)

1.1. Small Organisations

Small organisations have been found to be lacking in applying frameworks such as listed above (cognitive fit for network security), in strict normative compliance when compared to their larger counterparts and often '*play-by-ear*' (Loo, 2010). In trying to understand why small organisations lack such fit, we use and extend Cognitive Fit Theory. The Theory of Cognitive Fit suggests that a match between the problem representation and the task results in a better problem solving performance. In this paper we argue that the incapacity for small businesses to adequately deal with emergent wireless network security threats is as a result of a lack of match between understanding wireless network security threats (problem representation) and how to mitigate against such threats (problem solving performance). The main research questions have therefore been outlined as follows:

a) To what extent do network security practitioners in small organisations understand problem representations? (Wireless network security threats); and
b) How does congruence in problem representation in small organisations affect problem solving performance? (Wireless network security threat mitigation).

In trying to address and discuss the context and objectives of the research, this paper divides itself into eight sections. Section 1 has introduced and laid context for the key theme. Section 2 discusses wireless networks and security management in the context of small South African organisations. The proceeding and penultimate sections (sections 3-7) discuss the research methodology, data analysis and nature of findings while the conclusion of this paper follows thereafter in section 8.

2. Wireless Networks

A wireless network refers to any kind of computer network that is wireless and associated with a telecommunication network. Generally, there are three main types of wireless networks technologies that include; wireless personal area networks (wPAN), wireless local area networks (wLAN) and wireless wide area networks (wWAN). Large and small organisations typically use wLAN networks to broadcast data using radio frequencies. There are standards for security defined by Institute of Electrical and Electronics Engineers (IEEE) such as the IEEE 802.11 that specifies "*over the air*" broadcasts between access points and clients. The IEEE specification for wLANs comprises several 802.11 specifications. These specifications represent the manner in which wireless networks communicate with a wireless access point (AP) and are depicted in Table 2 below.

Wireless LANs → Characteristics ↓	802.11	802.11b	802.11a	802.11g
Spectrum	2.4 GHz	2.4 GHz	5 GHz	2.4 GHz
Maximum physical rate	2 Mbps	11 Mbps	54 Mbps	54 Mbps
Layer 3 data rate	1.2 Mbps	6-7 Mbps	32 Mbps	32 Mbps
Frequency selection	Frequency Hopping or Direct Sequence	Direct Sequence only	Orthogonal Frequency Division Multiplexing	OFDM
Compatible with	None	802.11	None	802.11 and 802.11b
Major advantage	Higher range	Widely deployed High range	Higher bit rate in a less crowded spectrum Smaller range	Higher bit rate in 2.4 GHz spectrum Higher range than 802.11a

Table 2: Multiple Versions of 802.11 (Source Varshney 2003b)

2.1. Wireless Network Security

Wireless network security is seen as a "*combination of physical, administrative and technical controls that ensure data is protected as it traverses broadcasted wireless networks*" (Loo, 2010). Wired Equivalent Privacy (WEP) is a security protocol designed to provide a wireless network that uses 802.11 with a level of security and privacy using encryption technology over data as it crosses wireless networks (Winget, Housley, Wagner, and Walker, 2003). WEP was introduced in 1997 to provide confidentiality. In WEP, data moving between computers and access points that apply 802.11x standards is encrypted using a 64 bit key algorithm (Winget *et. al.,* 2003). In 2001 cryptanalysts identified several WEP weaknesses. Despites its weakness, WEP is still widely used (Winget *et. al.,* 2003). Another security measure that is commonly being used and which eventually might supersede WEP due to inherent weaknesses is Wifi Protected Access (WPA). There are two versions of WPA namely WPA and WPA2 which are seen as the latest standard wireless network security measure that has rapidly gained acceptance with organisations.

2.2. Wireless Network Security Management in Small Organisations

There are various small organisations in South Africa that use wLANs for common business purposes. Security has often been a neglected attribute in small organisations and can be compromised through *war-driving* (Carter and Shumway, 2002; Loo, 2010). The act of war-driving typically resonates around driving around neighbourhoods searching weak wLAN security settings (particularly WEP use). The attacks range from trivialities such as accessing free internet to more serious issues that concern attacks on confidentiality and data integrity. *Wireshark* is an example of an application popularly used by hackers when *war-driving*. The application graphically displays access points and *ad-hoc* adapters in tabular format. It also detects the presence and/or use of Wired Equivalent Privacy (WEP) (Carter and Shumway, 2002).

3. Cognitive Fit and Wireless Network Security Management

Cognitive Fit Theory is a framework that assists in the understanding of relationships between information presented (problem representation) and how such information shapes problem-solving performance (Vessey, 1991). Cognitive Fit Theory posits that it is possible to model relationships between problem solving elements and problem-solving performance. These models can correspondingly be used to predict future problem-solving performance (Vessey, 1991). Within the domain of wireless network security, problem representation is seen as essential in influencing the management of wireless security networks which in turn shapes how threats are mitigated. We could argue that, the performance of a decision-making task such as threat mitigation in a wireless network using IT resources, will be enhanced and made effective if there is a cognitive fit between *internal and external problem representation on wireless network threats* and information required regarding wireless threat mitigation. We could further argue that larger organisations that exhibit cognitive fit, are organisations that are in a position to have information regarding wireless threats presented to them timely, and that information being both necessary and needed/required. This in turn will influence successful wireless network problem solving performance. We note that larger organisations are better placed to have the right information because these are financially endowed and are better placed to attract the right skills sets and procure the latest sets of technology. With the same reasoning we argue that small organisations lack such capacity, and lack the necessary resources to ensure that they have at their disposal, relevant *problem representation* regarding wireless threats that is needed at the right time. This argument is presented in Figure 1.

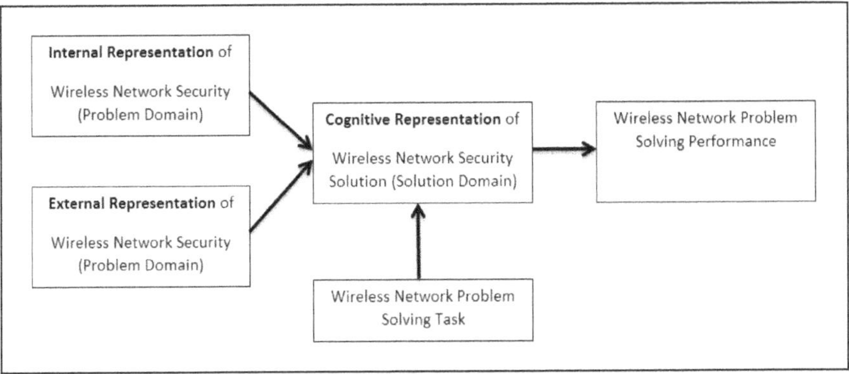

Figure 1: Cognitive Fit between problem representation and performance in Wireless Network Security, Adopted from Shaft and Vessey, (2006)

Underlying the reasoning in Figure 1, is the notion that, external (social, environmental and financial) and internal factors may shape the nature and value of problem representation which influences wireless network problem-solving performance. How small businesses perform will depend on Cognitive fit, (cognitive problem representation). In order to test the above model, a research was carried out. The next section explains the methodology and methods that underlie the extension of Cognitive Fit Theory into the Wireless Network Security domain.

4. Research Methodology

Welman, Kruger and Mitchel, (2007) define research as "*a systematic inquiry aimed at providing information to solve problems*" and differentiates between qualitative and quantitative research. Qualitative approach was the method chosen for the research to enable the understanding of congruence between problem representation of wireless network security threats and problem-solving performance within small organisations. Kaplan and Duchon (1988) define the qualitative approach as that which is an evolving process of data discovery, description and understanding. Kaplan and Duchon (1988) see qualitative research as an immersion in context. The research approach selected was the embedded case study (of 4 small organisations). The research aim was to gain knowledge by means of interviews, direct observation and testing. Direct observation is perceived as receiving knowledge of the outside world through senses or receiving of data using scientific instrument.

4.1. Data collection and Discussion

The first stage of the research involved interviews. From the interviews, was revealed on a number of cases selected that small organisations did not implement stringent wireless security (particularly WEP encryption). To confirm what was said during interviews the researchers observed wLAN settings using W*ireshark*. As an illustration, data from *wireshark* from a particular sampled region revealed more than **5** SSIDs being broadcasted as shown is Figure 2 below.

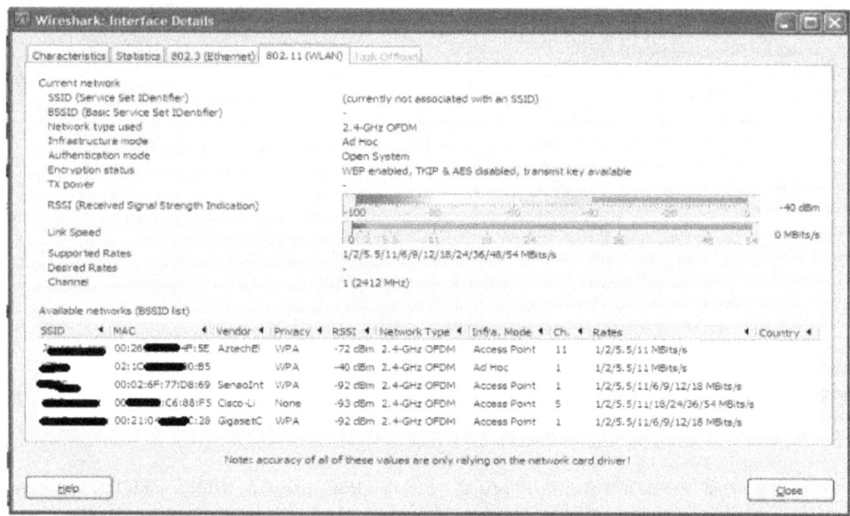

Figure 2: Wireshark data revealing one organisation with no Security

Figure 2 shows vendor names (SSIDs) being broadcasted and a quick review revealed the name of popular vendors. For most of these organisations the typical security and encryption standard was WPA. Figure 2 which hides the identity of the SSID for these organisations also shows one organisation ***with no encryption or security!*** A detailed review of how these small organisations perceive information *problem representation* is explained in the section below;

4.2. Organisation A

In organisation A, the SSID was not visible, (withheld) and the network required a password key. The organisation's WEP encryption was also not visible suggesting that the application could not pick the kind of security being used. This suggested that in this particular organisation, steps had been carried out to ensure that the network was secure. During the interview, assistant manager of this organisation [name withheld] said that "*they don't deal with information technology stuff*". The manager mentioned that they outsource from an organisation called [name withheld]. Whenever they have problems they report to this organisation. His honesty was revealed in the interview." *I will not be able to assist in anything to do with the wireless that we use, we never spend any time managing it because we outsource*". It remained clear for this specific organisation that any concern with security remained with third party providers. Outsourcing remains a popular option for some small organisations in Johannesburg, South Africa.

4.3. Organisation B

The interesting issue regarding organisation B was that *wireshark* picked that this organisation was still using its default SSID name "[name withheld]". It is a common practice for every organisation to change the default settings as soon wLAN is deployed. This was not the case for this organisation. On discussion with one of the interviewees, part of the reason for this was; "*We are a small health organisation, nobody would want to hack us*". It can be noted that when third party vendors sold their product to this small organisation, they neglected to mention or explain possible risks and vulnerabilities of using wireless technologies that come along with such products and the actual costs and commitment involved in making these system usable and secure. When asked about wireless security concerns and the underlying security procedure and posture which governed them, the interviewee responded as follows;

> *"We don't govern [either] cyber security or wireless [security] in our organisation..."*
>
> *"Who would want to harm our [health] organisation?"*
>
> *"When it was installed we implemented WEP... why waste time in governing it when we could do something else that would benefit our [health] organisation?"*

On further prodding the interviewee revealed that they had no knowledge on how the wireless was configured or how it was to be protected.

4.4. Organisation C

This organisation (a coffee shop) happens to broadcast free internet on the basis that customers who want coffee can browse the Internet for free. The researcher parked outside this organisation in a car and could receive these free broadcast signals (without the requirement of an SSID password). *Wireshark* picked its wireless adapter and identified the SSID broadcasting as "*free public wifi*". The security issue here was that the shop was broadcasting beyond range making it easily available to non-patrons of the coffee shop. The researcher interviewed the owner and explained the concerns. The interviewee mentioned that they "*were testing the signal strength*", and although they "*haven't restricted it*" they "*want to see how far it can go*". This did not make any sense to the researcher, since this was the very reason that would exposing this coffee shop and compromise its security. Possible risks could be outsiders browsing illegal sites or sites that infect its networks. Although a huge interest was shown by management towards this issue, it was clear that the management was not fully aware of the risks they were exposing the coffee shop to.

4.5. Organisation D

Organisation D remains a privately owned small organisation committed to promoting travel services for the Southern African region. Observation from this organisation revealed that they have set up stringent security measures on their wireless network. The SSID was not being picked up by *wireshark*. The interviewee was [name withheld] was the IT manager who described the network as "*a very small* network" in the sense that "*it has limited base station*", which uses standard technologies. Asked about the security management controls for wLAN, the interviewee responded that they "*don't have any formalised standards*". The interviewee mentioned that the IT department (which is fairly small) is the only department that "*knows the keys, there is no guest passwords [to network]*". Visitors that come in are allocated SSID passwords which are disabled when they leave. They have certain user access requirement that define authorisation regarding "*who gets access [to networks] and who doesn't*". The interviewee also stated that they have deployed WAP2, and thought of it as being "*robust*". The interviewee also mentioned that they moved from WEP (encryption security) because "*it was very insecure and, it was so easy to break*". The interviewee also mentioned that they "*monitor performance*" and that "*If there is more traffic than usual on the network we will be able to see if something is wrong*". They followed the standard known ways of configuring the wireless network. Asked about familiarity with war-driving, the interviewee seemed particularly knowledgeable and said that "*we are aware of war driving*" and that is why "*we have the [made] wireless [networks] to be indoors and not high powered*". The interviewee recalled a while back of an instance when Google "*was going around picking up wirelesses*". The security measure as described by this interviewee was that "*apparently if you disable your SSID, it makes it hard for hackers to hack*". They also seemed to be aware of a lot of best practice procedure that was available online and have a network policy that was created by the human resource department to meet their business requirements.

4.6. Problem Representation and Problem-Solving Performance

Based on empirical results obtained from Organisations **A**,**B**, **C** and **D**, it was clear that the selected respondents lacked an understanding of wireless network threats they faced (*poor problem representation*). By interpreting *qualitative data*, it was observed that only one organization represented congruence regarding problem representation (wireless security networks threats) and problem solving performance (wireless security threat mitigation). The rest of the smaller organisations exhibited risk in terms of poor problem representation. In short, from interviews conducted, smaller organisations *exhibited lack of cognitive fit,* in wireless network security management. These findings above can be summarised in Table 3 below.

	Cognitive Representation regarding Wireless Network Security Risk					
	SSID Visibility is understood	Use of WEP *vis a vis* WAP/WAP2 is understood	Public use of Network resources is understood *e.g. access point location, broadcast range*	Risk of third party outsourcing is understood	Problem Representation and Tasks are in Congruence is understood	Technical Representation , use of Intrusion Detection Systems (IDS) is understood
	Problem representation	*Problem representation*	*Problem representation*	*Problem representation*	*Problem-solving performance*	*Problem-solving performance*
Org **A**	✓	✓	✓	*Risk*	*Risk*	*Risk*
Org **B**	*Risk*	✓	✓	*Risk*	*Risk*	*Risk*
Org **C**	*Risk*	✓	*Risk*	*Risk*	*Risk*	*Risk*
Org **D**	✓	✓	✓	✓	✓	*Risk*

Table 3: Problem Representation, Wireless network threats against Problem-solving performance

Based on the above findings a framework that extends Cognitive Fit Theory into wireless network security management can be developed. The next section expounds on this.

5. Framework for Managing Wireless Network Security for Small Organisations

From the discussions in the previous sections, it can be noted that the main deficiencies in perceptions held by small organisations is the lack of ***awareness***, ***effective planning*** and ***stringent security implementation***. Due to the highlighted problems facing small organisations, we note that these perceptions have tended to influence problem representation for such organisations, and correspondingly this has affected their problem-solving performance (Vessey 1991; Vessey 2006). From a theoretical viewpoint, Cognitive Fit Theory, suggest that network security practitioners and decision makers in small organisations who lack understanding about wireless network threats will have a slower response rate towards dealing with emergent network threats and this will limit further their capacity to provide adequate solutions to those threats. A framework of Cognitive Fit Theory can be extended to incorporate these empirical findings as follows.

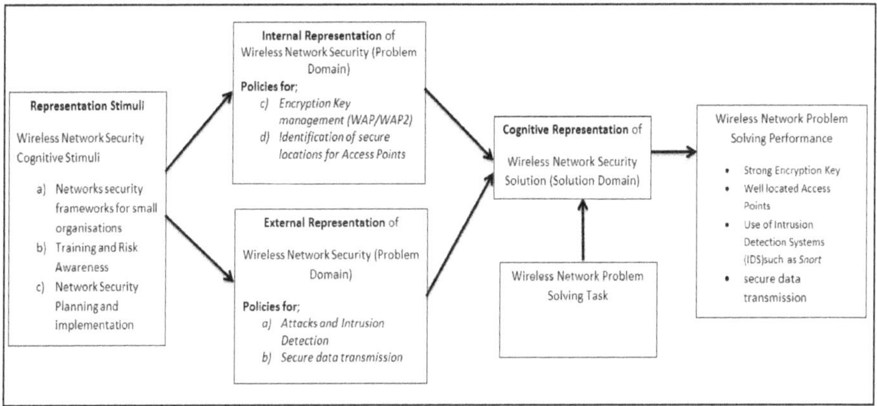

Figure 3: Extended Cognitive Fit Framework for Wireless Network Security for Small Organisations, Adopted from Shaft and Vessey (2006)

The framework presented by Figure 3 above is to be seen as further development of Cognitive Fit Theory and should provide a useful guide to small businesses that have implemented wireless network technologies. Based on Figure 3 above, it can be concluded that inferior problem representation can serve to influence problem solving performance. The aspects (***awareness***, ***effective planning*** and ***stringent security implementation***) embody what we will call "***representation stimuli***". This is the contribution to theory. We show that the correct representation stimuli will influence both internal and external problem representation for wireless network security that is bound to influence correct problem solving performance. We argue also that the converse also holds.

6. Conclusion

The research has raised concern about small organisations and the exposures and threats that these organisations face when they deploy wireless network systems. Lack of awareness regarding standard procedures for securing wireless systems has been noted to be a reason why small organisations constantly face threats to wireless networks. These findings are also confirmed by the National Cyber Security Alliance, (NCSA) which has raised concerns about the public including organisations not being fully and completely aware of the dangers of not implementing and governing wireless security (Loo 2010). As a contribution, we have proposed and extended Cognitive Fit Theory as a suitable framework that provides insights in the way management and network practitioners' awareness is raised. The aims and results of the research has been to present small organisations with useful insights about how to manage wireless networks securely. The research supports the need for small organisations to stringently implement and continuously govern wireless networks using stated and accepted best practice procedures commonly used by security professionals in larger organisations. It is hoped that this work has provided insights that will instil a sense of responsibility to smaller organisations on how they should carry out wireless security and risk management. It is hoped that the work has achieved this intended outcome and adds value to small organisations.

7. Reference

Bin T., Yi-xian Y., Dong L., Qi L. and Yang, X., (2010), A security framework for wireless sensor networks, *The Journal of China Universities of Posts and Telecommunications Vol* 17:2 pp. 118–122.

Carter, B., and Shumway, R., (2002), *Wireless Security End-to-End*, Wiley Publishing Indianapolis, IN.

Kaplan, B. and Duchon, D., (1988), Combining Qualitative and Quantitative Methods in Information Systems Research: A Case Study, *Ninth Annual International Conference on Information Systems*, November 30-December 3, Minneapolis.

Loo AW. (2010) Illusion of Wireless Security, *Advances in Computers,* Vol 79 pp. 119-167.

Shaft, TM. and Vessey I., (2006), The Role of Cognitive Fit in the Relationship between Software Comprehension and Modification, *MIS Quarterly,* Vol 30:1, pp. 29-55.

Varshney, U., (2003a) Wireless I: Mobile And Wireless Information Systems: Applications, Networks, And Research Problem *Communications Of The Association For Information Systems* VoL 12 pp. 155-166.

Varshney, U., (2003b) The Status and Future of 802.11-based WLANs, *IEEE Computer*, Vol 36:6 pp. 90-93.

Vessey, I., (1991), Cognitive Fit: A Theory-Based Analysis of the Graphs Versus Tables Literature. *Decision Sciences* Vol 22:2 pp. 219-240.

Vessey, I. (2006), The theory of cognitive fit: One aspect of a general theory of problem solving, in P. Zhang and D. Galletta (eds.), *Human-computer interaction and management information systems: Foundations, Advances in Management Information Systems Series*, Armonk, NY

Welman, C., Kruger, F. & Mitchel, B., (2007), *Research Methodology*, 3rd Edition, Oxford University Press Southern Africa, Cape Town.

Winget, N R., Housley, D., Wagner, and Walker J., (2003), Security Flaws in 802.11 Data Link Protocols, *Communications of the ACM*, Vol 46:5 pp. 35-39.

Mobile Ad-hoc Network Security Challenges under AODV Routing Protocol

E.O.Ochola, M.M.Eloff and J.A.van der Poll

School of Computing, University of South Africa, Pretoria, South Africa
e-mail: {ocholeo|eloffmm|vdpolja}@unisa.ac.za

Abstract

Mobile Ad-hoc Network (MANET) is a group of heterogeneous mobile nodes, forming a temporary network which is infrastructure less, multi-hop and dynamic in nature. MANET requires that nodes cooperate to be able to communicate. The nodes, which act as hosts as well as routers, communicate with each other through multiple hops due to limited transmission ranges. Security challenges in MANETs such as channel vulnerability, absence of infrastructure, node vulnerability, dynamic topology, cooperative routing protocols and limited resources, pose new kinds of security threats to such networks. Unlike other types of networks, MANETs are deployed without a centralised control unit. Therefore, the direct application of the conventional routing algorithms may not be feasible. Mutual cooperation amongst the participating entities forms the basis for determining the routes to the destination. This aspect makes MANETs vulnerable to various communication security related attacks. *Black Hole* attacks are launched by participating malicious nodes that agree to forward data packets to a destination but eavesdrop or drop the packets intentionally, which not only compromise the network, but also degrade network performance. Routing protocols, which act as the binding force in these networks, are a common target of malicious nodes. This paper analyses challenges with existing solutions to *Black Hole* attack in MANET and concludes that, better secure approaches can be achieved through utilisation of optimised threshold values during anomaly detections in routing control packets' characteristic changes.

Keywords

Mobile Ad-hoc Network (MANET), AODV Routing Protocol, Black Hole Attack

1. Introduction

Wireless networks are formed by routers and hosts, and use radio frequencies to transmit and receive data instead of using physical cables. Mobile Ad-hoc Network (MANET) (Poongothai and Jayarajan, 2008) is a group of wireless mobile hosts without the required involvement of any offered infrastructure or centralised access point such as a base station. Basic networking devices, such as routers or access points are lacking in a MANET. Thus, data transfer among the network nodes is realised by means of multiple hops, and every node acts as a router to establish and maintain routes rather than just serving as a single mobile terminal host. This presents many challenges, including secure routing protocols, to the research community.

Nodes within each other's radio range communicate directly via wireless links, while those that are far apart use intermediate nodes as relays. The functioning of mobile ad-hoc networks is dependent on the trust and cooperation between nodes. Thus, nodes help each other in conveying information about the topology of the network (Tamilselvan and Sankaranarayanan, 2007). A source node intending to transfer data to a destination node located beyond its transmission range do so through intermediate nodes. It is therefore an important issue in MANET to perform a quick route establishment from, a necessity capitalised on by *Black Hole* attack.

Tamilselvan and Sankaranarayanan (2007:118) agree that security is a major concern in all forms of communication networks. However, mobile ad-hoc networks are faced with greater challenges due to their inherent nature, which can be attributed to characteristics such as: dynamic topology, lack of centralised control, limited battery power and limited bandwidth (Kurosawa *et al.* 2007). Hence, there exist routing attacks that can be launched on mobile ad-hoc networks.

AODV is one of the most popular routing protocols, which has been extensively discussed in research papers (Cerri and Ghioni, 2008:121). Therefore, this paper focuses on *Black Hole* attack detection and prevention scheme on AODV-based MANETs. *Black Hole* attack is one of the Denial of Service (DoS) attacks, in which the communication between nodes is interrupted by ensuring that sent data packets do not reach their intended destination, as they are dropped whenever they have to be relayed by the *Black Hole* nodes.The existing *Black Hole* attack solution approaches do not explicitly address the issues of false positive and negative identifications (mistaken identifications) of *Black Hole* nodes, with tradeoffs on network performance metrics to achieve comparable results. Hence a need to explicitly address the issues through optimised threshold values during anomaly detections.

2. MANET Security Issues

Security is much more difficult to maintain in MANETs due to their vulnerability, than wired networks. The use of wireless links renders a mobile ad-hoc network susceptible to link attacks (Anjum *et al.* 2006). The MANET vulnerabilities include, but are not limited to the following (Kurosawa *et al.* 2007):

a) Dynamically changing network topology: mobile nodes join and leave the network arbitrarily, resulting in dynamic change of network topology. This allows for a malicious node to join the network without prior detection.
b) Lack of centralised monitoring: there is absence of any centralised infrastructure that prohibits any monitoring mechanism in the network. This makes the classical security solutions based on certification authorities and on-line servers inapplicable. Even the trust relationships among individual nodes also change, especially when some nodes are found to be compromised. Hence, security mechanisms need to be dynamic and not static.
c) Cooperative algorithms: MANET routing algorithms require mutual trust between neighbouring nodes, which violates the principles of network security.
d) The absence of a certification authority, as a result of none existing infrastructure.

e) The limited physical protection of each of the nodes: network nodes usually do not reside in physically protected places, such as locked rooms. Hence, they can more easily be captured to fall under the control of an attacker.
f) The intermittent nature of connectivity, as a result of the instability in bandwidth requirements.
g) The vulnerability of the links (open media): messages can be eavesdropped and fake messages can be injected into the network without the difficulty of having physical access to the network components. Eavesdropping might give an attacker access to secret information thus violating confidentiality.

The contemporary routing protocols for mobile ad hoc networks cope well with the dynamically changing topology but are not designed to accommodate defence against malicious attackers. No single standard protocols capture common security threats and provide guidelines to secure routing (Singh *et al.* 2010). Nodes exchange network topology information in order to establish routes amongst them, which is a potential target for malicious attackers. It is difficult to detect compromised nodes through routing information due to the dynamic topology of mobile ad hoc networks (Liu *et al.* 2007). The routing protocol should be able to bypass the compromised nodes, as long as there are sufficient numbers of valid nodes. However, this needs the existence of multiple, possibly disjoint routes between nodes.

3. AODV Routing

AODV is perhaps the most well-known reactive routing protocol for a MANET (Cerri and Ghioni, 2008). It provides a rapid, dynamic network connection, with low processing loads and low memory consumption. Nodes in the network exchange routing information only when they intend to communicate, and keep this information updated only as long as the communication lasts.

A node intending to send a packet to another node starts a route discovery process in order to establish a route to the destination node, by sending a route request message (RREQ) to its neighbours. Neighbouring nodes increment the hop count on receiving the RREQ, and similarly forward (broadcast) the message to their neighbours using a flooding approach. This continues until the destination node is found. The RREQ message forwarding has the side effect of making other nodes learn the *reverse route* to the source node. The RREQ message will eventually reach the destination node, which will react with a route reply message (RREP). The RREP is sent as a unicast to the source node along the *reverse route* established during the RREQ broadcast. Similarly, the RREP message allows intermediate nodes to learn a *forward route* to the destination node. Therefore, at the end of the route discovery process, packets can be delivered from the source node to the destination node and vice versa. A route error message (RERR) allows nodes to notify errors due to link breakage, such as when a previous neighbour moves to a new position and is no longer reachable. Each mobile node would periodically send Hello messages (HELLO), thus, each node knows which nodes are its neighbouring nodes within one hop. Routing messages are either path discovery (RREQ and RREP) or path maintenance (RERR and HELLO) messages. All routing information expires after a timeout in case of an inactive route, and is removed from the routing table.

AODV is a collaborative protocol, allowing nodes to share information about each other. RREQ messages do not necessarily need to reach the destination node during the route discovery process. That is, an intermediate node having a route to the destination simply generates the RREP without any further forwarding of the RREQ. This enables a quicker response to route availability, eliminating unnecessary further flooding of RREQs.

Sequence numbers are used by AODV to identify fresher routing information. Every node maintains its own sequence number, incrementing it before sending either a new RREQ or RREP message. The sequence numbers are included in routing messages and recorded in routing tables. AODV favours newer information, thus nodes update their routing table whenever they receive a message with a higher sequence number (a larger number refers to newer information) or a smaller hop count (smaller hop count refers to shorter path) than what exists in the routing table for a given destination. However, a sequence number is given a higher priority than a hop count. That is, a route with newer information is favoured even if it is longer.

Being a reactive routing protocol, AODV does not give nodes a complete view of network topology. That is, each node only knows its neighbours, and for the non-neighbours, it only knows the next hop to reach them and the distance in hops. However, the security of AODV is compromised by the *Black Hole* nodes, as it accepts the received RREP having fresher route.

The standard AODV routing protocol cannot fight the threat of *Black Hole* attacks, because during the phase of route discovery, malicious nodes may counterfeit a sequence number and hop count in the routing message; thereby, acquiring the route, eavesdropping or/and dropping all the data packets received for relay to intended next hop intermediate nodes.

4. Black Hole Attack

Due to the nature of instances that prompt the use of MANETs such as communication during natural disasters, on the battlefield, and business conferences, there is a need for guaranteed safety of data transfer between two communicating nodes. A *Black Hole* attack (Su, 2011) forges the sequence number and hop count of a routing message to forcibly acquire the route, and then eavesdrop or drop all data packets that are supposed to be relayed. A malicious (*Black Hole*) node impersonates a destination node by sending a spoofed RREP to a source node that initiated a route discovery.

A *Black Hole* node has two properties (Tamilselvan and Sankaranarayanan, 2007): (1) the node exploits the ad hoc routing protocol and advertises itself as having a valid route to a destination, even though the route is spurious, with the intention of intercepting packets, and (2) the node consumes the intercepted packets.

The behaviour of a *Black Hole* attack is depicted in Figure 1, where a source node S intends to establish a route to a destination node D. In an AODV routing protocol, a source node would broadcast a RREQ packet to establish a route to a destination; with the normal intermediate nodes receiving and continuously broadcasting the

RREQ, except the *Black Hole* node. Everything works well if the RREP from a normal node reaches the source node first; but the RREP from *Black Hole* could reach the source node first, if it is nearer to the source node. Moreover, a *Black Hole* node does not need to check its routing table when sending false RREP message; its response is likely to reach the source node first. This makes the source node to conclude that the route discovery process is complete, ignoring all other RREPs and beginning to send data packets. The *Black Hole* node would directly send a route reply (RREP) to the source node S, with an extremely large sequence number and hop count of 1, as shown in Figure 1(a). The destination node D would also select a route with a minimum hop count upon receiving RREQs from normal nodes, and send a RREP packet as illustrated in Figure 1(b). Based on the AODV protocol, a source node S would select the latest and shortest (i.e., largest sequence number and minimum hop count) route to send the data packets from the RREPs packets received. It implies that a route via the *Black Hole* node would be selected by node S. The received data packets by the *Black Hole* node will then be eavesdropped or dropped as in Figure 1(c). Therefore, source and destination nodes are unable to communicate with each other as highlighted in (Kurosawa *et al.* 2007).

The malicious (*Black Hole*) node always sends RREP as soon as it receives RREQ without performing standard AODV operations, while keeping the destination sequence number very high. Since AODV considers RREP having higher value of destination sequence number to be fresh, the RREP sent by the malicious (*Black Hole*) node is treated fresh. Thus, the malicious nodes succeed in injecting *Black Hole* attacks.

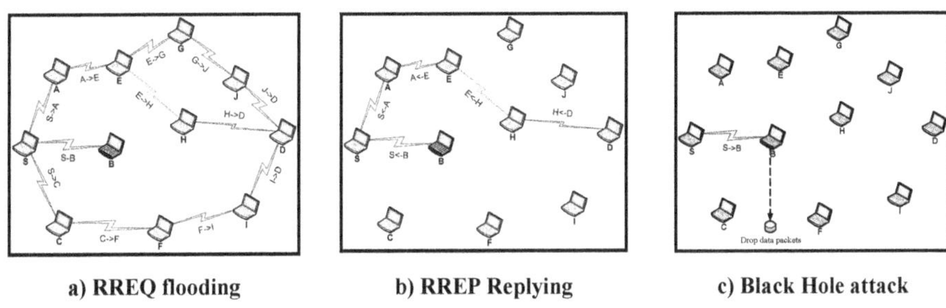

a) RREQ flooding b) RREP Replying c) Black Hole attack

Figure 1: A Black Hole attack illustration

5. Black Hole Attack Solution Challenges

Routing algorithms using sequence numbers and hop counts in determining best routes such as AODV are likely to experience *Black Hole* attacks. Numerous approaches have been proposed in the literature to guard the algorithms against such attacks. The AODV routing protocol was revised in (Dokurer *et al.* 2007) to reduce opportunities for a *Black Hole* node to acquire a route by the source node dropping the first two received RREPs, but selectively picking any subsequent RREP packets. This approach will likely be appropriate in cases where a *Black Hole* node is located nearer to a source node and is likely to underperform when it is located many hops away from the source node.

A proposal that a source node waits for a predetermined time value to receive other RREPs with next hop details from the other neighbouring nodes, without sending the DATA packets to the first RREP node at once is presented in (Tamilselvan and Sankaranarayanan, 2007). Upon the expiry of the timer, it checks in its routing table to find out any repeated next hop node. It then assumes that the paths are correct or the chance of malicious path is limited if any repeated next hop node is present in the RREP paths. And upon comparison of the received RREPs, it randomly selects a neighbour which has the same next hop as other alternative routes to send the data packets. This solution adds a delay and decreases throughput as more RREPs are waited for, and the process of finding repeated next hop is an extra overhead.

The PCBHA (Prevention of a Co-operative Black Hole Attack) proposed in (Tamilselvan and Sankaranarayanan, 2008) is another revised AODV routing protocol aimed at preventing cooperative *Black Holes* attack. It begins by providing each legal user with a default fidelity level. After broadcasting a RREQ, a source node waits for RREQs from its neighbours and then selects a neighbour with a higher fidelity level, which exceeds the threshold value, for data packets forwarding. The destination node sends an acknowledgement message (ACK) after receiving a data packet and the source node may increase the neighbour's fidelity level by 1, upon receiving the ACK response. A neighbour's fidelity level will be reduced by 1 if no ACK response is received by the source, which indicates a possible *Black Hole* node on the route, which drops data packets before reaching the destination node. The approach works well where the malicious node is not in a position to generate an ACK packet with a faked destination identity (ID). This implies that a source node has to counter check the IDs in the ACK table entities to verify that it is indeed from the destination node. However, the selection of an optimal threshold fidelity level still needs to be determined for accurate detection.

A dynamic learning method intended to detect a *Black Hole* node is proposed in (Kurosawa *et al.* 2007). It observes if the characteristic change of a node exceeds the threshold within a given time period. A node is declared a *Black Hole* node if its characteristic change exceeds the threshold. Otherwise, the latest observation data is added into dataset for dynamic updates. The characteristics observed are the number of sent RREQs, the number of received RREPs, and the mean destination sequence numbers of the observed RREQs and RREPs. However, there is no detection mode such as revising the AODV protocol, thus, *Black Hole* nodes are not isolated by this approach. Furthermore, this comes with increased processing overhead and the determination of optimal threshold values remains unresolved.

An attempt to address the survivability problem of the routing service when selective dropping attacks were launched, using trusted nodes to monitor neighbours is presented in (Marti *et al.* 2000). However, the method could not work well in a sparse network where there were no enough neighbours to act as the monitoring nodes. A proposal that each node overhears all traffic of its neighbours and then compares the values observed with some metric to detect abnormal behaviours in the network is made in (Huang and Lee, 2003). The approach requires nodes to be in promiscuous mode and process all overheard packets, which can be energy consuming, impacting negatively on energy constrained mobile nodes. Furthermore, nodes might not overhear neighbours' transmissions in a sparse network due to insufficient transmission power, which limits transmission ranges.

An improved ferry based detection method (MUTON) in which the transitive property was considered, achieving a better detection performance than FBIDM is proposed in (Ren *et al.* 2010). However, MUTON similarly uses trusted ferry nodes in its detection mechanism, thus, requiring additional devices to be deployed in the network, which may not be economical or feasible. The concept of encounter tickets to secure the evidence of nodes' communication is introduced in (Li *et al.* 2009). The nodes uniquely interpret the contact history by making observations based on the encounter tickets. However, the method can only prevent the attacker from claiming non-existent encounters, but cannot address the packet dropping.

Secure AODV (Zapata, 2002) defines a set of message extensions to RREQ, RREP and RERR messages in AODV. New messages also exist for detecting duplicate network addresses. The mechanism provides the authentication of the originator and destination nodes. However, it has weaknesses; nothing prevents a node from increasing a hop count arbitrarily or leaving it unchanged. Malicious nodes can acquire routes by consistently declaring high hop counts. Further weakness is that it does not protect the sender IP address field. A malicious (*Black Hole*) node can impersonate another node while forwarding a RREP to acquire routes. Hence, encryption solution approaches do not address packet dropping by a *Black Hole* node.

Two *Black Hole* attack detection approaches are proposed in (Ning and Sum, 2003): sending a ping packet to the destination to confirm the established route and waiting for the receipt of an acknowledgement, failure of which the presence of a *Black Hole* is deduced; and keeping track of sequence numbers since *Black Hole* nodes usually temper with them, sending packets with unusually high sequence numbers. However, the ping packet increases delay and traffic overhead.

A dynamic learning system (DPRAODV) which checks to detect the existence of a RREP sequence number (RREP_seq_no) that is higher than the threshold value is proposed in (Raj and Swadas, 2009). A node is then suspected to be malicious (*Black Hole*) if its RREP_seq_no is higher than the threshold value, and is added to the black list. The threshold value is dynamically updated at every time interval. And a node sends a control packet ALARM, to its neighbours whenever it detects an anomaly. The ALARM packet has the black list node as a parameter, notifying the neighbouring nodes to discard any RREP packet from any suspected malicious node (i.e., no processing is done to the packet). However, the dynamic update of the threshold value at every time interval leads to overheads. Similarly, the determination of an optimal threshold value is necessary for accurate anomaly detection.

A protocol requiring intermediate nodes to send RREP packets containing next hop information is proposed in (Deng *et al.* 2002). A source node receiving a RREP will send a RREQ to the next hop to verify the existence of a route to the RREP generator from the next hop, and another route from the next hop to the destination. When the next hop receives the route verification RREQ, it sends back a further reply to source node with check results. The source node finally judges the validity of the route based on the further reply information. This approach leads to an increased delay.

The existing solutions analyses show the loopholes in detections and eliminations of *Black Hole* attacks in AODV routing protocol. Hence, there is a need for the development of a 'perfect' *Black Hole* attack detection and elimination mechanism.

6. Simulation Performance Analysis

The simulation was done using OMNeT++ discrete events simulator, to analyse the AODV routing performance under the influence of a *Black Hole* attack, by varying the node mobility speed. Simulation setup illustrating the dynamic topology challenge in MANETs is shown in Figure 2.

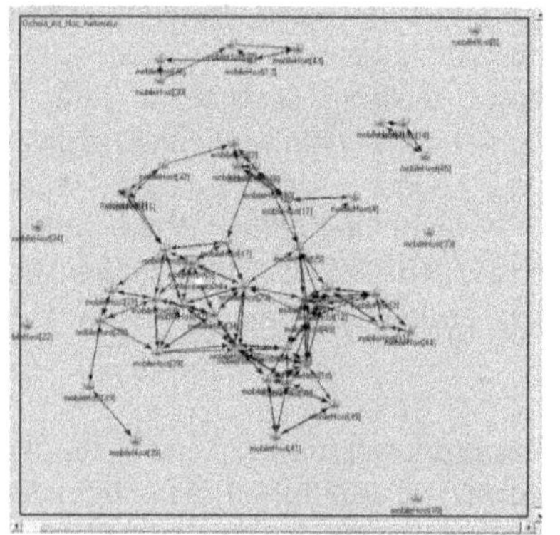

(a) Network topology at simulation time = 7200 sec.

(b) Network topology at simulation time = 90 sec.

Figure 2: Simulation setup showing MANET dynamic topology

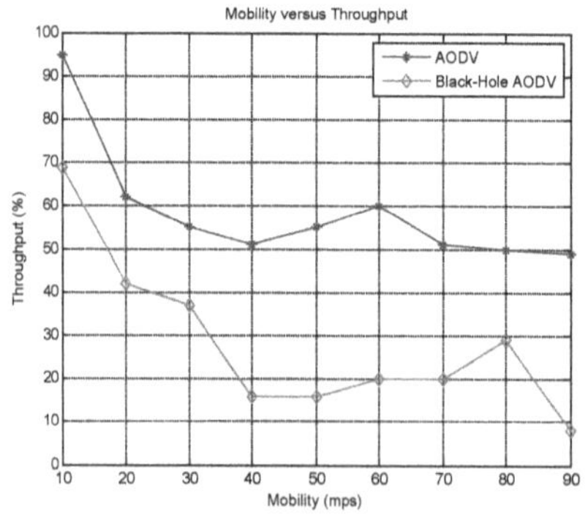

(a) Effect of Black Hole attack on the network throughput

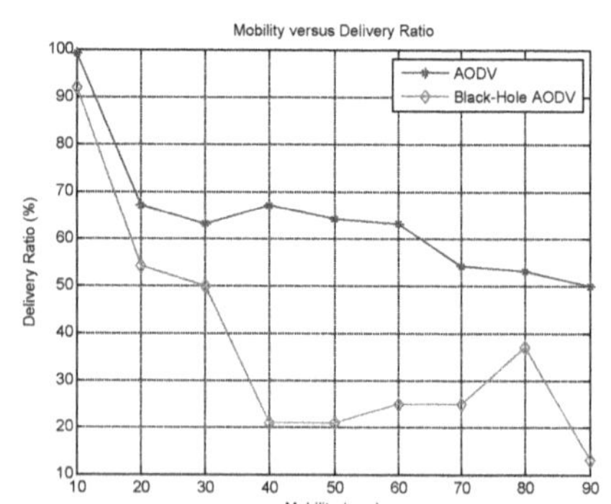

(b) Effect of Black Hole attack on the network packet delivery ratio

Figure 3: Effect of Black Hole Attack on the network performance

The metrics used to evaluate the routing performance are throughput and packet delivery ratio. The effect of a *Black Hole* attack on AODV routing protocol performance were evaluated as follows:

a) Throughput decreases in the presence of a *Black Hole* node in the network as shown in Figure 3 (a). The analysis shows that throughput is very high in AODV than *Black-Hole AODV* because of higher packet loss in the latter, as a result of packet dropping by the *Black Hole* node.
b) Packet delivery ratio decreases when there is a malicious (*Black Hole*) node in the network as shown in Figure 3 (b). This is because some of the packets are dropped by the *Black Hole* node and not received at the destinations.

7. Conclusion

Black Hole attack is one of the most serious security problems in MANET. It is an attack where a malicious (*Black Hole*) node impersonates a destination node by sending forged RREP to a source node that initiates route discovery, and consequently deprives data traffic from the source node. The paper analyses secure routing in MANET against *Black Hole* attack. The existing solutions affect the AODV routing protocol performance negatively in terms of throughput, delay and overheads. Although these may not be avoided in totality, there is a need for trade-offs to achieve a secure optimal performances. The analyses necessitate that optimal threshold values should be determined for accurate anomaly detections, with trade-offs in delays and overheads, during characteristic changes detections.

8. References

Anjum, F., Ghosh, A.K., Golmie, N., Kolodzy, P., Poovendran, R., Shorey, R. and Lee, D. (2006), "Security in Wireless Ad hoc Networks", *IEEE Journal on Selected Areas in Communications*, vol. 24, no. 2, pp. 217-220.

Cerri, D. and Ghioni, A. (2008), "Securing AODV: The A-SAODV Secure Routing Prototype", *IEEE Communications Magazine*, February 2008, pp. 120-125.

Deng, H., Li, W. and Agrawal, D.P. (2002), "Routing Security in Ad Hoc Networks", *IEEE Communications Magazine, Special Topics on Secuity in Telecommunication Networks*, vol. 40, no. 10, pp. 144-146.

Dokurer, S., Erten, Y.M. and Acar, C.E. (2007), "Performance Analysis of Ad-hoc Networks under Black Hole Attacks", *In Proceedings of the IEEE SoutheastCon*, 22-25 March 2007, Richmond, VA, pp. 148-153.

Huang, Y. and Lee, W. (2003), "A cooperative intrusion detection system for ad hoc networks", *In Proceedings of the 1st ACM workshop on Security of ad hoc and sensor networks (SASN '03)*, 27-30 October 2003, Washington, DC, USA, pp. 135-147.

Kurosawa, S., Nakayama, H., Kato, N., Jamalipour, A. and Nemoto, Y. (2007), "Detecting Black hole Attack on AODV-based Mobile Ad Hoc Networks by Dynamic Learning Method", *International Journal of Network Security*, vol. 5, no. 3, pp 338-346.

Li, F., Wu, J. and Srinivasan, A. (2009), "Thwarting black hole attacks in distruption-tolerant networks using encounter tickets", *In Proceedings of the IEEE INFOCOM 2009*, 19-25 April 2009, Rio de Janeiro, pp. 2428-2436.

Liu, K., Deng, J., Varshney, P.K. and Balakrishnan, K. (2007), "An Acknowledgment-Based Approach for the Detection of Routing Misbehavior in MANETs", *IEEE Transaction on Mobile Computing*, vol. 6, no. 5, pp. 536-550.

Marti, S., Giuli, T.J., Lai, K. and Baker, M. (2000), "Mitigating routing misbehavior in mobile ad hoc networks", *In Proceedings of the 6th annual international conference on Mobile computing and networking (MobiCom '00)*, 6-11 August 2000, Boston, MA, USA, pp. 255-265.

Ning, P. and Sum, K. (2003), "How to misuse AODV: A case study of insider attack against mobile ad hoc routing protocol", *In Proceedings of the IEEE Systems, Man and Cybernetics Society Information Assurance Workshop*, 18-20 June 2003, United States Military Academy, West Point, NY, pp. 60-67.

Poongothai, T. and Jayarajan, K. (2008), "A non-cooperative game approach for intrusion detection in Mobile Adhoc networks", *In Proceedings of the International Conference on Computing, Communication and Networking (ICCCn 2008)*, 18-20 December 2008, St. Thomas, VI, pp 1-4.

Raj, P.N. and Swadas, P.B. (2009), "DPRAODV: A Dyanamic Learning System Against Blackhole Attack In Aodv Based Manet", *International Journal of Computer Science Issues (IJCSI)*, vol. 2, pp 54-59.

Ren, Y., Chuah, M.C., Yang, J. and Chen, Y. (2010), "Muton: Detecting malicious nodes in disruption-tolerant networks", *In Proceedings of WCNC'2010*, pp. 1-6.

Singh, K., Yadav, R.S. and Ranvijay (2010), "A Review Paper on Ad Hoc Network Security", *International Journal of Computer Science and Security*, vol. 1, no. 1, pp. 52-69.

Su, M.Y. (2011), "Prevention of selective black hole attacks on mobile ad hoc networks through intrusion detection systems", *Computer Communications*, vol. 34, no. 1, pp. 107-117.

Tamilselvan, L. and Sankaranarayanan, V. (2007), "Prevention of Impersonation Attack in Wireless Mobile Ad hoc Networks", *International Journal of Computer Science and Network Security (IJCSNS)*, vol. 7, no. 3, pp. 118-123.

Tamilselvan, L. and Sankaranarayanan, V. (2008), "Prevention of co-operative black hole attack in MANET", *Journal of Networks*, vol. 3, no. 5, pp.13-20.

Zapata, M.G. (2002), "Secure ad hoc on-demand distance vector routing", *Mobile Computing and Communications Review*, vol. 6, no.3, pp. 106-107.

Chapter 4

Applications and Impacts

The Use of Customer Profiles for the Personalisation of User Interfaces

A.P.Calitz and S.Barlow

Department of Computing Sciences, Nelson Mandela Metropolitan University
P.O. Box 77000, Port Elizabeth, 6031, South Africa
e-mail: andre.calitz@nmmu.ac.za

Abstract

Businesses increasingly obtain data and information from customers in order to conduct customer profiling. On-line customer profiling has provided many benefits, including increased sales and the creation of personalised user interfaces. Customer profiling also provides the opportunity to provide product recommendations to customers and to improve customer relationships. Personalised user interfaces or product information displays (presentation modes) used on e-commerce websites are important factors that influence a customer's buying decisions. The provision of the most appropriate product information display, based on customer product knowledge can increase customer satisfaction and loyalty. Using customer profiling to personalise product information displays with Service Oriented Architectures (SOA) and Cloud Computing is increasingly being used by businesses which provide the ability to purchase products and services on-line.

In this research study an e-commerce website was designed and implemented using web services. The primary objective of this research was to determine whether a relationship exists between a customer's product knowledge level (novice, intermediate, expert) and a product information display preferred on an e-commerce website. The three most commonly used product information displays used are list, commented list and matrix layouts. The customer's product knowledge levels were determined using a decision model which was linked to the three different product information displays. The results indicated that a relationship exists between a customer's product knowledge level and the product information display preferred. The research findings supported related research indicating that customers with a novice product knowledge level prefer a matrix product information display which contained a large amount of detail.

Keywords

E-commerce, customer profiling, user interfaces, product information displays.

1. Introduction

Businesses today face many challenges in maintaining and sharing their product and customer information across different business units and subsidiaries, mainly because business units are located in different geographical locations (Han and Kamber, 2006). The Internet has however, changed the way people conduct business activities (Schneider, 2007). A popular trend in e-commerce is customer profiling, specifically integrating customer profiling with Customer Relationship Management (CRM) (Liu *et al.,* 2001). CRM is used by businesses to create personalised relationships between the business and the customer in order to improve customer loyalty and satisfaction (Liu *et al.,* 2001; Turban *et al.,* 2006).

A customer's knowledge of different product categories may vary significantly. This requires that the user interface and information provided about the product on the e-commerce website has to be adapted according to the customer's product knowledge. Product information displays or product presentation modes, such as product catalogues, should include more or less detail, based on the customer's product knowledge, as these factors may influence the customer's buying decision. Considering the available customer information in a customer profile, it is often difficult to determine the most appropriate product information display for a customer (Schafer, Konstan and Reidl, 2001).

Businesses increasingly use new technologies such as SOA and cloud computing in the e-commerce environment. In this research study, an e-commerce system was implemented using Service Orientated Architecture (SOA) principles, such as Web services for flexible and modular re-usage of computing services. This research designed and implemented an e-commerce website selling three different product categories (wine, groceries and electrical products) for three different business units. The three product categories were selected based on research conducted on the most popular products sold on the Internet (Ntawanga, Calitz and Barnard, 2008). It further used three different product information displays identified in literature, namely list, matrix and commented list to display the product information to customers, based on their product knowledge levels. The research implemented a stand-alone desktop application and then an e-commerce website with a Web service in a cloud service application. This used the Windows Azure environment for business units to maintain information using the desktop application.

In this research paper the background and related research is discussed in Section 2 and the focus of the research is presented in Section 3. The methodology followed in this research study is discussed in Section 4 and in Section 5 the evaluation procedure and results of the research are discussed. The research is then concluded in Section 6, where this section also highlights possible future research.

2. Background

E-commerce applications which use customer profile information to provide personalised services to customers have their own components. Using this customer profile information should make the product information displays on the e-commerce website more informative. Customer profile attributes are updated as the customer interacts with the website. This section discusses research related to the above mentioned terms, where customer profiling in e-commerce is highlighted.

2.1. Customer profiling in e-commerce

E-commerce is buying and selling products, services and information by using Internet technologies and electronic systems (Schneider, 2007). E-commerce has provided a way to build personalised relationships with customers by using a customer profile. A customer profile is a snapshot of the customer which provides customer information and specifically customer buying behaviour (Adomavicius and Tuzhilin, 2005). The demographical information about a customer includes attributes such as the customer's age, gender, name and geographical location. Behavioural information is captured while a customer is performing certain tasks on the website (Adomavicius and Tuzhilin, 2005). In this research, a customer profile, consisting of demographical information and the product knowledge levels was implemented. A customer's product knowledge level (novice, intermediate, expert) for each product category (wine, groceries, electrical products) was recorded according to the method used in the research conducted by Ntawanga, et al. (2008). The customer's product knowledge level is used in order to present a product information display (matrix, list, and commented list) for a product category whenever the customer chooses to view a product of a specific category.

A customer profile is established by implementing implicit and explicit feedback by on-line businesses (Jokela *et al.*,2001). Explicit feedback is simply determining factual information by asking customers to register their details on the website through the usage of an on-line questionnaire. Implicit feedback is completed by capturing information about the customer as he or she interacts with the e-commerce system. Well-known techniques are weblog mining and web cookies. The customer profile is then updated using the weblog files and by applying a decision model on the information captured. The potential uses of customer profile information in e-commerce are personalisation, customisation and recommendation (Hofgesang, 2007). Personalisation consists of the following phases: data collection, analysis of data and deciding the action (Eirinak and Vazirgiannis, 2003). Customisation is used for customers to receive a sense of ownership when obtaining a customised product or service. Recommendation is used to assist customers in their buying decision; by making suggestions about products they can purchase (Chang, Changchein and Huang, 2006).

2.2. Product information display interfaces

A customer who needs to purchase a product has many external and internal factors affecting the purchase decision. Information processing in the customer's memory plays a large role in the decision whether to acquire a product or not (Biiehal and Dipankar, 1983). Customer information processing (CIP) differs in the way in which product information is organised. Product information can be represented by brand or by product attribute, but product catalogues of e-commerce on-line stores should include more detailed information about products (Koenemann and Belkin, 1996). The three most commonly used product information displays used in e-commerce are:

- List layout (Figure 1) - contains a list of products with little detail about a product and is mostly used by e-commerce websites because the layout is easy for browsing (Hong, Thong and Tam, 2004).
- Matrix layout (Figure 2) - contains products which are displayed in a grid, where this layout contains a large amount of product information. This layout is mostly used to display technologic products and for searching (Hong, Thong and Tam, 2004).

- Commented list layout (Figure 3) - this is a layout which contains a list of products with a brief amount of product detail, and it is most often used in e-commerce for customers to add comments about products.

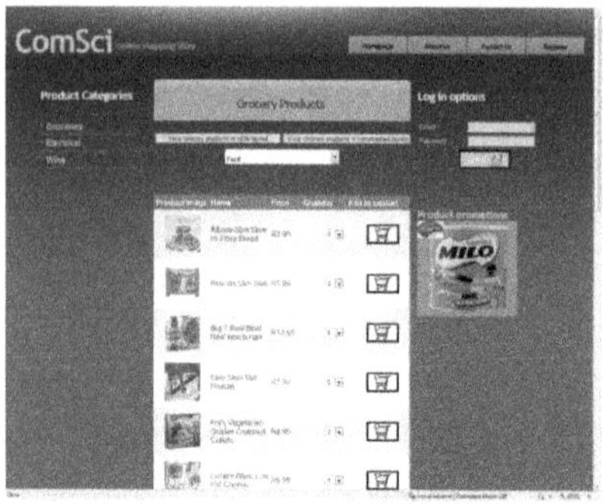

Figure 1: List layout used

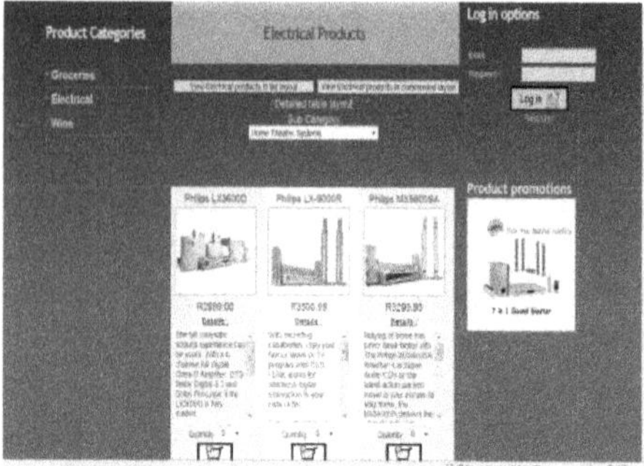

Figure 2: Matrix layout used

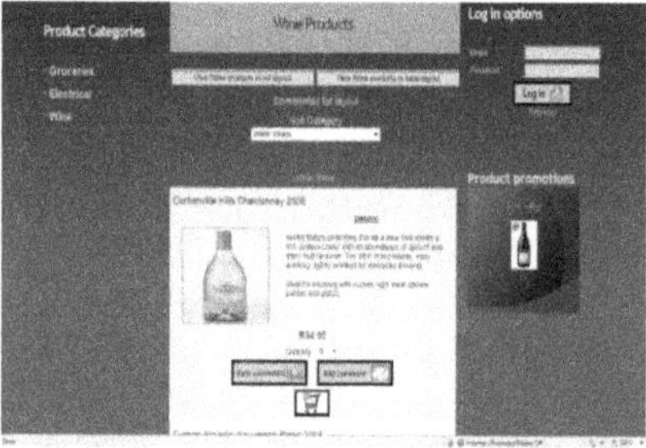

Figure 3: Commented List layout used

The presentation modes used could also contain image-based and text-based modes, where image-based has an image representing the product and text-based contains only textual descriptions of the product. Text-based is mostly used on sites accommodating users with low bandwidths. The research implemented the three product information displays and used them to present a product information display for the three product categories, namely wine, groceries and electrical products. These product categories selected, based on the research conducted by Ntawanga, et al. (2008), where the research highlighted that these product categories are popular products sold on e-commerce websites. The product information displays used play a large role in the focus of this research.

3. Focus of Research

E-commerce and customer profiling have opened the doors to the personalisation of relationships between customers and businesses. The customer profile information, consisting of many attributes, creates this possibility. A business can now provide each individual customer with a unique form of the current webpage being viewed based on the individual customer profile. Many challenges have been identified, as it is difficult to determine when a customer profile should be updated and what the decision model should be utilised. Another challenge is that some customer profile attributes are very personal and the receipt of this information illegally can lead to fraudulent activities. Further, it is hard to determine how to personalise the webpage perfectly for a specific customer. The presentation of the webpage plays a major role in a customer's buying decision. This research implemented an e-commerce customer profile website containing different product information displays; a web service using SOA techniques within a Windows Azure cloud environment and a desktop application linking it to the website using the web service. The paper will only focus on answering the following research questions which apply to the limitation discussed above:

Does a relationship exist between a customer's product knowledge level for a specific product category and the product information display layout which the customer prefers when purchasing products from this category?

4. Research Methodology

Researchers have identified many development methodologies in software development. This section discusses how the system was implemented and how the incremental prototyping methodology was used. This methodology was used because each component of the system was developed as a working prototype and then added to another, to form a working system. The system was developed on a Windows Azure platform.

4.1. E-commerce system

An online e-commerce website was developed and implemented as a *Web-Role (in Windows Azure.)* This was completed in order to capture the customers' profiles. It was then used to identify which attributes of the customer profile customers are willing to share on-line, in this environment. The customer profile was later used to determine whether product information displays on e-commerce websites have a relationship with customers' product knowledge levels. The e-commerce website was used to sell three categories of products, namely wine, groceries and electronic products. Each product category contained individual products, categorised into sub-categories. Each product contained product descriptions and other attributes which were mapped onto each of the three product information displays, namely list, matrix and commented list. The product information displays were then mapped to a customer's product knowledge level for the product category being viewed.

After completing an initial questionnaire, the customer's product knowledge levels for each product category is established. For example, a customer's product knowledge classification could be intermediate for groceries, novice for electronic goods and expert for wine. The mapping of the product knowledge levels, to product information displays, is as follows and the relationship between these will be evaluated:

- A Novice product knowledge level is mapped onto the Matrix layout which is shown in *Figure 2.* This includes the most detail about a product;
- An Intermediate product knowledge level is mapped onto the Commented List layout which is shown in *Figure 3.* This includes a fair amount of product detail and allows customers to view comments other customers made about the product being viewed;
- An Expert product knowledge level is mapped onto the List layout which is shown n *Figure 1.* This includes limited detail about a product, but includes the most important information about a product such as price, name and an image.

After the mapping, customers can change the product information display to view the same product's information in a different display mode. For example, if the customer needs more product information, he/she can change from a list layout to a matrix layout. The initial product knowledge levels for customers are assigned by the customers answering a product knowledge questionnaire based on the three product categories during the registration process. The questionnaire is based on research conducted by Ntawanga, *et al.* (2008). The product knowledge levels are then updated using the decision model previously developed and evaluated by Ntawanga, *et al.* (2008) with amendments to the number of products needing to be purchased and time spent on a product category.

4.2. Business unit application

A desktop application was developed for each particular product category, namely wine, groceries and electronic goods, to maintain product information and to retrieve relevant customer information. Each product category can be associated with an individual business unit to represent a real life business scenario. The three business units will then be able to see the entire customer's generic profile information. Where customers prefer information to be private, it will only be viewed by a specific business unit if the unit has a transaction history with the customer. This property is controlled by a flag attribute activated if a customer has purchased a product from a business unit before or not. The functionality of the business application was implemented as a web service within the cloud service of the e-commerce website, whereas the business unit application connected to this service and used its functionality through a web service.

5. Analysis and Results

5.1. Evaluation procedure

The evaluation of the proposed system was an ongoing process; in accordance with the incremental prototyping methodology selected. The user testing was completed in order to arrive at the answers to the research questions. User testing consisted of three tests. The first was completed to determine whether users find the different product information displays useful. The outcome was that they are useful except for the commented list layout. The second test was completed in order to test whether the system architecture can support this application. Expert users confirmed that the Window Azure environment can be used for this application. The third evaluation was a conducted on a convenient sample of 31 potential on-line customers. The participants consisted of male and female, undergraduate and postgraduate students, university staff and users in industry. Each participant was presented with a user test consisting of 5 Sections A to E. In Section A the researchers obtained basic demographical information of the participants, Section B computer experience and Section C on-line shopping experience. The tasks to be performed, namely purchasing of products, were presented in Section D. The post-test questionnaire was completed at the end of the session, acquiring information on participants' presentation layout preferences and product knowledge levels. The post-test questionnaire measured the various criteria using a 5 point Likert scale. The scale was represented as 1- Strongly disagree and 5- Strongly agree.

The researchers further tested the following hypotheses:

- H_0: No relationship exists between a customer's product knowledge levels and product information displays.
- H_1: A relationship between a customer's product knowledge levels and product information displays exists.

The convenience sample of participants consisted of at least 80% with computer experience of more than 6 years, 70% with Internet experience more than 6 years and 90% who spend an hour on the Internet per day. The participants (n=31) in the research study consisted of participants with a *novice* product knowledge level for wine (n=23), an *intermediate* product knowledge level for groceries (n=19) and electrical products (n=12) with only a limited number of participants being *experts* for the three product categories.

The participants evaluated the e-commerce application, completing the required tasks in their work environment. In order to eliminate prior learning the authors created two systems, A and B. Half of the sample used System A first and the remaining group, System B first. The difference between System A and B was that System A presented users with a default product information display when viewing products in a product category. System B presented a product information display based on the customer's product knowledge level for that specific category. The customers using both systems still had the freedom to change and choose a product information display of their choice when purchasing products in specific product categories. The task lists consisted of 9 tasks for each, which were basically, purchasing three products from each product category. The data collected by the application recorded the products purchased and which products the customer viewed using different product information displays. The data were finally used to determine which product information display is preferred by a customer with a certain product knowledge level.

5.2. Results

5.2.1. Task list results

The results shown in Table 1 are task success and task time for the activities for Systems A and B.

Task success			
System	**Observed count**	**Expected count**	**Chi-squared p-value**
A	229	237,5	0.44
B	246	237,5	

Table 1: Task success information (n=31)

The results tabulated in *Table 1* were calculated using the Chi-Squared test where the value obtained ($t_{30=}p=0.44$), using a 95% confidence interval, shows that there was not a significant difference between the task successes for the two Systems. In *Table 2* the task times were measured as interval data in seconds. In this table the data are represented as numbers 1-5 where 1 is < 30 sec, 2 is 31-60 sec, 3 is 61-90 sec, 4 is 90-120 sec and 5 is > 120 sec. The average time to complete tasks for System A was 2,63 seconds and 1,61 seconds for System B. When t-test on the task times were conducted, the following values were calculated ($t_{30}=14.66$, $p < 0.01$), this indicated that the task times were significantly different. The difference could be attributed to the learnability of the system or that the users performed better on System B which presented a product information display based on the customer's product knowledge level for that specific category. The average task time for system A's task 2 was the highest overall where this task was to purchase an electrical product. This can be because the users did not change the layout to the appropriate layout on in time. As the product category was electrical, it required a large amount of information and the product category could have influenced the preferred layout.

Task	Mean A	Mean B	Median A	Median B	Std.Dev A	Std.Dev B
1	2.81	1.97	3.00	2.00	0.91	0.80
2	2.90	1.77	3.00	2.00	0.79	0.80
3	2.71	1.42	3.00	1.00	0.78	0.62
4	2.71	1.42	3.00	1.00	0.69	0.67
5	2.61	1.65	3.00	1.00	0.92	0.75
6	2.68	1.58	3.00	1.00	0.75	0.67
7	2.26	1.42	2.00	1.00	0.73	0.62
8	2.45	1.87	2.00	2.00	0.77	0.72
9	2.81	1.45	3.00	1.00	0.98	0.72

Table 2: Task time information (n=31)

5.2.2. Post-test questionnaire results

The questionnaires were based on the evaluation of the system's metrics. *Table 3* indicates that participants were satisfied with the system and the product information displays with which they were presented. The direct comparison of System A and B illustrates that participants preferred to use System B which provided a product information display according to their product knowledge level. This illustrated that participants prefer a presentation which is personalised.

Question		Mean	Median	Std.Dev
Strongly disagree	Strongly agree			
1. The system speed was slow/fast?		4.68	5.00	0.48
2. I had enough information available to decide my purchase?		4.45	5.00	0.81
3. The layout of the product information matched my product knowledge level in System A?		3.42	3.00	1.03
4. The layout of the product information matched my product knowledge level in System B?		4.13	4.00	0.76
System A	System B			
5. I prefer System A which had default displays or System B which had a display according to my product knowledge level?		4.45	5.00	0.85
6. I enjoyed using System A or System B because it was easier to find the product I had to purchase?		4.26	4.00	0.77

Table 3: Post task questionnaire replies (n=31)

The analysis of the results indicated that participants mostly preferred the list layout when viewing grocery products. This could be due to the fact that most participants had an expert or intermediate product knowledge level for groceries. Comments made by participants were that, when they purchase groceries, they know what they need to purchase and do not require detailed product information.

After the completion of the post questionnaire, participants were requested to indicate which customer profile information they were willing to share. Twelve participants indicated that they were willing that their profile data, relating to product information display, be shared among business units. The participants generally felt that they would not want to share their contact number, email address, address, credit card number, passwords and identity number among business units.

The post-test questionnaire contained a section asking users whether they agreed with the updated customer profile attributes after interacting with the system. Table 4 indicates that users were satisfied with the updated profiles generated.

Product Category	Mean	Median	Std. Dev
Updated Grocery product knowledge	4.096774	4	0.83
Updated Electrical product knowledge level	3.967742	4	0.98
Update Wine product knowledge level	4.580645	5	0.62

Table 4: Satisfaction with updated product knowledge levels (n=31)

5.2.3. Participant interaction results

The results presented in this section are presented to support the goal of this research. Figure 4 (a) indicates that the 19% of the participants who were classified as novice for groceries, preferred the matrix layout for grocery purchases. Half of the 61% percent of the participants, classified as having an intermediate knowledge level for groceries, preferred the matrix layout. The 20% of participants that were classified as having an expert knowledge level for groceries were fairly evenly distributed between the three user interfaces.

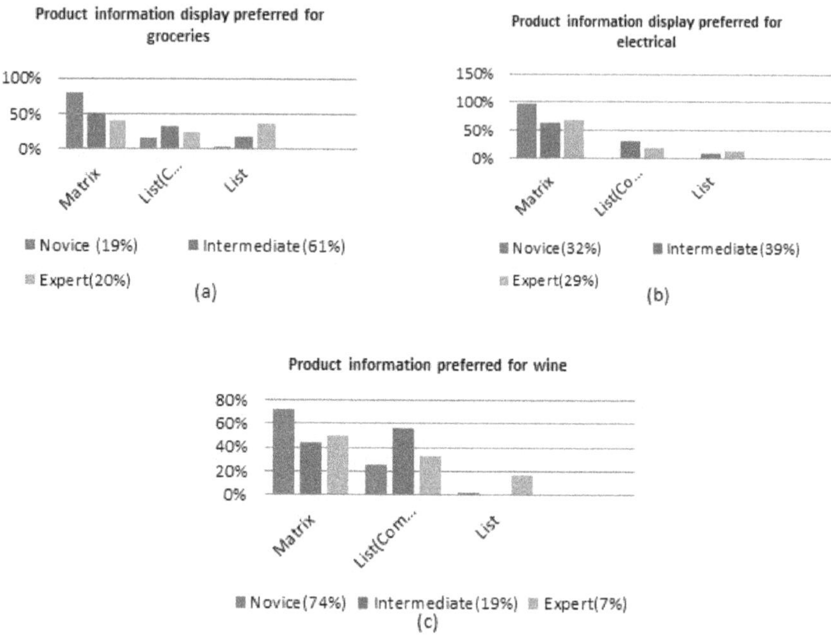

Figure 4: Preferred layout for product category (a-c) (n=31)

Figure 4 (b) indicates that for electrical products, regardless of their product knowledge classification, participants preferred the matrix layout to provide detailed information. Figure 4 (c) indicates that the majority of the 74% of participants that were classified as having a novice product knowledge level for wine, preferred the matrix layout. The participants, classified as having an intermediate product knowledge level for wine, preferred the commented list layout and the expert wine participants also preferred the matrix layout which provided a fair amount of product information. The reason for this could be that experts enjoy having a fair amount of information about the wine category, as wine drinkers enjoy seeing the most information possible about what they are going to be purchase.

In order to conduct data triangulations of results, a process and Apriori algorithm used in the evaluation of data mining results, was applied. The algorithm is presented with a rule and the support and confidence thereof is calculated. The strong support and confidence for *Rule 1in Table 5* emphasises that participants with novice product knowledge prefer the matrix layout.

Rule	Support	Confidence
1. A Novice product knowledge level implies that purchases will be completed in the Matrix layout.	42%	82%
2. An Intermediate product knowledge level implies that purchases will be completed in the Commented List layout.	38%	36%
3. An Expert product knowledge level implies that purchases will be completed in the List layout.	20%	22%

Table 5: Data Mining Rules (n=31)

The following tables *Table 6 to 8* tabulate the results of the Chi-squared test with a confidence interval of 95% on the data. The tables below show a statistically significant difference between the layout preferences for each class of participants. This is indicated by the p-values for the Chi-square tests being less than 0.05 for all classes of participants. Participants preferred a layout that was not equally split between the three layouts.

The results obtained after the analysis of the data showed clearly that participants preferred the matrix layout. This means that the null hypotheses, stating that there is no relationship between product information displays and customer product knowledge levels, cannot be completely rejected at this stage. The user interaction results section indicates that participants with any product knowledge level, preferred to use the matrix layout when purchasing a product from the groceries and electronic goods categories. This could be because the product category has an impact on the product information display preference. The wine category participants, with intermediate product knowledge levels, preferred the commented list layout for wine. This can be because the details provided about wines, in this product information display, were appropriate for task success.

The results could further indicate that participants with an intermediate product knowledge level had knowledge of the wine to be purchased. The Chi-squared tests used, showed that a significant difference existed between layout choices and that participants preferred the matrix layout overall. It can be deduced that there was a relationship between participants with a novice product knowledge level and the matrix layout. This result again highlights that the null hypotheses presented in Section 5.1 cannot be rejected completely. No statistically significant results have been identified between the other product knowledge levels and product information displays. All participants with the other product knowledge levels showed a preference for the matrix layout. These results indicated that the null hypothesis cannot be rejected as no relationship was found between customer product knowledge levels and all the product information displays, as the product categories could have played a role in the customer's preferences.

Layout	Novice(n=6)		Intermediate(n=19)		Expert(n=6)	
	Observed	Expected	Observed	Expected	Observed	Expected
List	33	33	35	35	17	33
List-com	17	33	24	35	33	33
Matrix	50	33	47	35	50	33
p-value	0.000259287		0.022692648		0.000259287	

Table 6: Chi-squared test for grocery product category (n=31)

Layout	Novice(n=10)		Intermediate(n=12)		Expert(n=9)	
	Observed	Expected	Observed	Expected	Observed	Expected
List	10	33	11	35	33	33
List-com	0	33	16	35	0	33
Matrix	90	33	78	35	67	33
p-value	9.42046E-33		5.18895E-18		1.68814E-15	

Table 7: Chi-squared test for electrical product category (n=31)

Layout	Novice(n=23)		Intermediate(n=6)		Expert(n=2)	
	Observed	Expected	Observed	Expected	Observed	Expected
List	2	37	17	36	0	33
List-com	17	37	8	36	0	33
Matrix	87	37	83	36	100	33
p-value	6.18041E-25		5.87645E-21		1.34796E-44	

Table 8: Chi-squared test for wine product category (n=31)

5.3. Limitations of the study

The system limitations were that the system had to run locally using a Windows Azure development storage account. The efficiency of cloud storage could not be measured accurately as the system was running locally. The evaluation had limitations which are listed below:

- There was no equal distribution of customers in the study with the different product knowledge levels;
- There was a small number of wine experts and those with intermediate knowledge;
- The system was evaluated in an artificial context where participants did not perform as they would have if they had to make real life purchases;
- The order in which the tasks was presented to participants using System A and System B.

6. Conclusions and Future Research

The development of e-commerce and customer profiling has become an integral part of business. The use of customer profiling in e-commerce has brought about personalisation which improves customer satisfaction levels and loyalty. The sharing of information, within a company consisting of various business units, has been challenging. A customer's profile, containing personal information as attributes, cannot be shared freely. The use of product information displays should include enough information to affect a customer's buying decision and lead to increases in sales. It has been identified that it is difficult to determine which product information display is most appropriate for customers. Therefore this research has implemented three different product information displays and used a customer's profile, containing product knowledge levels, to present a product information display relevant to the customer.

The results indicated that customers with a novice product knowledge level prefer a matrix product information display which contained a large amount of detail. The null hypotheses stating that there is no relationship between product information displays and customer product knowledge levels cannot be rejected. The research further concluded that the reason why there is no statistically significant relationship between product knowledge levels and product information displays is because customers know what products they want to purchase. In addition, there were not a large number of expert participants in product categories, such as wine and electrical products.

Future research to be implemented will include a recommendation for an e-commerce system using a customer's profile and evaluating whether the recommendations are useful. Future research could also implement an e-commerce website which is fully customisable by real-world customers and evaluate if the system increases customer satisfaction which is an important element when conducting on-line business.

7. References

Adomavicius, G. and Tuzhilin, A., (2005), Personalisation Technologies: A Process-Oriented Perspective. *Communications of the ACM* 48(10), pp 83-90.

Biehal, G. and Dipankar, C., (1983), Information Accessibility as a Moderator of Consumer Choice. *Journal of Consumer Research*, 10 (1), pp 1-14.

Canofora, G., Fasolini, A.R. and Tramontana, P., (2008), A wrapping approach for migrating legacy system interactive functionalities to SOA. *Journal of Systems and Software*, 81, pp 463-480.

Chang, S. E., Changchein, S.W. and Huang, R., (2006), *Assessing users' product specific knowledge for personalisation in e-commerce.* Expert Systems with Applications 30, pp 682-693.

Chappell, D., (2008), *Introducing the Azure Services Platform.* [Online] Available at: http://download.microsoft.com/download/e/4/3/e43bb484-3b52-4fa8-a9f9-ec60a32954bc/Azure_Services_Platform.docx [Accessed 28 April 2010].

Eirinaki, M. & Vazirgiannis M., (2003), *Web mining for web Personalisation.* ACM transactions on Internet Technology 3(1), pp 1-27.

Han, J. & Kamber, M., (2006), *Data mining concepts and techniques.* 2nd ed. San Fransisico: Morgan Kaufmann.

Hayes, B., (2008), Cloud Computing. Association for Computing Machinery.

Hofgesang, P.I., (2007), Web personalization through incremental individual profiling and support based user segmentation. In *Proceedings of the IEEE/WIC/ACM international conference on web intelligence.* USA, 2007. Silicon Valley.

Hong, W., Thong, J.Y. and Tam, K.Y., (2004). Designing product listing pages on e-commerce websites: and examination of presentation mode and information format. *International journal of HCS,* 1(1), pp 26-28.

Jokela, S., Turpein, M., Kurki, T., Savia,E. and Sulonen, R., (2001), The role of structured content in a personalised news service. Proceedings of the 34th annual Hawaii international conference on systems science (HICSS-34). Washington DC. IEEE Computer Society: 7.

Koenemann, J. and Belkin, N.J., (1996), A case for *interaction*: a study of interactive information retrieval behaviour and effectiveness. In *Conference on Human Factors in Computing Systems*. Canada, 1996. ACM.

Liu, D., Lin, Y., Chen, C. and Huang, Y., (2001), Deployment of personalised e-catalogues. An agent-based framework integrated with XML metadata and user models. Journal of Network and Computer Applications (24), pp 201-228.

Microsoft, (2009), *Windows Azure Portal*. [Online] Available at: www.microsoft.com/ windowsazure/windowsazure. [Accessed 27 March 2010].

Ntawanga, F., Barnard, L. and Calitz, A., (2008), Maintaining Customer Profiles in an E-commerce. In *SAICIT 2008*. South Africa. ACM.

Sanders, D., Hamilton, J. A. and Macdonald, R. A., (2008), Supporting A Service-Oriented Architecture. Association for Computing Machinery.

Schafer, A.I., Konstan, J., and Reidl, J., (2001). E-commerce recommendation applications. Data Mining and Knowledge discovery, 5 (1-2), pp 115-113.

Schneider, G.P., (2007), *Electronic Commerce*. 7th Annual edition. Boston: Thomson.

Thomas, E., (2009), *What is SOA*. [Online] Available at: e-commerce://www.whatissoa.com. [Accessed 28 June 2010].

Turban, E., Leidner, D., McLean, E. and Wetherbe, J., (2006), *Information* Technology for Management, Transforming Organisations in the Digital *Economy*. 5th Ed, John Wiley & Sons, INC.

Vaquero, L.M., Rodero-Merino, L., Caceres, J. and Lindner, M., (2009), A break in the clouds. In definition, T.a.c., ed. *ACM SIGCOMM Computer Communication Review*.

Using Complex Adaptive Systems and Technology to Analyse the Strength of Processes and Cultural Indicators: A Method to Improve Sustained Competitive Advantage

E.Ehmann[1], N.Houlden[2] and V.Grout[2]

[1] Otterman's Consulting Pty Ltd, Sydney, Australia
[2] Creative and Applied Research for the Digital Society, Glyndwr University Wrexham, United Kingdom
e-mail: Ehmanne@ottermans.com.au; {N.Houlden|V.Grout}@glyndwr.ac.uk

Abstract

This paper generalises and strengthens the investigation of capturing intangible data for the benefit of organisations encouraging learning environments and self-organisation practices. It suggests current technological and algorithmic analysis may aid an organisation's quest for sustained competitive advantage through the identification of previously unobservable data including cultural nuances. However, the implementation of such an approach presents challenges of which we summarise in our conclusion.

Keywords

Resource based view, change readiness, competitive advantage, knowledge transfer, ant colony optimisation, self-organisation.

1. Introduction

In the 21st Century, organisations are forced to strive for competitive advantage while reacting to the relentless advent of technology, globalisation and diminishing natural resources. Achieving sustained competitive advantage requires more than conserving the milieu we know; it entails a relentless quest for innovation in divergent products and markets that are currently beyond our imagination (O'Reilly and Tushman, 2004).

The achievement of competitive advantage depends greatly on an organisation's capacity to be agile; how quickly and effectively it is able to respond to its environment. Crucial to this capacity is the organisation's human resource. Not only is its knowledge of routines and culture important, but its ability to share this knowledge between current individuals, as well as subsequent generations, allowing an organisation increased buoyancy in the face of change.

This paper presents a nascent idea using technology to gather and monitor knowledge that is currently systematically unobservable, along with the knowledge pertaining to more tangible routines and processes. Using systems based on nature to analyse relationships between employees, managers and other relevant stakeholders, we propose a model that allows comparison between various routines, processes and cultural indicators to identify similarities which we envisage will enable more effective self-organisation within corporations.

In section one; we outline the challenges faced by organisations around the transfer of knowledge. Section two presents a model for a new biologically inspired system that captures tangible and intangible knowledge. In section three we review the implications and outline future work. Finally, section four presents our conclusions.

2. The need for knowledge transfer

In order to achieve agility, a number of factors need to be present within the organisation. Barney (1991) suggests that organisations will achieve agility, and therefore sustained competitive advantage, if it adopts a resource based view (RBV) of its business. RBV includes myriad resources, tangible and intangible, and are not limited to "training, experience, judgment, intelligence, relationships, an insight of individual managers and workers in a firm" (Barney 1991 p101). Of course, processes, routines and coordinating systems are also resources, as are the casual interactions within groups.

When drawing a relationship between RBV and sustained competitive advantage, Barney suggests that not only are firms generating economic value through a unique strategy within their industry at a certain time, but their competitors are incapable of replicating their strategy's success. While Barney's discussion does not stipulate a calendar time frame for competitive advantage to qualify as *sustained* competitive advantage, our suggested model's potential for identifying and measuring unique resources, we believe, can precipitate sustained competitive advantage over calendar time.

While many organisations have frameworks in place to measure the effectiveness of tangible resources, for example, processes and routines, our paper suggests a novel method for identifying and monitoring the intangible unique resources, which by definition are more difficult to replicate and therefore could offer sustained competitive advantage over an even longer calendar timeframe.

Identifying an organisation's resources allows management to cross-pollinate processes and routines, organisation-wide, enabling agile realisation of opportunities (Prahalad and Hamel, 1990). Prahalad and Hamel further suggest that the "collective learning" (p.82) of an organisation represents its core competencies; the coordination of skills along with the amalgamation of myriad technologies, or quite simply, communication. Garud and Nayyar (1994) refer to this communication of internal knowledge as a firm's transformative capacity. Lichtenthaler and Lichtenthaler (2009) adapted this definition to include the *retention* of this knowledge within the organisation. This knowledge must be "actively managed" (p. 1320) for it to flourish (Lane et al 2006). If organisations do not identify, monitor and communicate processes and routine, organisational competencies become bound and individuals' skills degenerate (Prahalad and Hamel, 1990). As Prahalad and Hamel rightly propose, "unlike physical assets, competencies do not deteriorate as they are applied and shared. They grow." (p82).

Firms possess myriad cultures within the greater organisational culture. Management has the task of identifying and developing these capacities to ensure organisational agility (Robertson 2011). The traditional hierarchical organisation structure does not complement an organisation's need for agility and, therefore, coordination of competencies. Organisations can promote a learning environment that encourages collaboration and risk taking in an effort to achieve innovation quickly.

For organisations to realise a learning environment team members at the coal-face must be empowered to make decisions and adapt quickly to consumer demands. Of course, hierarchical managers indoctrinated with the belief that they hold, and are expected to hold, all knowledge, must overcome this mind-set and allow their team members to not only use their knowledge to execute their own work, but to share their knowledge (Espinosa et al 2007) and contribute to emergent strategies (Burgelman 2002) rather than be controlled solely by management.

An organisation's ability to achieve effective change in dynamic environments, or the organisational *capacity for change (OCC)* (Benn and Bolton, 2011), is vital for organisations to understand. Benn and Bolton suggest a RBV of cultural characteristics that facilitate change readiness, including the preparedness and "employee wellbeing" (p163). As they note, literature around RBV is predominantly focused on evolving and ground-breaking resource building. Interestingly, Bolton (2004) raises the potential for RBV to identify resources that are resilient to change and, therefore, potentially deleterious.

The ability for an organisation to improve its OCC and promote learning at all levels, rather than just at senior management levels for top-down dissemination (Senge 1990; Daft 2009), represents a *complex adaptive system (CAS)* (Holland 1992) that encourages and allows communication and learning throughout the organisation. Holland initially proposed CAS based on the study of naturally occurring systems. These types of self-organising systems are not so easy to model in a simulator, although with *High Performance Computing (HPC)* this is becoming more of a reality.

CAS provides an explanation of patterns that occur within an organisation. It suggests that all parts of the system are intricately related to one another and therefore those pieces of the system that share similarities, or patterns, are attracted and, therefore, present as self-organisation (Olsen and Eoyang 2001). This suggests homogeneous change mechanisms across the across the organisation, if not the wider industry.

Tangible data, or information around routines and processes, are fundamental to an organisation and are generally captured in an organisation's policies and procedures. With the advent of technology, more of this information is contained on technological systems. Intangible data, likely to be cultural data, is less likely to be captured as part of a formal system. We believe CAS offers an opportunity to model the capturing of tangible data through legacy systems and intangible data through social media applications, or networks, and to use this data to identify patterns within the firm, assisting self-organisation, thereby enabling far greater agility and sustained competitive advantage.

3. A new model

Over the last decade, substantial work has been done analysing the biological world. The principle of the needs of the many out weighing the needs of a few, or the one, is a common adage that few have managed to realise. In the biological world, a collective group is stronger when each individual works for a single, greater, purpose, in effect, self-organising. This phenomenon is studied by academics from many disciplines.

Self-organisation is not solely about 'pulling together'. Systems can easily have organisation imposed upon them, for example, managers, policies, pre-existing patterns in the environment etcetera. This is common place in businesses, computer networks and many other areas however it is more useful to have a system that is self-organising.

Camazine et al (2004) suggests that self-organisation, in the context of a biological system, is a process in which patterns at the global level of a system emerge solely from the numerous interactions among the lower-level constituents of that system. Furthermore, they affirm that the rules dictating the interactions among the system's components are carried out using only local information without reference to any global pattern.

As the lower components interact, these patterns emerge without any guiding influence from the global level. The emergent properties cannot be examined by looking at the system's individual components alone but by considering the interactions between the system's components.

This is not a new concept. Grout and Houlden (2005) have already proposed that from a networking perspective, the collective good is a potential solution to the problem of routing. Their theory draws on the natural behaviour of ants. Ants work in unison for the good of the colony as they forage for food. If a food supply is found, pheromones are laid down which enables other ants to follow to find the food source; the richer the food source the greater amount of pheromone is applied.

One of the most successful algorithmic techniques based upon ant behaviour, is *Ant Colony Optimisation (ACO).* Grout and Houlden (2005) state that ACO is a paradigm for designing metaheuristic algorithms for combinatorial optimisation problems. Metaheuristic algorithms can be best described as:

> *"... algorithms which, in order to escape from local optima, drive some basic heuristic: either constructive heuristic starting from a null solution and adding elements to build a good complete one, or a local search heuristic starting from a complete solution and iteratively modifying some of its elements in order to achieve a better one."*

Ant colonies are complex adaptive systems and, as with many social insect societies, they are a distributed system that, in spite of the simplicity of their individuals, they present a highly structured social organisation (Maniezzo et al 2004). It is this organisation that allows ant colonies to accomplish complicated tasks that in many cases are far beyond the individuals' capabilities.

To focus on ants' systems may seem simplistic however it is an ideal starting point to attempt to model complex adaptive systems. Ants communicate between themselves, or with the environment, by producing chemicals called pheromones. Different species of ants work in different ways. Some species use a trail pheromone which marks pathways, for example from food to nest, which other ants then sense the stronger pheromone trail left by others before them and consequently deposit more pheromone thereby increasing its strength even more. It is the principle of collective trail laying and trial following, based upon chemical path that has inspired ACO.

The ability of ants to work as a cohesive group can be demonstrated with the double bridge experiment. In this experiment Goss et al (1989) establish a long route and a short route for the colony to a food source, ants leave the nest to explore the environment and arrive at a decision point where they have to choose one of the two routes. Because the two branches initially appear identical to the ants, they choose randomly, as the ants reaching the food source will arrive quicker over the shorter route upon their return journey they will follow the route with the 'heavier' pheromone, the shorter one. This trail is then used by successive ants each laying down pheromone.

This simple experiment shows how groups acting together can achieve something for the good of the colony, in this case the shortest route to a food supply. This simplicity has already been applied to other problems, in particular the problem of routing in a computer network. ACO has already proven to be successful in various fields of optimisation.

In particular, Dorigo and Stützle (2004) show how the ACO algorithm can be applied to an *NP*-complete problem like the *Travelling Salesman Problem* (*TSP*). The TSP is a static combinatorial optimisation problem, where the characteristics of the problem are given when the problem is defined and do not change, such as the number of miles between cities. Routing, however, is a dynamic problem where whatever metric we are using for cost could, and probably will, vary. Effective ACO approaches to dynamic routing are beginning to appear (Johnson and Perez, 2005).

It is from the principle of nature, particularly the use of laying down a trail of pheromones, which can be followed, or even just re-used to lead to a goal to help others that our model starts to evolve. Obviously, humans are unable to follow pheromone trails, but we do and can produce digital trails. We often do this when using the Internet and social networking sites, recording what we did and when we did it. Could the exploitation of this type of data allow us to record the intangible? The presence of certain data showing our 'mood' or location when we did something that was successful or not so successful could be extrapolated and then potentially re-used to achieve the same outcome, if desired. The current data held by social networking would not be enough to represent the complex relationships between individuals. However, by using other forms of technology we could capture and analyse some of the intangible resources within an organisation.

The use of technology in self-organising teams may start to help organisations become more agile as changes in business need to come from the bottom up. By using current technology, such as smart phones, tablets and simple devices for measuring brain waves, such as the NeuroSky Mindwave™ to record temperature, light levels, voice patterning and utilising algorithms to monitor different nuances, data can be captured and measured against the outcome of a particular operational routine.

Data, both tangible and intangible, can be gathered at source and then fed in to a data warehouse to be stored. The warehouse also contains each individual operational routine, but not just only what the routine is but it will be broken down to much lower components and a pattern stored. This pattern will be used once data has been gathered as a matching system between similar operational tasks.

The incoming data will be marked as either positive or negative for a particular operational routine, depending upon the outcome of that task; this will then be stored as good (positive) data and will be fed back to the task reinforcing that layer of pheromone.

However, as negative data is gathered from a particular routine, a routine that did not succeed in its outcome or did not reach a pre-established level, then the pheromone is deducted, creating a negative trail.

An algorithm looks at each operational routine and attempts to find one of similar style, using the pattern of that routine that has been stored. If this new routine has strong layers of pheromone attached to it these will be fed in to the routine that has the negative pheromone to try to rectify the problems that it has.

Collecting tangible data is relatively easy when compared with the collection of intangible, but since the relationship has been captured it can be attempted to be reproduced. CAS use this in a very natural way by automatically correcting their environment. Our model to improve self-organisation enables corrections based on proven solutions.

```
1. Input Capture_data {Capture the stream of incoming data}
2. If Capture_data = + then {Is it positive or negative}
        2.2 Operational_routine_ph = Operational_routine_ph +
1{increment the layer of pheromone}
Else
        2.3 Operational_routine_ph = Operational_routine_ph –
1 {decrement the layer of pheromone}
3. End;
```

Figure 1: High level data capture algorithm

Figures 1 and 2 present two algorithms, one showing the data capture routine and the other showing the operational routine comparison.

1. Input Poor_routine, PR← Poor_routine *{This is the complete operational routine}*
2. Input Good_routine , GR← Good_routine
3. Input number_of_Ki *{Number of key indicators to test}*
4. For x = 1 to max_number_of_routines_to_compare do *{Test all routines}*
    4.1. For *i* = 1 to number_of_Ki do
        4.1.1. Score ← 0
        4.1.2. Input PR_i *{PR_i is the key indicator i}*
            4.1.2.1. If $PR_i = GR_i$ then *{Are the key indicators the same}*
            4.1.2.2. Score ← Score + 1
        4.1.3. Output *i*, Score

    4.2. If Score > number_of_Ki/2 then
        4.2.1. Output GR 'Apply this to ' PR
    4.3. Else if
        4.3.1. Output 'No match'

Figure 2: Operational Routine Comparison

These routines are very high level and are designed to give an idea of how the data will be captured and how an operational routine that is not achieving reasonable results will be compared to one that is achieving better results.

The key indicators used by the algorithm could be a number of datum that can be considered intangible, for instance this could be the amount of daylight, temperature, particular nuances of a person's voice etc.

4. Future Work

While this work is still in its infancy, the usefulness of nature's ideas is well proven. The next steps in this research are establish tests in order to capture data from an array of devices, measuring a wide range of factors, then storing this data and comparing it to the task's outcome. The algorithms themselves need to be refined and tested. From a technical standpoint the data could be stored in an RDBMS (Relational Database Management System) such as Oracle and utilise PLSQL in order to implement the algorithms.

From an organisational perspective, we consider two levels: operational and leadership level.

Operational testing will involve the specification of routines and processes (tangible data). For a series of specified processes or workflows, we will gather an individual's perceived skill level and perceived attitude to the process. This will be matched and compared with actual skill level, through quality assurance processes and actual attitude, using a device such as NeuroSky Mindwave™ . The results of which will be applied to the algorithm (Figure 2) to ascertain a score. By overlaying the analysis of currently unobservable emotional responses we aim to determine which processes are less effective or generating apathy.

The second branch of testing, leadership, will identify cultural behaviours and pathways, outside of routine and processes, ascertaining which have a positive effect on the organisation and perhaps providing actual measurables around organisational leadership styles and psychological profiles. Again, these tests will include comparison of perceived leadership skills with actual skills and then contrasting these results with perceived attitude with actual attitude using a device such as NeuroSky Mindwave™ . This measurement is somewhat more personal and, as such, we will be incorporating a psychological profiling mechanism in an effort to place more predictive ability behind measuring desired leadership and cultural attributes.

For both levels, we will incorporate standard, well-communicated, processes as well as uncertain and ambiguous communication. We will also be looking for dilution of results as we extrapolate the data to an organisational application.

From a cultural perspective, we plan to use social media to establish an environment for test participants to interact with one another, and an unknown researcher, to collect and score intangible cultural information in a perceived 'safe' environment pertaining to the organisational or leadership testing.

5. Conclusion

In conclusion, for an organisation to achieve competitive advantage, it must be equipped with meaningful data that allows greater understanding of its resources including those which, historically, have been unobservable. For an organisation to achieve sustained competitive advantage, the understanding of patterns and which ones need to be perpetuated or halted may provide longevity to their position in the market. With the burgeoning use of social networking, mobile and other devices, the collection of this ethereal information is becoming more accessible.

As our model suggests, the methods of data collection may be considered invasive, therefore any future studies will involve university ethical approval and volunteers being observed in laboratory conditions rather than real world environments. Our intention is to collaborate with organisational behavioural psychologists to propose a model that includes existing psychological profiles.

6. References

Benn, S & Bolton D, 2011, *Key Concepts in Corporate Social Responsibility*, Sage, USA.

Bolton, D 2004, 'Change coping and context in the resilient organisation', *Mt Eliza Business Review*, vol. 7, no.1, pp. 57-66.

Burgelman, RA 2002, *Chapter One, Strategy is Destiny; how strategy making shapes a company's future*, The Free Press, NY.

Camazine, S, Deneubourg, JL, Franks, NR, Sneyd, J, Theraulaz, G & Bonabeau, E., 2001, (Eds) *Self-Organization in Biological Systems*, Princeton, NJ, Princeton University Press.

Daft, RL 2009, *Organization Theory and Design*, 10th Ed. Thomson South Western.

Senge, P 1996, 'Leading Learning Organizations', *Training & Development*, vol. 50, no.12, pp.36-37.

Dorigo M & Stützle T, 2004, *Ant Colony Optimization*, MIT Press, Cambridge, Massachusetts, pp. 65 – 69.

Espinoza, A, Harnden, R & Walker, J 2007, 'Beyond hierarchy: a complexity management perspective', *Kybernetes*, vol. 36, no. ¾, pp. 333-347.

Garud, R & Nayyar, PR 1994. 'Transformative capacity: continual structuring by intertemporal technology transfer', *Strategic Management Journal*, vol. 15, pp. 365–85.

Goss, S, Aron, S, Deneubourg JL & Pasteels, JM 1989, 'Self-organized shortcuts in the Argentine ant', *Naturwissenschaften*, vol. 76, pp. 579-581.

Houlden, N & Grout, V 2005, "Principles of Optimal Interior Routing", *Proceedings of the 1st International Conference on Internet Technologies and Applications (ITA 05)*, Wrexham, North Wales, UK, 7th-9th September 2005, pp. 274-281.

Johnson, CM & Perez E 2005, 'An Ant Colony Optimization Algorithm for Dynamic, Multi-Objective Network Routing', *Proceedings of the International Conference on Internet Technologies and Applications (ITA 05),* 7th-9th September 2005, Wrexham, UK.

Lane, PJ, Koka,BR & Pathak, S 2006, 'The reification of absorptive capacity: a critical review and rejuvenation of the construct', *Academy of Management Review*, vol. 31, pp. 833–63.

Lichtenthaler, U & Lichtenthaler, E 2009, "A Capability-Based Framework for Open Innovation: Complementing Absorptive Capacity", *Journal of Management Studies*, December, pp. 1315-1338.

Maniezzo V, Gambardella LM, De Luigi F, 2004, *Ant Colony Optimization*, New Optimization Techniques in Engineering, by Onwubolu, G. C., and B. V. Babu, Springer-Verlag Berlin Heidelberg, 101-117.

Olson, E & Eoyang, GH 2001, *Facok ilitating Organization Change: Lessons from Complexity Science*, Jossey-Bass/Pfeiffer A Wiley Company, San Francisco ISBN-10: 078795330X.

O'Reilly III, CA & Tushman, ML 2004, 'The Ambidextrous Organization', *Harvard Business Review*, vol. 82, no. 4, pp. 74-81.

Prahalad, CK & Hamel, G 1990 'The Core Competence of the Corporation', *Harvard Business Review*, May-June, pp. 79-91.

Mobile Banking Services in South Africa: The Case of M-Pesa

S.K.Kabanda, A.Downes and S.Baltazar dos Ramos

Department of Information Systems, University of Cape Town, South Africa
e-mail: salah.kabanda@uct.ac.za; andrea.downes@myuct.ac.za; sbdosramos@gmail.com

Abstract

Mobile banking systems have revolutionised business transactions in developing countries by paving the way for the conduct of electronic commerce transactions via mobiles. As a result, people in developing countries can now participate and partake in the global digital exchange which they were previously denied due to the digital divide. An example of a mobile banking technology that has been very successful in most parts of Africa and used for sending and storing money is M-Pesa. This study investigates the M-Pesa phenomena, amongst the rural township communities in the Western Cape of South Africa with the purpose of understanding the perceptions of the township community towards mobile payments – specifically M-Pesa. The results indicate that although M-Pesa services have shown to be easier to use and less riskier than traditional means of financial transacting; to ensure M-Pesa success, there is a need for (i) an aggressive continuous awareness programs necessary to publicise the service; and (ii) additional functionalities to allow customer retention and use of the service given the presence of competitors service such as money market transfer systems. To arrive at these findings, the study followed an interpretive approach in which in-depth interviews were conducted.

Keywords

Developing countries, mobile banking, M-Pesa

1. Introduction

E-Commerce has for the past years been nonexistence in developing countries due to contextual challenges of technological, social and institutional factors. One of the technological factors that have deterred the growth of E-Commerce in developing countries has been the lack of suitable payment instrument and corresponding payment system such as debit and credit cards, e-banking, and electronic checks (Dani and Krishna 2001). Although developing countries try to implement and use electronic payment systems, the task appears to be incomprehensible as such systems remain complex and difficult to implement and maintain, especially for developing countries that do not have the infrastructure, necessary institutional arrangements and financial resources to cover the costs associated with the implementation (Po et al 2007).

However with the introduction of mobile phones, electronic transactions seem possible via mobile banking. Mobile banking is the provision of banking services such as depositing, withdrawing, sending and saving money, as well as making payments via mobile networks using mobile phones (Bångens and Söderberg 2008). This paper investigates the use of a mobile banking technology called M-Pesa, amongst the rural township communities in the Western Cape of South Africa. The focus is in understanding the perceptions of the township community towards mobile payments. These communities are usually the unbanked and are "predominantly rural poor people that live in a cash-based economy which is highly informal" (Bångens and Söderberg 2008). To carry out the study, an interpretive approach using semi-structured interviews to collect data was adopted because the approach allows for the explicit recognition to the world of consciousness and humanly created meanings and shows evidence of investigation of the phenomena within the specific cultural and contextual settings from the perspective of participants (Ngwenyama and Lee, 1997). In this study, M-Pesa participants are viewed as active sense-makers, engaged participants, and creators of life in their settings and their identities emerge from discourse (Alvarez, 2002). An interpretive approach therefore provides this study with a rich realm of resources from which the M-Pesa phenomenon can be investigated. The rest of the paper is organised as follows: Section 2 presents related work on Mobile electronic payment system. The methodology and analysis of the study is carried out in section 3. The findings of the study are depicted in section 4, followed by the discussion in section 5. Section 6 concludes the study.

2. Mobile Banking: M-Pesa

The fast diffusion of mobile telecom networks has enabled mobile banking service operators to deliver basic financial services to the financially excluded poor by drawing on the geographic coverage of mobile networks and diverse needs of the client base (World Economic Forum 2011, Bångens and Söderberg 2008). Mobile services for example mobile payments have been suggested as a solution to facilitate micropayments in electronic and mobile commerce, and to provide an alternative for the diminishing use of cash at point of sale (Mallat 2007). Although mobile payments are still restricted to a few geographies, largely because of strict banking regulations and large populations of the unbanked (Medhi et al 2009); they are still suitable for proximity and micro-payment and have the potential to revolutionize methods for paying products and services (Ondrus and Pigneur 2006).

One example of a mobile technology that has revolutionised the practices of doing business in Africa has been M-Pesa - an innovative mobile banking technology targeted to serve the unbanked market which have consequently no formal earnings, rely on farm income, live on 'welfare' from friends and family, have irregular income or earnings too small to save (Hughes and Lonie 2007, Finscope 2007, 2006). M-Pesa allows millions of previously unbanked people to move money quickly, securely and across distances, thereby allowing them to take advantage of services that are considered out of reach in many parts of the world. M-Pesa not only facilitates the safe storage and transfer of money, but "by allowing money to flow electronically rather than physically, M-Pesa lessens, and in some cases eliminates, many of the spatial and temporal barriers to money transfer" (Morawczynski and Pickens 2009). The technology facilitates trade, making it easier for people to pay for, and to receive payment for, goods and services such as electricity bills which "can be paid with a push of a few buttons instead of traveling to an often distant office with a fistful of cash and waiting in a long queue; consumers can quickly purchase cell phone credit ("airtime") without moving" (Jack et al 2011). With M-Pesa, no bank account is required as subscribers can deposit and withdraw money at a number of M-Pesa agents. As a result of the accessibility of this service, M-Pesa adoption rate has increased quickly, and has become one of the most successful mobile payment systems in Africa (Mas and Morawczynski 2009). In South Africa however, M-Pesa is relatively new with only three years in operation. Although new, it is believed that it can play a critical role among the migrants who migrate from poor rural areas to large metropolitan cities for work purposes. According to Cross (2003), "these migrants remit considerable amounts of money to their families". Traditionally the money is sent via traditional financial systems which poses a problem for most family members in rural areas because owning a bank account is luxury that they cannot afford. Against this background, M-Pesa could serve as a solution to not only migrant workers and their families but to all unbanked South Africans.

3. Research methodology and data analysis

The study was explorative in nature and followed an interpretive stance so as to better understand the user's social reality through the contextual interpretations of multiple, dynamic realities of the mobile payment phenomena (Avgerou 2001, Ritchie and Lewis 2003). Interviews were used to gather data using open ended questions in order to facilitate descriptive responses. Two groups were interviewed: M-Pesa users and M-Pesa agents who are M-Pesa service providers within the community. Due to the limited number of users and the newness of the service, only 11 M-Pesa users agreed to partake in the study. The M-Pesa agent sample consisted of 25 participants ranging from senior managers, M-Pesa champions as well as those whom were responsible for servicing M-Pesa customers within the communities. Although the sample size is small, given the newness of the technology; it is important to note that the study is interpretive in nature and such studies do not restrict themselves to such generalisation as would have been possible if the study had been strictly based upon statistical sampling. Interpretivist research does not 'prohibit the researcher from extending his or her theory to additional settings', but, instead, allows for generalisation in its own right (Lee and Baskerville 2003).

The data analysis followed a general inductive approach because of the newness of the technology in the community. Analysis commenced with the transcription of the audio interviews. This process firstly involved the translation of all interviews conducted in Xhosa and Afrikaans into English; and secondly ensuring verbatim documentation of those interviews. For each interview, the process of transcription followed immediately after the interview so as to take advantage of recall memory and thus increase accuracy of non-verbal transcriptions. After transcription, the corpus of data was subjected to rigorous pattern identification process of reviewing the data, making notes, and sorting the data into more structured categories (themes) that can explain the data. The focus was on identifying themes and patterns that emerge as being important to the description of the M-Pesa phenomenon through a process of carefully reading and re-reading the data. This analysis approach has the power to report people's experiences, perspectives, and meanings, whilst examining the ways in which events, realities, meanings, and experiences come about (Braun and Clarke 2006). The themes generated from this inductive approach follow a process in which data coding is done "without trying to fit it into a pre-existing coding frame, or the researcher's analytic preconceptions" (Braun and Clarke 2006). As such, the process was highly data-driven to allow "research findings to emerge from the frequent, dominant or significant themes inherent in raw data without the restraints imposed by structured methodologies" (Thomas 2003).

4. Research findings

Five main themes emerged from the data analysis as depicted in Table 1. The findings are discussed below.

Theme	Explanation
Awareness	Cognizance of M-Pesa potential opportunities
Perceived usefulness and relative advantage	observing the direct benefits and indirect benefits of using M-Pesa in comparison to existing innovation; degree to which M-Pesa is perceived as being better than its precursor
Perceived ease of use	Complexity, problems and convenience with usability; not difficult to understand
Risk and trust	secure financial transactions in electronic environment (confidentiality, data integrity, authentication, and non-repudiation, anonymity and privacy)
Market pressure	pressure from trading partners such as consumers and suppliers

Table 1: Emerging themes

4.1. Awareness of M-Pesa services

M-Pesa users became aware of M-Pesa services through a friend, family member or a colleague. It was established that if a person saw a friend or family member making use of a new service they also were more inclined to use the same service as well. This however was still subject to how beneficial the service was and to community leader peer pressure. Peer pressure was a contributing factor to both awareness and adoption because according to M-Pesa $agent_{20}$, *most rural communities still have the mind-set that they do only what the elders tell them to do. So they don't want to move away from the old way of doing things and therefore end up not making use of the new products that are out on the market such as the M-Pesa payment service... It's all about the community and what the community elder says goes - understand?* Thus perception of the service and user's attitudes towards it was highly affected by social influences of family members, friends and community leaders.

Although friends, families and community leaders played a significant role in the awareness of M-Pesa; users insisted on a thorough awareness campaign by the M-Pesa providers. They recommended that the M-Pesa logo on the container shop be amplified because it is *too small and people find it difficult to locate which of the containers in the community actually offer the M-Pesa service* ($User_{11}$). These sentiments were confirmed by M-Pesa agents who collectively indicated that the advertising was not very clear and consumers were confused about what the service actually does and how best it can benefit them. The agents established that without a thorough awareness programs such as M-Pesa focus days, promotion programs which are currently taking place, M-Pesa adoption was likely to dwindle. They also cautioned that awareness must not be geared towards promotions only but should also focus explaining how M-Pesa actually works and how it would be beneficial if adopted.

4.2. Perceived usefulness and relative advantage

As for those who had adopted M-Pesa, their perception of the service was that it was to provide them with an alternative inexpensive method to traditional financial services irrespective of location. M-Pesa was used for numerous activities ranging from saving accounts ($User_{1,8}$), money transfer to and from family members ($User_5$) *because it was an easier and more convenient way than traditional banking* ($User_4$). $User_3$ explains: *most of us have families in Eastern Cape who don't have bank accounts...they can now go to any M-Pesa Agent and get the money that we send them from this side.* In addition to convenience, users found the service affordable and *actually cheaper than your normal bank accounts* ($User_9$). However, 27% of users perceived M-Pesa as a service from which they could obtain free airtime and text messages (sms). $User_{10}$ explains: *initially people sign up for the free services such as airtime and sms, but later once we are aware of the benefits we sometimes continue using the service for other activities or simply abandon it...but most of us started with the need for the free services.*

M-Pesa agents were in agreement with user's perception that the services was aimed more at consumers who were not in proximity of financial services or banking facilities; and to those who found traditional financial services an expensive method of banking ($Agent_{11}$). $Agent_{21}$ explains: *I think its coz most of the people here in Khayelitsha come from Eastern Cape. They then have to send money back home but the financial facilities aren't as prevalent as they are here in the Western Cape. Therefore, the user feels more comfortable using the M-Pesa service as his family have access to a mobile phone making it more convenient for them to receive the money.* M-Pesa services were also frequently sort out for and used by asylum seekers or foreigners with no South African identity documents which are a prerequisite for traditional banking. The general tendency as observed by $Agent_{11}$ was that *some users did have the wrong intentions when opening an M-Pesa account and that was to obtain the initial benefits of the free services.* $Agent_{23}$ explains: *they open accounts to get the free airtime and the free sms's offered after you register for the service...customers who sign up get 20 sms's ... as a result, some users open M-Pesa accounts initially but don't use them afterwards... ...but this does not mean that all of them wouldn't use them. No, others just don't have the need for the account as of now, but could so in the near future.* These observations support $User_{10}$'s report that some users start off with the intention of obtaining free services and later on could potentially be transformed into loyal M-Pesa users.

4.3. Perceived ease of use

Although all M-Pesa users found the service relatively easy to use compared to other financial services such as banking and mobile banking; M-Pesa agents were not convinced because they *were confronted with consumers who just don't know how to use their phone and would therefore not be comfortable or confident when making M-Pesa transactions.....and when this happens they tend to use competitors services such as money transfer as they only need their ID* ($Agent_{16}$). Some agents indicated that when such customers come for registration, agents engage with them in training on how to make transactions. $Agent_6$ indicates that with sufficient training users will eventually be able to utilise the benefits that M-Pesa offers.

4.4. Risk and trust

Issues associated with risk and trust of M-Pesa services were not perceived to have a significant factor to adoption as they were mentioned by only 18% of users. The remaining 80% showed complete trust in the service and its infrastructure. $User_2$ explains: *it [M-Pesa service] uses the PIN number and is very safe... my money is safe. You see, no one would want to steal a phone as compared to money...so I put the money in M-Pesa for safekeeping when I travel 'cause I know its safe there - it reduces the risks of losing my money in case of a robbery.* The risks associated with remembering traditional bank account number was minimised via M-Pesa because it was perceived easier to remember a person's mobile phone number than a bank account number. This benefit minimised the risk of sending money to a wrong account. In addition, M-Pesa users didn't have to present their identity document whilst making a transaction and as such felt more comfortable as the risk of losing one's identity document or bank card was reduced: *I can simply do banking without my bank card or ID* ($User_2$), *I don't have to carry it [ID] - I am scared that I could lose it you know* ($User_3$).

4.5. Market pressure

45% of M-Pesa users indicated that the services are very limited and they would like to have more services. For example, $User_{10}$ explains that *additional functionalities that would be more useful are to buy electricity and airtime as well as to pay my other accounts using my mobile phone.* $User_4$ also emphasises this point: *I think they need to add electricity purchases in the future.* $User_3$ adds the need for a further functionality: *I would prefer to get paid my salary through M-Pesa.* M-Pesa agents confirmed the need for M-Pesa to diversify their services due to consumer needs. $Agent_{23}$ specifically indicated that diversification could ensure customer retention. He explains: *There were competitors who offered some of the services which consumers are in need of, for example, I know competitor X is already doing so and our customers always come in and ask us why we are not providing the same service...you see, other financial services available to customers are much easier to make use of and therefore the customer would rather make use of them, for example money transfer markets instead of M-Pesa. With money transfer markets all the user needs is their ID and then they send the money to the relevant person. That person will get a reference number that will need to be presented on requesting the money. People find this method of transferring money much easier as they don't have to learn anything as there will be someone else doing the whole transfer for them.* It was apparent that the incorporation of other services was of paramount important to M-Pesa's success given the competition from other financial services such as money market services. Money markets are retail money transfer services that allow a user to transfer money to another retail partner across a geographical area using an Identity document.

5. Discussion

The findings indicate that M-Pesa awareness in rural communities was low due to the poor visibility of the M-Pesa service providers (the agents shop) as a result of the M-Pesa advertising logo sign. Awareness has been reported as a challenge in other countries as well and has in fact been regarded as one of the key factors for ensuring M-Pesa success (Mas et al 2010). In this study, awareness was also positively influenced by family, friends and community leaders. The impact which social relations have on awareness and ultimately adoption is significant. Thus creating awareness should be one of the top priorities of M-Pesa service providers. Awareness could result in adoption but continuous use of services can be effected if users found the service relatively easy to use and beneficial. The findings indicate that M-Pesa users were comfortable with using M-Pesa services. However this was contradictory with the agents who service those customers. A possible explanation to this could be that most users were still at the initial stage of enjoying the free services and had not transformed into habitual loyal users who actually use the service for what it was designed for. Whilst enjoying the free services, users engage only in the process of sending short text messages and making phone calls – a process that they are already conversant with. However in order to perform an M-Pesa transaction, more is required. Nevertheless users who had traversed to performing financial transactions using M-Pesa still found the service easy to use and this is what made them recommend the service to their families and friends. Ease of use has been documented in literature as one of the factors that ensured customer take-up or acceptance of a given innovation (Daniel 1999). They also found the service beneficial and better than alternative methods of traditional banking. Based on the usefulness of the service, consumers recommended the service to their families and friends who were also equally eager to adopt the technology. These findings confirm that the fact that users will accept an innovation if they perceive it would help them to attain desired performance (Par et al 2004, Teo et al 2004). M-Pesa in this study was able to reduce the distance between users and their families, specifically between migrant workers and their families in rural areas.

However as indicated by the World Economic Forum (2011) "other intangibles such as perceived trust in a service provider's brand, personal relationship an individual holds with their local agent and the endorsement from relevant peers all play a role in adoption" (World Economic Forum 2011). These intangibles were quite visible in our study. One of them was the issue of risk associated with using the service. Risk has been described as an important factor that consumers consider before adopting an innovation is the level of risk involved (Sathye 1999). In this study, M-Pesa users found the service risk free and were able to trust the services because bank cards and account numbers were no longer necessary whilst performing a transaction and thus the risk of losing those items was minimised. By not requiring bank cards and the remembrance of account numbers, M-Pesa improves its customer's confidence and trust by keeping to a minimum the personal data required from the consumer (Par et al 2004). However to remain competitive, M-Pesa needs to reconsider the differentiation of its services because the pressure from trading partners such as consumers and suppliers has a significant impact on technology adoption behaviour. Consumers in this study have distinctive expectations of the services such as paying for utility expenses and receiving salary via their M-Pesa accounts. This market pressure could require that M-Pesa service providers provide these features due to the specific request for it by their trading partners in the industry sector (Van Akkeren and Cavaye 1999) or a strategic necessity to maintain competitiveness in the industry (Teo et al 2004).

6. Conclusion

Developing countries lag towards E-Commerce has been as a result of a lack of suitable payment instruments. However, with the introduction of mobile payment instruments such as M-Pesa, E-Commerce is paving way for mobile commerce. Such instruments, specifically M-Pesa, allow for both money transfer service as well as payment for traditional e-commerce transactions because M-Pesa as a mobile banking service provides services such as depositing, withdrawing, sending and saving money, as well as making payments via mobile networks using mobile phones (Bångens and Söderberg 2008). Mobile banking systems have now become appropriate tools for transforming banking as they provide services tailored to fit the currently unbanked in developing countries. This study investigated the perception of mobile banking, specifically M-Pesa in South Africa. Although M-Pesa is relatively new in South Africa in comparison to other countries, the result indicate the need for (i) continuous awareness programs necessary to publicise the service; and (ii) additional functionalities to the service. Because rural communities tend to have limited financial resources, they would be more reluctant to adopt M-Pesa if they do not perceive the potential benefits. With limited services offered by M-Pesa, users are likely to switch to competitors where they perceive they could obtain positive effects of their technology. Thus for M-Pesa to be successful, awareness and differentiation of services are two important factors necessary for customer retention and continuous use of the service. The contribution of this paper is on alerting Mobile banking providers to pay attention to these two critical factors that could potentially allow them to increase financial access to the low income and often unbanked consumers and thereby, ensuring effective social and financial development amongst the low income and unbanked market.

7. References

Abdulla B.V (2009). The Electronic Payment System (EPS) As an E-Commerce Enabler: The Macedonian Perspective. Working Paper: MPRA Paper No. 13996, Available from URL: http://mpra.ub.uni-muenchen.de/13994/1/mpra_paper_13996.pdf

Alvarez R. (2002). Confessions of an Information Worker: A Critical Analysis of Information Requirements Discourse. Information and Organization 12 (2002) 85–107

Avgerou, C. (2001). The Significance of context in Information Systems and organizational change. Information Systems Journal, 11(1), 43-63.

Bångens L and Söderberg B. (2008). ICT4D: Mobile banking – financial services for the unbanked? SPIDER: The Swedish program for ICT in developing regions. ISBN: 978-91-85991-01-3

Boateng R., Heeks R., Molla A., and Hinson R (2008). E-commerce and socio-economic development: conceptualizing the link. Internet Research Vol. 18 No. 5, 2008 pp. 562-594

Braun V and Victoria Clarke V. (20006) Using Thematic Analysis in Psychology. Qualitative Research In Psychology 2006; 3: 77 -101

Cross C. (2003). Migrant Workers Remittances and Micro-finance in South Africa. ISBN : 92-2-114913-7. Available from URL: http://ilo-mirror.library.cornell.edu/public/english/employment/finance/download/cross.pdf

Dani, A.R., and Krishna, P.R. 92001). An E-Check Framework for Electronic Payment Systems in the Web-Based Environment, Electronic Commerce and Web Technologies Lecture Notes in Computer Science, 2115/2001, 91-100.

Daniel, E. (1999), "Provision of electronic banking in the UK and the Republic of Ireland", International Journal of Bank Marketing, Vol. 17 No.2, pp.72-82.

FinScope. (2009). FinScope Survey South Africa. Johannesburg: FinMark Trust.

Hadjimanolis A. and Dickson K. (2001). Development of national innovation policy in small developing countries: the case of Cyprus. Research Policy 30 (2001) 805–817

Hughes, N., and Lonie, S. (2007). M-PESA: Mobile money for the “unbanked” turning cellphones into 24-hour tellers in kenya. Innovations: Technology, Governance, Globalization, 2(1), 63-81.

Jack W., Suri T and Sloan M. (2011). Mobile Money: The Economics of M-PESA. Available from URL: http://www9.georgetown.edu/faculty/wgj/papers/Jack_Suri-Economics-of-M-PESA.pdf

Mallat, N. (2007). Exploring consumer adoption of mobile payments – A qualitative study. The Journal of Strategic Information Systems, 413-432.

Mas I., Ng’weno A., and Bill and Melinda Gates Foundation. (2010). Three keys to M-PESA’s success: Branding, channel management and pricing. Available from URL: http://mmublog.org/wp-content/files_mf/keystompesassuccess4jan.pdf

Mas, I., and Morawczynski, O. (2009). Designing mobile money services lessons from M-PESA. Innovations: Technology, Governance, Globalization, 4(2), 77-91.

Medhi I., Gautama S.N.N., and Toyama K. (2009). A Comparison of Mobile Money-Transfer UIs for Non-Literate and Semi-Literate Users. CHI 2009 ~ Mobile Applications for the Developing World April 8th, 2009 ~ Boston, MA, USA

Meso P., Musa P and Mbarika V. (2005). Towards a model of consumer use of mobile information and communication technology in LDCS: the case of Sub-Saharan Africa. Info Systems J (2005) 15 , 119–146

Morawczynski, O. and Pickens M. (2009). “Poor People Using Mobile Financial Services: Observations on Customer Usage and Impact from M-PESA.” CGAP Brief, August (Washington, DC: CGAP).

Ngwenyama J O and Lee A.S. (1997). Communication Richness in Electronic Mail: Critical Social Theory and the Contextuality of Meaning. MIS Quarterly/June 1997. pp 145-167.

Ondrus J, Pigneur Y (2006) A multi-stakeholder multi-criteria assessment framework of mobile payments: an illustration with the Swiss public transportation industry. In: The 39th annual Hawaii international conference on system sciences (HICSS)

Park J., Lee D., and Ahn J. (2004). Risk-Focused e-Commerce Adoption Model - A Cross-Country Study. Journal of Global Information Technology Management; 2004;7,2; ABI/INFORM Global pg6-30

Po C.C., Fong S., and Lei P. (2007). On Designing an Efficient and Secure Card-Based Payment System Based On ANSI X9.59-2006. IEEE International Workshop on Anti-Counterfeiting, Security, Identification. Xiamen, Fujian, 16-18 April 2007 pp 427 - 430

Ritchie, J., & Lewis, J. (2003). Qualitative research practice: a guide for social science students and researchers. Thousand Oaks: SAGE.

Sathye M. (1999). Adoption of Internet banking by Australian consumers: an empirical investigation. International Journal of Bank Marketing. Volume: 17, Number: 7, Year: 1999, pp: 324-334

Teo L.T., Chan C., and Parker C. (2004). Factors affecting e-commerce adoption by SMEs: a meta-analysis, in ACIS 2004 : Proceedings of the 15th Australasian Conference on Information Systems, Australasian Conference on Information Systems, Hobart, Tasmania.

Thomas D.R. (2003). A General Inductive Approach for Qualitative Data Analysis. Available from URL: http://Www.Fmhs.Auckland.Ac.Nz/Soph/Centres/Hrmas/_Docs/Inductive2003.Pdf

Van Akkeren J.K. and M Cavaye A. L. (1999) Confusion with Diffusion? Unraveling IS diffusion and innovation literature with a focus on SMEs. AJIS Vol. 7 No. 1 Sept 1999

World Economic Forum (2011). The Mobile Financial Services Development Report. Available from URL: http://www3.weforum.org/docs/WEF_MFSD_Report_2011.pdf

Model Driven Engineering in Systems Integration

M.Minich[1], B.Harriehausen-Mühlbauer[2] and C.Wentzel[2]

[1]Centre for Security, Communications and Network Research,
Plymouth University, Plymouth, UK
[2]Department of Computer Science, University of Applied Sciences Darmstadt,
Darmstadt, Germany
e-mail: info@cscan.org

Abstract

Software development in systems integration projects is still reliant on craftsmanship of highly skilled workers. To make such projects more profitable, an industrialized production, characterized by high efficiency, quality, and automation seems inevitable. While first milestones of software industrialization have recently been achieved, it is questionable if these can be applied to the field of systems integration as well. Besides specialization, standardization and systematic reuse, automation represents the final and most sophisticated key concept of industrialization, represented by Model Driven Engineering (MDE). The present work discusses the most prominent MDE approaches, while considering the particularities of systems integration. It identifies Generative Programming as being most suitable and integrates it into previous works on Software Product Lines and Component Based Development in Systems Integration.

Keywords

Software Industrialization, Automation, Systems Integration, Software Product Lines, Generative Programming, Model Driven Engineering

1. Introduction

Compared to other high tech industries, software engineering shows only marginal improvement in terms of productivity, quality, and cost efficiency. It is still characterised by a high degree of craftsmanship to develop software from scratch with labour-intensive methods. By applying industrial methods and thus enhancing an organization's productivity, we possibly can increase quality and product complexity, and at the same time reduce cost and production time. Key industrial methods can be defined as specialization, standardization, systematic reuse, and automation (Encyclopaedia 2005). In the field of software engineering, Software Product Lines (SPL) represent specialization as the first and probably most important industrial principle. By concentrating on a limited scope, production assets can be much more power- and useful, which is especially important for standardization and systematic reuse as the second industrial principle. Both are available within Component Based Development (CBD), an approach to exchange and systematically reuse software artefacts in a standardized fashion. The final aspect of industrialization, automation, can be achieved with Model Driven Engineering (MDE). Using models as a description of software and utilizing domain specific languages, the degree of freedom and possible contexts available to a software developer is reduced. Without such limitation it would hardly be possible to provide formal model transformation engines and code generators, as they would have to cover an indefinite number of possible implementations for e.g. a single business concept.

In today's business world, IT faces high demands in quickly adopting to new requirements. As legacy systems often do not offer the flexibility to do so, new systems are implemented which need to interact with the existing IT landscape. This situation inevitably leads to systems integration efforts, joining the different subsystems into a cohesive whole, in order to provide new business functionality or data access (Fischer, 1999; Leser and Naumann, 2007). Systems integration deals with the steps required to move an IT system from a given degree of integration to a higher one by merging distinct entities into a cohesive whole, or integrating them into already existing systems (Riehm, 1997; Fischer, 1999).

Although several literature on the different industrialization concepts and their practical implementation is available (Clements and Northrop, 2007; Herzum and Sims, 2000; Stahl and Bettin, 2007), it seems questionable if they are suitable for all areas of software development, such as systems integration with its high heterogeneity or single-use development projects. The present work therefore takes the position of a large systems integrator, who provides enterprise application integration (EAI) services and solutions to his customers. Research was done with support of a German company active in the field, providing a variety of integration solutions to its customers. The objective was to identify different possibilities for model driven engineering while considering the particularities of the company: Taking into account that such providers are usually involved in different industries; a high heterogeneity must be assumed. This anticipates the formation of standards and is reinforced by the fact that integrated systems are often connected on a peer-to-peer basis with each other. Due to high acquisition cost, they are also not replaced frequently (Hasselbring, 2000).

It must be assumed, that for such heterogeneous, volatile, and customer specific projects, conventional industrialization approaches are hardly feasible. For Software Product Lines and Component Based Development, we have developed a methodology in our previous works about an Organizational Approach for Industrialized Systems Integration (Minich *et al.*, 2010), and Component Based Development in Systems Integration (Minich *et al.*, 2011). The present work deals with the implementation of the third and final industrial key principle, i.e. automating development with the help of Model Driven Engineering. With the given situation and existing MDE concepts, it must be assumed that such intent will never break even, as no considerable economies of scale or scope exist to justify expenses for domain specific language, transformer, and generator development. To overcome this challenge, either reusability or cost efficiency must significantly be increased.

2. Automating Software Development

In automated software development, software engineers specify what to do, but not how. It is up to model transformers or code generators to interpret descriptive models of the intended system and create either intermediate models to be further refined, or source code. Different approaches exist or are currently being researched. The following are the most discussed ones in literature:

- Model Driven Architecture (MDA): An initiative from the Object Management Group (OMG), MDA defines a model driven development approach which is based on a separation of functional and technical concerns (Object Management Group, 2003). It therefore specifies UML as its modelling language, and the Meta Object Facility as its describing model (meta model) for all specification models. These are the Computation Independent Model (CIM), the Platform Independent Model (PIM), the Platform Specific Model (PSM), and the Platform Specific Implementation (PSI). The CIM describes the required systems from hard- and software independent point of view. It can be represented as a high level UML class diagram containing the key concepts and terms of the respective domain. The CIM is further elaborated with conceptual information and transforms into a PIM, describing the required system on a formal and precise level, containing elements like entities, attributes, or data types (Petrasch and Meimberg, 2006). The PIM is the first model which may automatically be transformed by transformation engines or code generators and thus needs to be as precise as possible (Singh and Sood, 2009). Subsequently, it is transformed into the PSM, formally describing the application for the specified platform. Several iterations are possible, until the final result is the Platform Specific Implementation, i.e. an executable artefact reflecting the requirements previously depicted in the CIM.
- Generative Programming (GP): Based on the work of Czarnecki and Eisenecker (Czarnecki, 2005), Generative Programming aims at automating the development of a family member within a Software Product Line. It therefore defines a problem space expressed by a Domain Specific Language and the solution space consisting of "implementation-oriented abstractions, which can be instantiated to create implementations of the specifications expressed using the domain-specific abstractions from the problem space" (Czarnecki, 2005). The mapping between both contains the configuration knowledge such as illegal feature combinations, default settings, default dependencies, construction rules and grammar, or optimizations. These mapping rules are implemented within a generator returning the solution space, which may either be an intermediate model or executable program code.
- Software Factories (SF): An approach introduced at Microsoft by Greenfield and Short (Greenfield *et al.*, 2004) which, similar to GP, utilizes Software Product Lines and Component Based Development, along with a highly customized IDE. It is based on Software Factory Schemes, which describe certain viewpoints required to develop a system. Such viewpoints express concerns regarding the business logic and workflows, data model and data messaging, application architecture, and technology, and may be present on all levels of abstraction. All together the schemes with their viewpoints exactly define what needs to be done and how to manufacture a family member. In order to provide a customized IDE, the schema with its viewpoints is represented by a Software Factory Template. The template can be loaded into an IDE, providing wizards, patterns, frameworks, templates, domain specific languages, and editors. Complete definitions of domain specific languages furthermore allow (semi-) automatic model to model transformations and code generation.

Compared to MDA, Generative Programming has a domain oriented focus which is usually found in Software Product Lines. MDA in turn does not necessarily rely on a clearly delimited problem domain. GP furthermore allows to create DSL, generator, and other artefacts required "on the fly" during regular software development. This reduces the necessity of high upfront investments and leads to artefacts tailored exactly to the needs of the implementing company. In contrast to GP and MDA, Software Factories are currently based on proprietary IDEs and modelling frameworks from Microsoft. Furthermore, most of the infrastructure needs to be in place before software development may start, leading to high upfront investments. Comparing MDE with previous advances of software development, such as compilation technology or 3rd generation languages, further advancing the level of abstraction and thus increasing automation seems obvious.

However, even after almost 30 years of research in Computer Aided Software Engineering (CASE) and similar approaches as the ones introduced above, this has not yet happened. In an article on automation and model based software engineering (Selic, 2008), Bran Selic names some of the most significant reasons for the lack of acceptance of automated software development in the industry. Foremost, the biggest advantage of fourth generation programming languages (i.e. Domain Specific Languages) is also their biggest drawback: A limited scope makes them very powerful, but also reduces the economies of scale for any infrastructure development such as IDEs, transformation engines, or code generators. Development tools are either built in-house and commercially hardly break even, or by a very small number of vendors, leading to a vendor lock-in. In addition, software developers sufficiently skilled in a particular language or toolset are highly specialized and not easily available on the market. However, even with such available, there are still some more pragmatic issues such as usability of large graphical models, interoperability between tools, or current development culture (Selic, 2008).

In conclusion it can be said that with Model Driven Architecture, Generative Programming, and Software Factories, there are some interesting and promising approaches being developed. However, their way into industrial practice is still prone to "a great deal of improvisation, invention, and experimentation and still carries with significant risk" (Selic, 2008). Major improvements in standardization and availability of tools must be made to further advance model driven engineering beyond academia. The authors therefore do not believe that for the time being a full-fledged model driven engineering approach in an industrial setting is feasible. This especially applies to the field of systems integration with particularities like one-off development, high heterogeneity, and multiple systems to be integrated. These and their implications on automated software development will be discussed in the following.

3. Characteristics of Systems Integration

Systems Integration comes with certain particularities, distinguishing it from conventional or single-system software development. It has to challenge a multiplicity of technologies, business processes, and other aspects, such as regulatory requirements. Considering the fact that most system integrators are active in multiple industries with multiple customers, chances that one project is similar to another are extremely small. However, the industrialization of software development requires some sort of specialization, standardization, and automation to be beneficial. While specialization can be found in Software Product Lines and standardization in Component Based Development, automation requires an approach similar to the ones introduced in chapter 2.

As with every new technology, implementation cost are associated with model driven engineering. First, one has to define a domain specific language in which the different applications of a product line will be modelled in. For systems integration, such a DSL needs to represent not only the system that is to be modelled, but also parts of those systems the new one is to be integrated with. Subsequently, respective model transformation engines and code generators must be developed, a task far from being trivial. Depending on the type of integration, such generators need to generate code for different platforms. Once all this is in place, automated software development may begin. Preparations therefore require a certain effort to be completed and must be considered from a cost benefit analysis. However, in the context of systems integration, implementation costs seem contradictory to model driven engineering. With the given situation and existing MDE concepts, it must be assumed that such intent will never break even, as no considerable economies of scale or scope exist to justify expenses for DSL, transformation engine and code generator, and IDE development. Furthermore, one has to consider shortcomings of current tools and development culture as introduced at the end of chapter 2. To overcome these challenges, either reusability or cost efficiency must significantly be increased, as well as suitable tools need to be available.

4. Combining MDE with Industrial Systems Integration

In our previous work (Minich *et al.*, 2010), we presented an organizational model for industrialized systems integration, which was done as a first step towards industrialization. It assumes that integration of different IT systems mostly occurs within the boundaries of a certain business domain, as the automotive industry, for instance. Herein, a large number of concepts, such as the logical entities car, supplier, or customer, remain the same for all applications and product lines. The model therefore consolidates similar activities of different product lines within a super ordinate layer, i.e. the Business Domain Layer. The advantage of this consolidation lies in a simplified integration of products from the underlying product lines, and a more efficient implementation approach due to the consolidation of redundant activities. In a subsequent step, we adapted the Business Component Model by Herzum and Sims (Herzum and Sims, 2000) as the second key principle of industrialization (Minich *et al.*, 2011). Herein we have shown how the different aspects of the model can be adapted to systems integration by matching them to an integration meta model. In addition we have shown where the required process steps of the Business Component Model are best situated within our Organizational Model for Industrialized Systems Integration.

This leaves us with automation as the final step, represented by model driven engineering. Given the MDE approaches introduced above, we chose Generative Programming as the basis for our work due to its focus on automating the development of a family member within a software product line (Czarnecki, 2005) and its ability to be implemented concurrently with the actual product being developed. Development within a product line allows for specialization as one of the key principles of industrialization. Advancing the approach while developing an actual product removes the necessity of high upfront investments. In the following sections we will show where in our previously developed organizational model the GP processes are best situated and how they relate to the Business Component Model.

4.1. Development Processes of Generative Programming

Generative programming (GP) includes the following eight main development processes (Czarnecki and Eisenecker, 2000) to define scope and functionality, infrastructure and core assets, as well as automation artefacts:

1. **Domain Scoping** identifies the domain of interest, stakeholders, goals, and defines the scope of the GP approach. It is influenced by e.g. the stability and maturity of potential solutions, available resources to implement them, and the potential for reuse during production (Czarnecki and Eisenecker, 2000).
2. **Feature & concept modelling** identifies the distinguishable characteristics of a system within a certain domain and models them within a feature model (Czarnecki and Eisenecker, 2000).
3. **Common architecture & component definition** depends on the previously developed feature model. Each identified area of functionality requires one or more components, whereas their component model, interaction, type, and distribution will depend on the architecture chosen for the system (Czarnecki and Eisenecker, 2000).
4. **Domain Specific Language design** specifies a language by defining its syntax and semantics. This may be done in different ways, ranging from simple translational semantics (i.e. defining a translation scheme to an implementation language) to complex axiomatic semantics (i.e. defining a mathematical theory for proving programs written in a given programming language) (Czarnecki and Eisenecker, 2000).
5. **Specification of configuration knowledge** defines how the problem space will be transformed into the solution space by utilizing the features and concepts identified above. It shields the developer from knowing all components and features by specifying illegal combinations, default settings, dependencies, or construction rules.
6. **Architecture & component implementation** implements the architecture and components identified above. The technology in which both are implemented depends on the scope of the domain.
7. **Domain Specific Language implementation** takes the DSL specification from the DSL design process and derives a concrete implementation. Here GP differentiates between separate DSLs (e.g. SQL or T_EX), embedded DSLs (e.g. template meta programming in C++), and modularly composable DSLs (e.g. embedded SQL, or aspect oriented programming) (Czarnecki and Eisenecker, 2000).
8. **Configuration knowledge implementation in generators** allows advancing the problem specified with the help of a Domain Specific Language into executable program code. To do so, generators apply validation of the input specification,

complete a given specification with default settings, perform optimizations, and eventually generate the implementation. Generators may be implemented as stand-alone programs, using built-in meta programming capabilities of a programming language, or by using a predefined generator infrastructure (Czarnecki and Eisenecker, 2000).

Comparing the eight process steps with the concepts of Software Product Line and Component Based Development, Generative Programming can be clearly subdivided into the industrial key concepts of specialization (steps 1 and 2), standardization (steps 3, 5 and 6), and automation (steps 4, 7, and 8).

4.2. GP and the Organizational Model for Industrialized Systems Integration

Software Product Lines and Component Based Development already cover the large parts of the GP processes. In the following we will therefore describe how our previously developed approach for Software Product Lines in systems integration needs to be adjusted to incorporate the requirements of Generative Programming.

4.2.1. The Business Domain Layer

The Business Domain Layer was developed to align domain wide functionality and utilize economies of scope due to similar concepts and core assets among different product lines of a given domain. It therefore contains the Software Product Line processes domain analysis & portfolio definition, architecture development & roadmap definition, and core asset development.

As to Generative Programming, the above processes already cover the GP processes 1 and 2, such as development of a domain or feature model (Minich *et al.*, 2010). Furthermore, the activities of GP processes 3 and 4 are already enclosed in Architecture Development & Roadmap Definition, and Core Asset Development. However, as the Business Domain Layer only features concepts suitable for more than one product line, we have to differentiate between global (business domain wide) and local (product line specific) aspects of GP. This means that there will for instance be DSL design activities in both, the Business Domain and the Software Product Line Layer. In the former, the overall structure and domain wide syntax and semantics are defined, whereas the latter covers product line specific syntax and semantics, such as "bill of materials" for a shop floor system produced in a particular software product line. The distribution is illustrated in Figure . Combining the activities introduced in (Minich *et al.*, 2010) with the respective ones from Generative Programming, the Business Domain Layer in its final stage consists of the following core processes:

- **Business Domain Analysis** explores the typical IT landscape of the business domain in scope and identifies areas of expertise required to develop and provide the products and services under consideration. Similar to software product lines but on a higher level, it identifies recurring problems and known solutions.
- **Portfolio Definition & Domain Scoping** evaluates the information from the domain model and develops a product portfolio for the particular business segment. The portfolio covers typical applications and solutions for the most

important business services of the segment and identifies the portfolio elements and resulting software product lines.

- **Architecture & Feature Definition**. Once the scope is defined, a basic product line and integration architecture, a component framework, and an overall feature model, applicable for all product lines are developed. As different product lines have different functional and technical requirements, this architecture may also exist in an abstract form and be instantiated within the product line subsequently. This approach allows for a later integration of products from different product lines of the same business domain.
- **Core Asset Development** develops reusable assets, applicable to all or many software product lines within the business segment. Such joint core assets may for instance be development tools and processes, or joint software development patterns. Core Asset Development may also include the production of reusable software components equal to each product line. To additionally support Generative Programming, Core Asset Development now also contains the definition of an abstract syntax for a domain wide specification language. This DSL may then be extended within the underlying software product lines in order to support more specific concepts.

4.2.2. The Software Product Line Layer

The Software Product Line Layer consists of several software product lines identified in business domain analysis and portfolio definition processes of the business domain layer (Minich *et al.*, 2010). The most obvious variance to a conventional software product line is the lack of the business domain analysis process, and a simplified domain requirements engineering process. These functions are now incorporated in the business domain layer and provide their findings to the subsequent product lines. All other processes remain the same but must adhere to the specifications and utilize the provided core assets from the business domain layer.

As to Generative Programming, we can find all but the first development process within the Software Product Line Layer. However, due to the separation of domain wide and product line specific concerns, the GP processes 2 to 4 only handle product line related concerns. A systems integrator's feature model for the automotive industry may for instance define the entity car with several features, such as model, engine, transmission, colour, price, owner, and so on. These features exist in all products of the underlying product lines. A product line for shop floor systems may however extend this feature model by adding features like electronic control unit (ECU) type, brake type, or parts list. As this has no implication on the functionality of the car itself or the customer, these features are not necessary to be known in other product lines. A financial system does not need to know what type of ECU is built into a car, but it does need to know the price and the owner of the car. This same principle applies to Common Architecture & Component Definition and Domain Specific Language Design. GP processes 5 to 5 are carried out in the software product lines only. Combining the activities introduced in our Organizational Model for Industrialized Systems Integration with the respective ones from Generative Programming, the Product Line Layer in its final stage consists of the following core processes:

- **Requirements Engineering & Feature Modelling** defines the scope of the intended software product line by identifying its products and documenting their commonalities and variability within a feature model. The process has to conform to the Portfolio Definition & Domain Scoping artefacts of the superior business domain layer, but may extend them with product line specific features.
- **Architecture, Component & DSL Design** transforms the scope defined in requirements engineering into a technical architecture and specification for the product line and its products. The architecture decomposes a software system into common and variable functional parts, and specifies the configuration knowledge in terms of component dependencies, default configurations, construction rules, illegal combinations, and rules for their implementation. Each identified area of functionality requires one or more components with an architecture specific component model, interaction scheme, and distribution mechanism. All programming artefacts are finally described within a Domain Specific Language. The process' activities must adhere to the specifications from the business domain layer, but may extend it with product line specific features.
- **Core Asset Development** provides the design and the implementation of reusable software assets (Pohl *et al.*, 2005). This implementation includes the overall framework, software components, executable code, and other product line assets, such as development processes and tools. In terms of Generative Programming, core asset development is also responsible for the implementation of the DSL as specified in the previous process. In a later and more mature stage, Core Asset Development will implement the configuration knowledge within generators to advance the system specified with the help of a DSL into intermediate models or executable code. As this can be extremely complex, we suggest postponing this activity until reasonable experience with the DSL and the product lines has been gathered.
- **Domain Testing** develops test cases and inspects all core assets and their interactions against the requirements and contexts defined by the product line architecture. Domain testing also includes validation of non-software core assets, such as business processes, product line architecture or development policies.
- **Software Integration** in the context of product line development occurs during pre-integration of several software components. They form blocks of functionality common to all products and contexts of a product line. Furthermore, the integration process ensures the interoperability of all reusable assets and provides the required integration mechanisms.

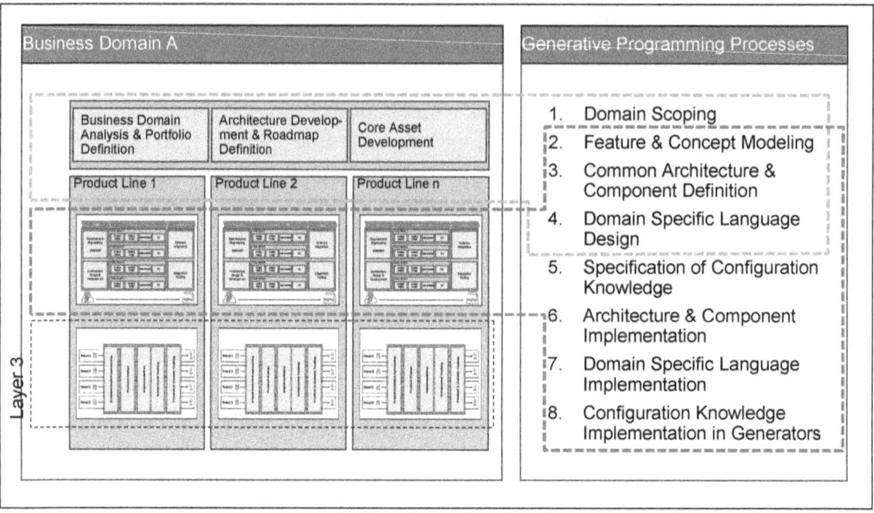

Figure 1: Mapping of GP Processes to Organizational Structure

4.3. GP and the Business Component Model

The Business Component Model is a methodology to model, analyse, design, construct, validate, deploy, customize, and maintain large scale distributed systems, developed by Herzum and Sims (Herzum and Sims, 2000). It consists of five dimensions: Architectural Viewpoints, Component Granularity, Development Process, Distribution Tier, and Functional Categories. In our previous work we have already shown how to align the Business Component Model with our Organizational Model to reflect the particularities of Systems Integration. The following sections will show how these five dimensions fit together with Generative Programming, assuming that development of components occurs with GP.

4.3.1. Architectural Viewpoints

The first dimension consists of four architectural viewpoints, which are the Project Management Architecture (PMA, concerned with organizational decisions, tools, and guidelines), the Technical Architecture (TA, defining the execution environment, component and user interface frameworks, and other technical facilities), the Application Architecture (AA, describing development patterns, guidelines, or standards), as well as the Functional Architecture (FA, identifying the features and functional aspects of a system and their relationships).

With regards to the Project Management Architecture, Generative Programming does not make any statements about the organization or structure of a development project within its processes. The PMA from the Business Component Model is therefore regarded beneficial to the GP approach. In our organizational model, the PMA is found in the Business Domain Layer, whose organizational decisions, tools, and guidelines will influence the development in GP. The remaining three, rather technical viewpoints, are concerned with the execution infrastructure and programming frameworks (Technical Architecture), development patterns, guidelines, and programming standards (Application Architecture), as well as the functional aspects of a system including its implementation (Functional Architecture). Generative Programming in turn only offers the generic process common architecture & component definition. We therefore suggest replacing the respective GP process with the actual implementation of the much more detailed architectural viewpoints from the Business Component Model. For Generative Programming, this replacement offers a more comprehensive view on different aspects of the architecture, while for CBD it ensures coverage of more component related artefacts, such as the component infrastructure or execution environment.

4.3.2. Component Granularity

Generative Programming does not explicitly refer to well defined components as known from e.g. Enterprise Java Beans or Corba. Also it doesn't conceptually concentrate on business processes and therefore does not know reasonable levels of granularity. An artefact may for instance be a generic and reusable data container for C++, allowing handling domain specific types of information. It may also be a reusable programming library providing a complex business concept like a bank account. Generative Programming rather concentrates on technologies and means to develop reusable artefacts of variable sizes, depending on the intended usage. This way of partitioning a problem into reusable artefacts is known as *continuous recursion*. One iteratively partitions a problem into different but reasonable granularities. The Business Component model in turn follows a *discrete recursion* approach. It therefore defines five levels of granularity: the language class, the distributed component (a component in its common sense, e.g. an EJB or CORBA component), the business component (still independently deployable, consisting of distributed components and glue code, representing a business process), and the system level component (a set of business components providing business functionality). The highest level of granularity is the federation of system-level components (i.e. system level components federated to provide multiple complex business services).

We believe that discrete recursion and thus partitioning of the problem is more beneficial in an environment with systematic reuse. For each layer of recursion, a developer has to define scope, characteristics, packaging, and deployment (Herzum and Sims, 2000). In an environment where components are to be reused as much as possible, it seems more beneficial to define these layers of recursion on a common basis. A middleware messaging adaptor for a specific ERP system will most likely exist as a distributed component as introduced above. A developer can rely on this concept and build his application accordingly. We therefore suggest to introduce discrete recursion to the Generative Programming approach if it is to be used within component based development and systematic reuse in mind.

4.3.3. Development Process

The Business Component Model encompasses a set of manufacturing processes, which support component, system, and federation of systems development. However, as most organizations are in a transitive state towards CBD, Herzum and

Sims suggest a process called rapid system development (RSD). It is following the well known V-Model, whereas requirements to implementation denote the left, and component, system, and acceptance testing the right side of the V (Herzum and Sims, 2000). RSD allows subsequently engineering reusable artefacts based on customer specific requirements and eventually building the respective end product. The advantage is that reusable artefacts evolve on the fly. The disadvantage is that, beginning with the requirements of one specific customer, one may easily miss important variation points or even take architectural decisions which may conflict with the overall scope of the product line. Generative programming in turn focuses much more on domain engineering activities and the technical implementation of reusable artefacts, rather than development of the end product. It puts explicit focus on feature modelling processes such as FODA or FeatuRSEB (Czarnecki and Eisenecker, 2000), as all GP artefacts rely on a detailed domain model. As research in the field has progressed, we also considered PLUSS (Product Line Use Case Modelling for Systems and Software engineering) (Eriksson *et al.*, 2006) being a viable alternative for precise domain modelling. The advantage of PLUSS over FODA or FeatuRSEB is that besides a feature model it also allows to allocate use cases, use case variations, and cross-cutting concerns to each feature. In the context of the present work we follow the rationale of Generative Programming to define a precise model of the product domain before implementing any reusable artefacts. This seems especially important if domain specific languages and generators are to be built, although they will be rather simple in the beginning. We therefore suggest to enhance the Requirements, Analysis, and Design activities of Herzum and Sims' rapid system development process with Feature Modelling and Use Case Development of Eriksson et.al.'s PLUSS approach (Eriksson *et al.*, op. 2005). The result will be a detailed feature model, including a variety of use cases for the required feature combinations. Based on these artefacts, the customer specific application can be built and reusable components derived.

4.3.4. Distribution Tier

In their model, Herzum and Sims separate between user, workspace, enterprise, and resource tier. The user tier presents the component on the screen and communicates with the user. It may be stand-alone, plug in, or non-existent at all. The local business logic is implemented by the workspace tier, which will interact with the enterprise tier. Typical business logic may for instance include transaction management utilizing several enterprise-level resources. The latter are implemented by the enterprise tier, providing business rules, validation, and interaction between components. It typically forms the core functionality of business components of a complex, large-scale component based system. The resource tier manages access to shared resources, such as databases, files, or communication infrastructures and shields all higher layers from their technical implementation.

Such detailed differentiation of reusable components and their internal structure is not provided by the Generative Programming approach. Being more generic, GP leaves such decisions on the target architecture of the product line, which is in turn depending on the overall feature model (Czarnecki and Eisenecker, 2000). With regard to the Business Component model, feature model and architecture will already be available and are furthermore influenced by the conceptual structure of business components. In combination with GP, we see no issues when implementing the four distribution tiers with the means of Generative Programming.

4.3.5. Functional Categories

The final dimension defines utility, entity, process, and auxiliary business components (Herzum and Sims, 2000). Utility components can most generally be reused and represent autonomous concepts, such as unique number generators, currency converters, or an address book. Entity business components represent the logical entities on which a business process operates and are specific to a particular business domain. Examples are item, invoice, address, or customer. The actual business *process* is implemented within a process business component. Usually unique for one industry or customer, it is hardly reusable. The fourth category, auxiliary business components, provides services usually not found within a process description. Such may be performance monitoring, messaging, or middleware services.

As with the distribution tier above, Generative Programming does not know any functional categories. However, a detailed feature model in connection with component granularity, distribution tiers, and functional categories, will provide a structured and standardized approach to generative development of business components. As such we believe it is more likely to yield systematic reuse than a structure that is flexible from component to component.

5. Conclusion & Further Research

As we have explained in chapter 3, systems integration comes with certain particularities requiring a highly efficient and cost effective way of implementing industrial key concepts. The low number of similar products in SI seems contradictive to Model Driven Engineering with its Domain Specific Languages, Model Transformers, and Code Generators. However, with integrating GP into our organizational model and combining it with CBD, we can save efforts for domain scoping, feature and concept modelling, architecture and component definition, configuration knowledge specification, and component implementation. All these activities, although slightly adapted, have already been completed, once it comes to the implementation of MDE.

Together with the Business Component Model, a standardized component and implementation architecture is available which allows us to systematically reuse functionality already developed. If a middleware adaptor will always be implemented as an auxiliary business component at the resource distribution tier, it is much more likely to be reused than a freely implemented one. We therefore believe that in order to get the most out of Generative Programming, it must be combined with a component based development approach. Based on our previous work (Minich *et al.*, 2011), we found the Business Component Model to be most beneficial, especially in the context of systems integration.

The present paper completes the development of a concept for industrialized systems integration. It consists of the organizational model for software product lines in systems integration, reflecting specialization as the first industrial key principle. Subsequently, the alignment of Herzum and Sims' Business Component Model with Vogler's Integration Meta Model describes how to divide a system into a set of reusable artefacts, reflecting the particularities of systems integration. With the present work, Generative Programming has been identified as a potential way towards automation as the final industrial key principle. What is left to be done is a concluding description of the overall concept including the presentation of a field study across all three principles: Beginning with Business Domain design and subsequent Software Product Line definition, over the development of a detailed feature model and component structure, up to the definition and implementation of an initial Domain Specific Language and the according generators with the help of Generative Programming. It is intended to exemplarily develop at least one example of each artefact required for a successful industrialization of systems integration.

6. References

Clements, P. and Northrop, L. (2007), *Software product lines: Practices and patterns,* [Nachdr.], Addison-Wesley, Boston.

Czarnecki, K. (2005), "Overview of Generative Software Development", in Banâtre, J.-P., Fradet, P., Giavitto, J.-L. and Michel, O. (Eds.), *Unconventional Programming Paradigms, Lecture Notes in Computer Science*, Vol. 3566, Springer Berlin / Heidelberg, pp. 97-97.

Czarnecki, K. and Eisenecker, U. (2000), *Generative programming: Methods, tools, and applications*, Addison Wesley, Boston.

Encyclopaedia Britannica (2005), "Industrial Revolution", in *Encyclopaedia Britannica: In 32 volumes,* Vol. 6, 15. ed., Encyclopaedia Britannica, Chicago, London, New Delhi, Paris, Seoul, Sydney, Taipei, Tokyo, pp. 304–305.

Eriksson, M., Börstler, J. and Borg, K. (op. 2005), "The PLUSS Approach - Domain Modeling with Features, Use Cases and Use Case Realizations", in Obbink, H. and Pohl, K. (Eds.), *Software product lines: 9th international conference, SPLC 2005, Rennes, France, September 26-29, 2005 proceedings*, Springer, Berlin, New York, NY, pp. 33–44.

Eriksson, M., Börstler, J. and Borg, K. (2006), "Software Product Line Modeling Made Practical", *Communications of the ACM*, Vol. 49 No. 12, pp. 49–53.

Fischer, J. (1999), *Informationswirtschaft Anwendungsmanagement*, Oldenbourg, München, Wien.

Greenfield, J., Short, K. and Cook, S. (2004), *Software factories: Assembling applications with patterns, models, frameworks, and tools*, Wiley, Indianapolis, Ind.

Hasselbring, W. (2000), "Information System Integration", *Communications of the ACM*, Vol. 43 No. 6, pp. 32–38.

Herzum, P. and Sims, O. (2000), *Business component factory: A comprehensive overview of component-based development for the enterprise*, John Wiley, New York.

Leser, U. and Naumann, F. (2007), *Informationsintegration: Architekturen und Methoden zur Integration verteilter und heterogener Datenquellen,* 1. Aufl., dpunkt-Verl., Heidelberg.

Minich, M., Harriehausen-Mühlbauer, B. and Wentzel, C. (2010), "An Organizational Approach for Industrialized Systems Integration".

Minich, M., Harriehausen-Mühlbauer, B. and Wentzel, C. (2011), "Component Based Development in Systems Integration", in *GI Lecture Notes in Informatics 2011: Informatik schafft Communities*, Ges. für Informatik, Bonn, p. 470.

Object Management Group (2003), *MDA Guide Version 1.0.1.*

Petrasch, R. and Meimberg, O. (2006), *Model Driven Architecture: Eine praxisorientierte Einführung in die MDA,* 1. Aufl., dpunkt, Heidelberg.

Pohl, K., Böckle, G. and Linden, F. (2005), *Software product line engineering: Foundations, principles, and techniques ; with 10 tables*, Springer, Berlin.

Riehm, R. (1997), "Integration von heterogenen Applikationen", Dissertation, Universität St. Gallen, St. Gallen, 1997.

Selic, B. (2008), "Personal reflections on automation, programming culture, and model-based software engineering", *Automated Software Engineering*, Vol. 15 3-4, pp. 379-391.

Singh, Y. and Sood, M. (2009), "Model Driven Architecture: A Perspective", in IEEE Computer Society (Ed.), *Proceedings of the 2009 IEEE International Advance Computing Conference*, IEEE Computer Society, Patiala, pp. 1644–1652.

Stahl, T. and Bettin, J. (2007), *Modellgetriebene Softwareentwicklung: Techniken, Engineering, Management,* 2., aktualisierte und erw. Aufl., dpunkt-Verl., Heidelberg.

*i*SemServ: Facilitating the Implementation of Intelligent Semantic Services

J.Mtsweni, E.Biermann and L.Pretorius

School of Computing, University of South Africa, Pretoria, South Africa
e-mail: mtswejs@unisa.ac.za; bierman@xsinet.co.za; pretol@unisa.ac.za

Abstract

The process of developing semantic services is viewed by service developers as being complex, and tedious. The main barriers that have been identified include a steep learning curve for emerging semantic models and ontological languages, the lack of integrated tool support for developing semantic services, and lack of interoperability between emerging semantic technologies and matured Web service technologies. In addition, current efforts that are meant to ease the implementation of semantic services are fragmented; that is, developers are required to use a combination of disconnected tools to realize semantic services. Moreover, existing semantic technologies are tightly coupled to specific semantic models and service architectural styles; leading to restrictive development environments. In this paper, an *iSemServ* framework is proposed, and implemented as an Eclipse plug-in with the core objective to facilitate, unify, and accelerate the process of developing intelligent semantic services using semantic models and service architectural styles of choice. Experimental evaluations demonstrate that a solution, such as *iSemServ* has the potential to minimize some of the barriers associated with building intelligent semantic services.

Keywords

iSemServ, Eclipse, Semantic Web Services, Ontologies, Intelligent Agents, Model-driven

1. Introduction

The applicability and benefits of employing Semantic Web Services (SWS) also referred to as *semantic services* in this paper are well studied and documented in academia and industry. In (Bachlechner, 2008, de Bruijn et al., 2005a, Janev and Vranes, 2010), the benefits that could be relished by businesses from utilizing semantic technologies are highlighted. These include: (1) improved representation, sharing, searching, reasoning, and re-use of data and services on the Web, (2) anywhere and anytime dynamic connection of business partners through services, and (3) automation of various tasks on the Web such as service discovery, selection, composition, choreography, orchestration, execution, and monitoring.

Nevertheless, in spite of all the benefits, the practical uptake and real-world implementation of semantic services has remained minute to date. A number of scholars (Bachlechner, 2008, Agre et al., 2007, Cardoso, 2007, Daniel et al., 2010) have identified some major challenges that are contributing to this lack of implementation and usage. Some of the major issues that are common include the lack of unified semantic service development tools, non-integration of semantic technologies into existing matured Web services technologies, steep learning curve for emerging semantic models, complex semantic description languages, and the lack of standardisation within the semantic services domain. In addition, existing platforms do not support the development of semantic services that are intelligent beyond the application of ontologies as envisaged within the Semantic Web Services Architecture (SWSA) (Burstein *et al.*, 2005). Other observations are that existing semantic tools are fragmented and tightly coupled specific semantic models and languages; leading to prolonged service development process, and restrictive environments.

In this paper, we thus attempt to address some of the identified challenges by proposing a unified semantic service creation framework that support multiple semantic description models, and service architectural styles called *iSemServ* (from: *I*ntelligent *Sem*antic *Serv*ices). The key objective of the proposed framework is to facilitate the process of implementing intelligent semantic services through a unified, interoperable, and extensible environment.

The remaining sections of this paper are structured as follows. Section 2 provides background information related to intelligent semantic services and its fundamental building blocks. Section 3 discusses the underlying *iSemServ* framework that provides a blueprint for facilitating the process of building intelligent semantic services. Section 4 demonstrates the implementation of the proposed *iSemServ* framework as an Eclipse plug-in. In Section 5, the evaluation results for the suggested solution are presented with the main focus on performance, and Section 6 concludes the paper with a summary and possible future research.

2. Intelligent Semantic Services

Semantic services are geared towards addressing the drawbacks of syntactic services by mapping syntactic descriptions with semantic descriptions (Lu et al., 2007). Semantic descriptions purport to describe what a service does (i.e. service capability), how does it achieve its functionalities (i.e. service behavior), and how to access its functionalities (i.e. orchestration and choreography) (de Bruijn et al., 2005a). Within the semantic services domain, a number of conceptual ontology models have been proposed on how to map semantic descriptions; which are derived from ontologies (Gruber, 1993), into syntactic services. Some of the prominent semantic models to date are heavy-weight models such Web Ontology Language for Services (OWL-S) (Martin et al., 2004) and Web Service Modeling Ontology (WSMO) (Roman et al., 2006).

The main objective of the heavy-weight semantic models is on exploiting commonly agreed upon vocabularies in a form of domain and service ontologies (Kuropka et al., 2008) to represent and describe different aspects of Web services (WS) separately from syntactic descriptions.

OWL-S is one of the first heavy-weight semantic efforts based on the Web Ontology Language (OWL). It provides a structure for defining semantic descriptions through the use of *service profiles*; which semantically describe what a service is capable of offering to prospective consumers, *service model*: describes the specific behavior of a service in terms of its input, output, pre-conditions, and effect, and *service grounding*: describes how a semantic service can be invoked and executed. Comparably, WSMO is an ontology-based model for describing semantic services - based on the WSML (Web Services Modeling Language) (de Bruijn et al., 2005b). WSMO focuses on four elements that are essential in describing semantic services. These are: (1) *Ontologies*: provide formal concepts that can be used by other WSMO elements (2) *Web Services*: describe functional, non-functional, and behavioral aspects of a service, (3) *Goals*: semantically capture users' request that could invoke the service capability, and (4) *Mediators*: handle incompatibilities and mismatches between terminologies used by WSMO elements.

In the context of this paper, an *intelligent semantic service* (IsS) extends and leverages conventional Web services with intelligentt characteristics adopted from the domain of intelligent agents (Mtsweni et al., 2010). This is done to realize the emergence of services that are machine-processable and interpretable; thus leading to minimal human intervention when it comes to service provisioning on the Web (García-Sánchez et al., 2011). The intelligence concept is commonly associated with autonomy, reactive, proactive, and collaborative or social ability properties. Henceforth, adopting the core intelligent agent properties found in (Jennings and Wooldridge, 1998, Protogeros, 2008), and the Semantic Web key enablers found in (Studer et al., 2007, de Bruijn et al., 2008), an *intelligent semantic service is defined as a semantically enabled software unit representing some business functionality that could be accessed through the Web, and is capable of being: (1) Autonomous, (2) proactive, (3) reactive (4) machine-processable and understandable, as well as (5) collaborative* (Daniel et al., 2010).

Furthermore, the fundamental building blocks that comprise intelligent semantic services are: (1) *syntactic descriptions*, (2) *domain ontologies*, (3) *semantic descriptions*, and (4) *intelligence*. These building blocks are essential as they provide a base on how intelligent semantic services could be simply developed within a unified service-creation environment. The following section delves into the suggested framework that is meant to facilitate the realisation of these fundamental building blocks within a unified environment.

3. iSemServ: The proposed framework

In Figure 1, the proposed *iSemServ* framework is demonstrated. The framework adopts a model-driven engineering (MDE) (Qafmolla and Cuong, 2010) technique to enable modelling, specification, and description of intelligent semantic services.

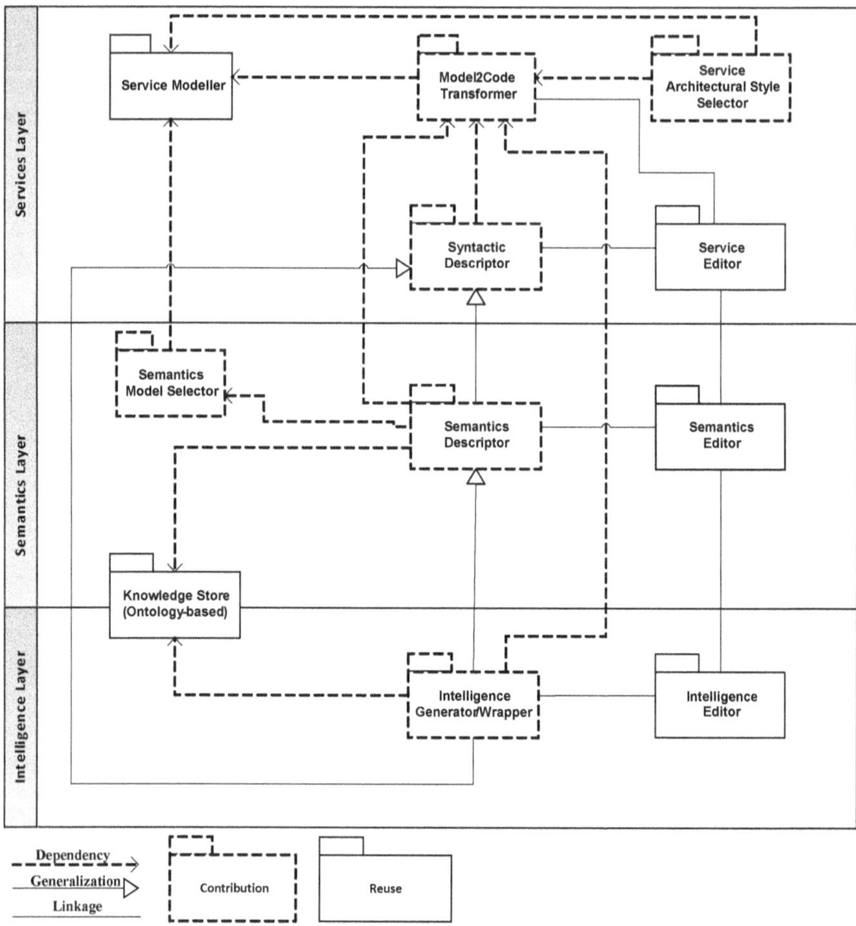

Figure 1: iSemServ framework

The framework is designed based on the overarching principles of uniformity, simplicity, interoperability, decoupling, multiple language support, and intelligence. These principles were identified through an in-depth literature review of related work (Daniel et al., 2010, Mtsweni et al., 2010), and from the challenges that the *i*SemServ framework purports to address. The framework is presented in a multi-layered format for supporting the development of service descriptions, semantic descriptions, and the intelligence functionality in an independent manner. The core layers are: *services layer*, *semantics layer*, and *intelligence layer*. The following subsections explain the purpose of each layer without focusing on the technologies that could be used to implement these layers. Section 4 will highlight some of the technologies that could be used to implement the specific modules of the suggested framework.

3.1. Services Layer

This layer deals with the initial core phases of producing conventional Web services - without semantics and/or intelligence. The first step involves creating structured and annotated service models that represent the functional and non-functional aspects of intended services, and this process is facilitated by the *Service Modeller* module. The service model serves as a basis for other layers as well, particularly for automatically generating relevant service source code stubs (e.g. semantic descriptions), thus reducing service development time. The *Model2Code* transformer uses the defined templates and transformation rules to automatically translate service models into syntactic descriptions assisted by the *Syntactic Descriptor* module; which houses different description templates. In addition, the *Model2Code* transformer translates the service model into partial service logic (e.g. Java). The key in this layer is that services of different architectural styles such as SOAP or RESTful (Filho and Ferreira, 2009) can be auto-generated with the help of the *Service Architectural Style Selector (SASS)* module. New architectural styles or standards could easily be accommodated by simply defining and integrating new templates and transformation rules into the *Model2Code* transformer.

3.2. Semantics Layer

This layer uses the *Service Modeller* module, and relies on the *Model2Code transformer* module to automatically generate domain ontologies and semantic descriptions. Since there are a number of semantic models that could be used to semantically describe Web services, the proposed framework provides the developer with the ability, through the use of a defined UML profile with key stereotypes (e.g. <<WSMO>>), to choose the preferred semantics model. Depending on the annotations; semantic descriptions and domain ontologies can be automatically generated – using the *Model2Code* transformer and the *Semantics Descriptor* module. Because the semantic descriptions and ontologies auto-generated could be incomplete depending on the defined service models; the service engineer is provided with a *Semantics Editor* module, in order to visualize, edit, augment, and validate the generated semantic descriptions and/or ontologies. In this layer, an ontology-based *knowledge store* is also provided, so that developers could also re-use existing ontologies to semantically describe services – where applicable. Additionally, the knowledge store is shared with the intelligence layer, as depicted in Figure 1, for purposes of using the same domain and service knowledge to embed semantic services with intelligence.

The key in this layer is also that service developers are not restricted in terms of semantic models to use for deriving semantic descriptions. The developer needs to only annotate the service model with the relevant stereotypes that corresponds to the semantic model of choice. The *Model2Code transformer* and the *Semantics Descriptor* will then use the defined templates and transformation rules to auto-generate the relevant code. New semantic models could also be easily accommodated in the framework by defining new templates and transformation rules.

3.3. Intelligence Layer

The *Intelligence Generator/Wrapper* module, as depicted in Figure 1, is responsible for generating all the necessary *intelligence logic* (e.g. automatic service execution) for the developed semantic services and wrapping of semantic descriptions and syntactic descriptions with intelligent properties. The module also relies on the service model and re-usable *intelligence logic* (i.e. agents' behaviour and operations) available through the Intelligence Editor. The properties that are essential for completely realizing the *intelligence* for semantic services are those that implement *autonomous, proactive, reactive,* and *collaborative* behaviours.

4. iSemServ Implementation: an Eclipse Plug-in

The *i*SemServ framework was partially implemented as a unified plug-in within the Eclipse platform; which encompasses a variety of re-usable service engineering components, such as the UML2 SDK (for enabling service models development, UML profile with specific stereotypes), Acceleo (model-to-text language generation framework was used for implementing the *Model2Code* transformer – templates and transformation rules) and JADE (a Java-based agent development environment was used for implementing the intelligent features) and JESS (a Java-based rule engine for realizing other intelligent features, such as reasoning) (Balachandran, 2008). Eclipse is touted as a mature, well-designed, and extensible architecture (Rivières and Wiegand, 2004). The Eclipse environment was chosen because of its openness, and wide acceptance in the service development domain. Figure 2 depicts a user interface for the *iSemServ* Eclipse plug-in; which is meant to facilitate the implementation of intelligent semantic services in a simpler and unified approach.

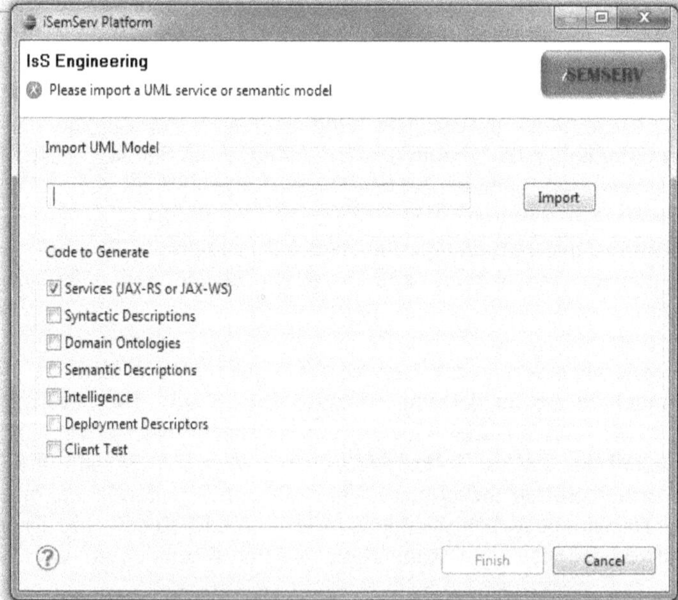

Figure 2: iSemServ Eclipse plug-in

This plug-in integrates with a number of technologies and templates that makes it possible for the service engineers to only design and import an annotated service model, select the different artefacts (e.g. domain ontologies) that are preferred for the new or existing Web services, and click finish to initiate the auto-generation process. Once the different artefacts have been generated into Eclipse project workspace, the service developer would then use Eclipse integrated editors and other tools to augment, edit, and validate some of the artefacts before deploying the final intelligent semantic service into available semantic service repository for discovery and consumption. A use case scenario implemented in (Mtsweni et al., 2011) demonstrates the type of an annotated service model, semantics models used, and the samples of the generated code (e.g. RESTful services and WSMO-based semantic descriptions).

5. Evaluation

Using real-life project scenarios (Mtsweni et al., 2011), a number of service models were designed in order to experiment and evaluate the usefulness and performance of the *iSemServ* Eclipse plug-in. The models comprised 6 to 1152 classes. In Figure 3, an overall graph is depicted highlighting the performance of the plug-in under varying service model sizes. The overall execution times, presented in seconds (s) illustrate the time it took by the platform to generate the artefacts involved in engineering intelligent semantic services.

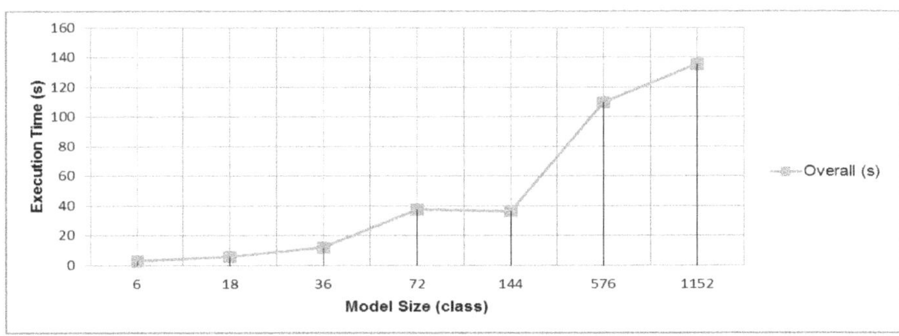

Figure 3: Overall performance of the plug-in

The graph suggests that, as the size of the service model grows, so does the amount of time required to automatically transform the model to different artefacts. For instance, processing a service model with 144 classes required about 36 seconds. An average of 73 seconds was additionally required to generate a total number of 576 Java classes and mapped building blocks, such as semantic descriptions. The code generation execution time increased to 135 seconds for processing a service model made up of 1152 classes. Further evaluations revealed that the auto-generation of syntactic descriptions in the services layer took most of the processing time as compared with other artefacts in the semantics and intelligence layer, as the service model size became bigger. Moreover, it was derived that the auto-generation process can be split into different phases, thereby minimizing the processing load and improving the performance of the plug-in as it is not a requirement that all artefacts need to be auto-generated at the same time. From the experiments, it was evident that the times to generate different artefacts that make up an intelligent semantic service are significantly smaller as compared to when the service developers have to manually generate all the relevant intelligent semantic services' components. The plug-in was developed in a manner that ensures uniformity, simplicity, interoperability, decoupling, and multiple language support. Hence, as it can be noted in Figure 2, the developer only needs to import an annotated model and select all the necessary artefacts that need to be generated. The process that is not accommodated within the plug-in is that of editing the generated artefacts. That process is generally accommodated by the different editors within the Eclipse environment.

6. Conclusion

Semantic services are seen as the main building blocks for the dynamic Web, where user intervention is kept to a minimum. However, there are still a number of challenges that need to be addressed in order to make semantic services commercially relevant. The main hindrance tackled in this paper is the lack of unified tool support for developing semantic services. In addressing this challenge, a model-driven *iSemServ* framework has been proposed that purports to facilitate the implementation of intelligent semantic services independent of a particular semantic model or service architectural style.

The proposed framework follows a top-down approach, where semantic services are modeled, and seamlessly transformed into specific service implementations, syntactic service descriptions, semantic descriptions, and intelligence using transformation rules and templates implemented specifically for the suggested approach. The approach was implemented through a simple Eclipse plug-in with the support of a number of matured tools, such as the UML2 SDK and Acceleo. The plug-in was then evaluated through real-life project scenarios for performance and utility. It was deduced that the suggested approach is one possible solution in minimizing the current hindrances of semantic services, especially due to its principles of standards independency, and automatic code generations.

The main contributions emanating from the suggested and implemented are: (1) an end-to-end approach of developing intelligent semantic services, thus enabling the developer to use one platform to realize all the modules comprising intelligent semantic services, (2) enable service engineers to focus on developing intelligent semantic services in a structured and extensible, and platform-independent manner, (3) support different architectural styles and semantic models by exploiting template-based code generators, and (4) intelligence mapping of services at message and knowledge levels for the purposes of automatically processing semantic service requests and responses by machines with minimal user intervention. Nevertheless, further research points to improving our approach with regard to multiple-language support as currently the framework only relies on templates and transformation rules, which need to be developed for each semantic model or service architectural style.

7. References

Agre, G., Marinova, Z., Pariente, T. & Micsik, A. (2007), Towards Semantic Web service engineering. *Workshop on service matchmaking and resource retrieval in the semantic Web (SMRR 2007)* CEUR

Bachlechner, D. (2008), Semantic Web service research: current challenges and proximate achievements. *International Journal of Computer Science and Applications,* 5, 117-140.

Balachandran, B. M. (2008), Developing Intelligent Agent Applications with JADE and JESS. *12th international conference on Knowledge-Based Intelligent Information and Engineering Systems, Part III.* Zagreb, Croatia, Springer-Verlag.

Burstein, M., Bussler, C., Finin, T., Huhns, M. N., Paolucci, M., Sheth, A. P., Williams, S. & Zaremba, M. (2005), A semantic Web services architecture. *IEEE Internet Computing,* 9, 72-81.

Cardoso, J. (2007), *Semantic Web Services: theory, tools and applications*, IGI Global.

Daniel, F., Facca, F., Mtsweni, J., Biermann, E. & Pretorius, L. (2010), iSemServ: Towards the Engineering of Intelligent Semantic-Based Services. *Current Trends in Web Engineering.* Springer Berlin / Heidelberg.

De Bruijn, J., Fensel, D., Keller, U. & Lara, R. (2005a), Using the web Service modelling ontology to enable semantic ebusiness. *Communications of the ACM,* 48.

De Bruijn, J., Fensel, D., Kerrigan, M., Keller, U., Lausen, H. & Scicluna, J. (2008) *Modeling Semantic Web Services: The Web service modeling language*, Springer-Verlag Berlin Heidelberg.

De Bruijn, J., Lausen, H., Krummenacher, R., Polleres, A., Predoiu, L., Kifer, M. & Fensel, D. (2005b), The Web Service Modeling Language WSML. . *WSML Final Draft.* DERI.

Filho, O. F. F. & Ferreira, M. A. G. V. (2009), Semantic Web Services: a RESTful approach. *IADIS International Conference WWW/Internet 2009* Rome, Italy.

García-Sánchez, F., Sabucedo, L. Á., Martínez-Béjar, R., Rifón, L. A., Valencia-García, R. & Gómez, J. M. (2011), Applying intelligent agents and semantic web services in eGovernment environments. *Expert Systems*, 1-21.

Gruber, T. R. (1993), A translation approach to portable ontologies. *Knowledge Acquisition,* 5, 199-220.

Janev, V. & Vranes, S. (2010), Applicability assessment of Semantic Web technologies. *Information Processing & Management.*

Jennings, N. R. & Wooldridge, M. (1998), Applications of intelligent agents. *Agent technology: foundations, applications, and market.* Springer-Verlag New York, Inc.

Kuropka, D., Troger, P., Staab, S. & Mathias, W. (Eds.) (2008), *Semantic Service Provisioning.*

Lu, J., Zhang, G. & Ruan, D. (Eds.) (2007), *E-Service Intelligence: Methodologies, Technologies and Applications*, Springer-Verlag Berlin Heidelberg.

Martin, D., Burstein, M., Hobbs, J., Lassila, O., Mcdermott, D., Mcilraith, S., Narayanan, S., Paolucci, M., Parsia, B., Payne, T., Sirin, E., Srinivasan, N. & Sycara, K. (2004), OWL-S: Semantic Markup for Web Services X, W3C.

Mtsweni, J., Biermann, E. & Pretorius, L. (2010), Toward a service creation framework: a case of intelligent semantic services. *2010 Annual Research Conference of the South African*

Institute of Computer Scientists and Information Technologists. Bela Bela, South Africa, ACM.

Mtsweni, J., Biermann, E. & Pretorius, L. (2011), Engineering RESTful semantic services on the fly. *Proceedings of the South African Institute of Computer Scientists and Information Technologists Conference on Knowledge, Innovation and Leadership in a Diverse, Multidisciplinary Environment.* Cape Town, South Africa, ACM.

Protogeros, N. (2008), Agent and Web services technologies in Virtual Enterprises. IN PROTOGEROS, N. (Ed.), IGI Global.

Qafmolla, X. & Cuong, N. V. (2010), Automation of Web services development using model driven techniques. *The 2nd International Conference on Computer and Automation Engineering (ICCAE).* Singapore IEEE.

Rivières, J. D. & Wiegand, J. (2004), Eclipse: a platform for integrating development tools. *IBM Systems Journal,* 43, 371-383.

Roman, D., De Bruijn, J., Mocan, A., Lausen, H., Domingue, J., Bussler, C. & Fensel, D. (2006), WWW: WSMO, WSML, and WSMX in a nutshell. In R. MIZOGUCHI, Z. S., and F. GIUNCHIGLIA (Ed.) *1st Asian Semantic Web Conference* Beijing, China, Springer-Verlag.

Studer, R., Grimm, S. & Abecker, A. (Eds.) (2007), *Semantic web services: concepts, technologies, and applications*, Springer-Verlag Berlin.

Data Compression for Tele-Monitoring of Buildings

A.Salatian[1], F.Adepoju[1], B.Taylor[2] and L.Oborkhale[1]

[1] School of Information Technology and Communications, American University of Nigeria, Yola, Nigeria
[2] Scott Sutherland School, Robert Gordon University, Aberdeen, UK
e-mail: {apkar.salatian|rancis.adepoju@aun.edu.ng}, b.taylor@rgu.ac.uk, lawrence.oborkhale@aun.edu.ng

Abstract

In Africa there has been an increase in construction of new buildings. In many cases, these buildings are constructed at a rate where the local authorities have no capacity to enforce any building code, ethics or standards. To compound this problem, there is a predominant lack of qualified staff on the ground to conduct proper physical inspections in the building sites. One solution to this problem is to utilise tele-monitoring of buildings whereby building data is transmitted over a network for remote interpretation by an expert in a different location. A common form of telecommunication is broadband which is not always straightforward to use in Africa. In this paper we propose wavelet analysis as a data compression technique to transform the building monitor data into trends to address the challenges of broadband in Africa for data transmission and allow qualitative reasoning at the receiving site for building decision support.

Keywords

Wavelets, data compression, building, tele-monitoring

1. Introduction

In Africa, there is a lack of building expertise and a lack of standards in the construction industry (Wells, 1986; Abate, 1997). One solution to this problem is to use tele-monitoring of buildings whereby building data is transmitted over a network for remote interpretation by an expert in another location. One of the mediums for tele-monitoring of buildings is broadband, which, in turn, presents further challenges in Africa which need to be addressed. Due to the capital costs, a common problem associated with broadband in Africa is the lack of telecommunication infrastructure. Consequently, bandwidth demand can easily outstrip the revenue realizable that is needed to pay for the network infrastructure investment (Freeman, 2005). As a result, many rural areas in Africa generally have lower bandwidth than urban areas because it is cheaper – this makes data transfer slow. Moreover, there will be service contention on the restricted bandwidth even if core bandwidth exists to deliver the services because aggregate bandwidth will be generally greater than can be delivered over the access connection (Stallings, 2007). One approach to deal with these challenges is to use data compression. Data compression can be defined as the act of encoding large files in order to shrink them down in size and in doing so the intelligence present in the information is preserved (Ahmad, 2002).

In this paper we propose wavelet analysis as a lossy data compression technique to help alleviate the challenges of broadband in Africa for building operators. The data compression in the form of trends will serve 2 purposes: better use of broadband for transmission of monitored building data since smaller files take up less room and are faster to transfer over a network; and to facilitate qualitative reasoning of the trends by building operators and specialists at the receiving site for building decision support.

The structure of this paper is as follows. Section 2 describes the wavelet analysis algorithm for data compression. Section 3 discusses the results of applying wavelet analysis to data taken from the monitors of a building. A discussion of how wavelets analysis can be used to address the challenges of building operators and the challenges of broadband is given in section 4. Final conclusions are given in section 5.

2. Wavelet Analysis

Wavelet analysis is a mathematical technique that can be used to extract information from many different kinds of data. A wavelet is a wave-like oscillation with amplitude that starts out at zero, increases, and then decreases back to zero. It can typically be visualized as a *brief oscillation* like one might see recorded by a building monitor.

Wavelet analysis is a lossy data compression technique which concedes a certain loss of accuracy in exchange for greatly increased compression. Wavelets can be adjusted to different quality levels, gaining higher accuracy in exchange for less effective compression.

In wavelet analysis, the scale that we use to look at data plays a special role. Wavelet algorithms divide a given function or continuous-time signal into different scale components. One can assign a frequency range to each scale component. Each scale component can then be studied with a resolution that matches its scale. If we look at a signal with a small window, we would notice small features. Similarly, if we look at a signal with a large window, we would notice gross features. There has been a requirement for more appropriate functions than the sines and cosines that comprise the bases of Fourier analysis, to approximate choppy signals.

Generally, Wavelet transform of signal f using wavelet Ψ is given by:

$$W_{\psi}(f)(a,b) = \frac{1}{\sqrt{a}} \int_{-\infty}^{\infty} f(t)\psi\left(\frac{t-b}{a}\right)dt \qquad (1)$$

where the variable a is the dilation factor, variable b is the translation factor and a and b are real numbers.

The wavelet analysis procedure is to adopt a wavelet prototype function, called an analyzing wavelet or mother wavelet. Temporal analysis is performed with a contracted, high-frequency version of the prototype wavelet, while frequency analysis is performed with a dilated, low-frequency version of the same wavelet. We will now describe the wavelet method.

Assume that $Y(t)$ is the value of an observable time series at time t, where t can take on a continuum of values. $Y(t)$ consists of two quite different unobservable parts: a so-called trend $T(t)$ and a stochastic component $X(t)$ (sometimes called the noise process) such that

$$Y(t) = T(t) + X(t) \qquad (2)$$

where it is assumed that the expected value of $X(t)$ is zero. There is no commonly accepted precise definition for a trend, but it is usually spoken of as a nonrandom (deterministic) smooth function representing long-term movement or systematic variations in a series. Priestly (1981) refers to a trend as a tendency to increase (or decrease) steadily over time or to fluctuate in a periodic manner while Kendall (1973) asserted that the essential idea of a trend is that it shall be smooth. The problem of testing for or extracting a trend in the presence of noise is thus somewhat different from the closely related problem of estimating a function or signal $S(t)$ buried in noise. While the model $Y(t) = S(t)+X(t)$ has the same form as equation (2), in general $S(t)$ is not constrained to be smooth and thus can very well have discontinuities and/or rapid variations.

The detection and estimation of trend in the presence of stochastic noise arises in building monitor data as presented in this paper. Wavelet analysis is a transformation of $Y(t)$ in which we obtain two types of coefficients: wavelet coefficients and scaling coefficients - these are sometimes referred to as the *mother* and *father wavelet coefficients* respectively. The wavelets are scaled and translated copies (*father wavelets*) of a finite-length or fast-decaying oscillating waveform (*mother wavelet*).

The mother and father wavelets coefficients are fully equivalent to the original time series because we can use them to reconstruct $Y(t)$. Wavelet coefficients are related to changes of averages over specific scales, whereas scaling coefficients can be associated with averages on a specified scale. The information that these coefficients capture agrees well with the notion of a trend because the scale that is associated with the scaling coefficients is usually fairly large. Trend analysis with wavelets is to associate the scaling coefficients with the trend $T(t)$ and the wavelet coefficients (particularly those at the smallest scales) with the noise component $X(t)$.

Generally, in wavelet analysis, sets of wavelets are needed to analyze data fully. A set of *complementary* wavelets will deconstruct data without gaps or overlap so that the deconstruction process is mathematically reversible – this is useful for our application because the receiver of the compressed data can perform decompression to obtain the original signal albeit with some information missing.

3. Results

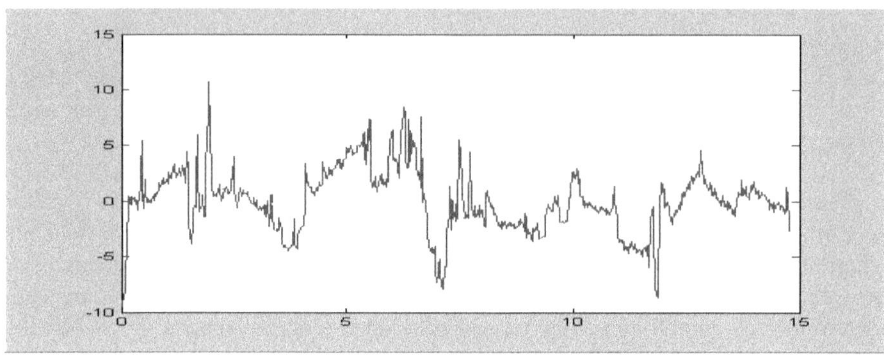

Figure 1: Original/Raw Data Set

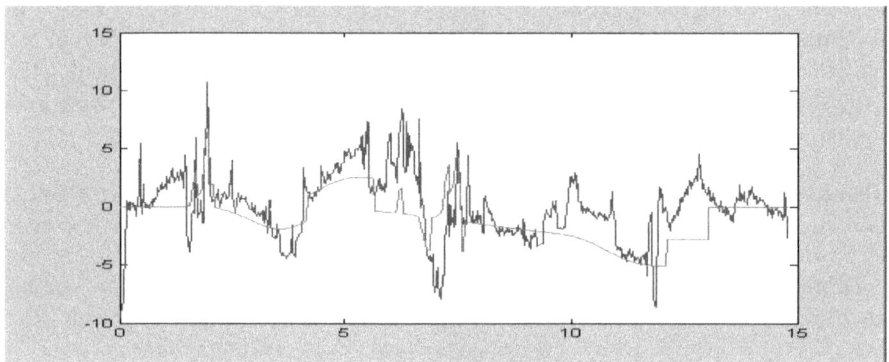

Figure 2: Compressed Data after Wavelet Analysis

To demonstrate the results of wavelet analysis, figure 1 shows the waveform of a Heat Flux signal at 15 - 20Hz recorded in a building in the UK. The bandwidth required for transmission of this digital signal is 20Hz. Heat flux was measured in a building in the United Kingdom with unfired clay bricks for two reasons: to determine the u-value of the wall (how well insulated the wall is); and to determine the admittance of the wall (change in heat flow at the surface ÷ change in wall surface temperature).

The final trends after applying wavelet analysis are shown in figure 2. Trend analysis with wavelets is to associate the Father coefficients (red) with the trend T(t) and the wavelet coefficients (blue). Figure 2 clearly marks the data trend when the data was analyzed with Shannon and Daubechies wavelets. It can be seen that wavelet analysis removes redundancy in the data such as noise caused by external events. It is these trends that are transmitted over the network to the receiver site for interpretation by building operators or specialists. The compression will reduce the bandwidth of the signal and the transmission channel can therefore accommodate more signals which will make better use of resources.

4. Discussion

There are a number of data compression techniques that have been used to make better use of network resources - they include pipelined in-network compression (Arici et al, 2003), coding by ordering (Petrovic et al, 2003) and distributed compression (Kusuma et al, 2001). It has also been shown that data compression for network data transmission cuts the bandwidth needed, improves response size and response delays in networks (Mogul et al, 1997).

We have shown that wavelets analysis can be used as a lossy data compression technique for tele-monitoring of building data. Wavelet analysis allow for more efficient use of network resources because the resulting compressed data reduces storage requirements and makes better use of bandwidth since smaller files take up less room on the access pipe and are therefore faster to transfer over a network. Data compression is therefore ideal for tele-monitoring of building data in Africa because it makes better use of lower bandwidth and contention of services at the monitored building site. In our results we have also shown that our approach serves to remove redundancy in the data such as noise caused by external events.

Since a set of complementary wavelets deconstruct data without gaps or overlap, their mathematical properties make the deconstruction process reversible, albeit with loss of data. If the receiver does not wish to perform decompression then they can perform qualitative reasoning of the trends for building decision support. In (Salatian and Taylor, 2011) it has been shown that qualitative reasoning of trends can be used for fault detection of buildings - here an expert system using associational rules applied to trends was developed to determine periods when there was a fault in the monitored building. Likewise, in (Salatian et al, 2011) the trends generated by wavelets was used to create a conceptual model of a building - this model allows specialists and building operators to determine the current state of a building under observation in order to make informed decisions.

5. Summary and Conclusions

There is a lack of building expertise in Africa which can be addressed by transmitting building data over a network for remote assistance by an expert in another location. However, the transmission of data is not straightforward because there are problems associated with broadband in Africa, especially in rural areas. To address these challenges we have proposed in this paper using wavelet analysis as a data compression technique to transform the building monitor data into trends.

Wavelet analysis is a lossy data compression technique to provide qualitative measurements in the form of trends from the voluminous, high frequency and noisy data that is generated by the monitors in a building. The transmitted trends make better use of restricted broadband and facilitate building specialists at the receiving site to perform qualitative reasoning of the trends for building decision

6. References

Abate, B. (1997) "Domestic Contractors and their Role in the Economic Development of the Country", *Addis Tribune*, 28 November 1997.

Ahmad, A (2002) "Data communication principles For Fixed and Wireless Networks", Kluwer Academic Publishers, 2nd Edition, ISBN: 1402073283.

Arici, T., Gedik, B., Altunbasak, Y. Liu. L. (2003) "PINCO: A Pipelined In-Network Compression Scheme for Data Collection in Wireless Sensor Networks", *In Proceedings of 12th International Conference on Computer Communications and Networks*, Dallas, Texas, 22-22 October 2003, pp 539 – 544.

Freeman, R. L. (2005) "Fundamentals of Telecommunications", John Wiley & Sons, Inc., Hoboken, New Jersey, 2nd Edition, ISBN: 0471710458.

Kendall, M. (1973) "Time Series". London: Charles Griffin, ISBN: 0852642202.

Kusuma, J., Doherty, L., Ramchandran, K. (2001) "Distributed Compression for Sensor Networks", *In Proceedings of 2001 International Conference on Image Processing*, Volume 1, Thessaloniki, Greece, 7-10 October 2001, pp 82 – 85.

Mogul, J.C., Douglis, F., Feldmann, A., Krishnamurthy, B., (1997) "Potential Benefits of Delta Encoding and Data Compression for HTTP", *In Proceedings of the ACM SIGCOMM '97 Conference on Applications, Technologies, Architectures, and Protocols for Computer Communication,* Cannes, France , September 14-18, 1997, pp 181-194.

Petrovic, D., Shah, R.C., Ramchandran, K., Rabaey, J. (2003) "Data Funneling: Routing with Aggregation and Compression for Wireless Sensor Networks", *In Proceedings of First IEEE International Workshop on Sensor Network Protocols and Applications*, Anchorage, Alaska, May 2003, pp 156 – 162.

Priestley, M.B. (1981) "Spectral Analysis and Time Series (Volume 1): Univariate Series". London: Academic Press, ISBN: 0125649223.

Salatian, A., Taylor, B. (2011) "ABSTRACTOR: An Expert System for Fault Detection in Buildings", *In Proceedings of 1st International Conference on Intelligent Systems & Data Processing (ICISD 2011)*, Vallabh Vidya Nagar, India, January 24 - 25, 2011, pp 7-11.

Salatian, A., Adepoju, F., Taylor, B., Odinma, A. (2011) "Using Wavelets to Create Conceptual Models from Building Monitor Data", *In Proceedings of the 2nd International Multi-Conference on Complexity, Informatics and Cybernetics (IMCIC 2011)*, Volume 1, Orlando, Florida USA, March 27th - 30th, 2011, pp 235-240.

Stallings, W. (2007) "Data and Computer Communication", Pearson Educational Inc. 8th Edition, ISBN: 0132433109.

Wells, J. (1986) "The Construction Industry in Developing Countries", London, Croom Holm, ISBN: 0709936265.

A Service-Oriented Approach to Implementing an Adaptive User Interface

E.K.Senga, A.P.Calitz and J.H.Greyling

Department of Computing Sciences, Nelson Mandela Metropolitan University
P.O. Box 77000, Port Elizabeth, 6031, South Africa
e-mail: andre.calitz@nmmu.ac.za

Abstract

Service-Oriented Architectures (SOA) are increasingly being adopted to integrate the disparate computational assets in organisations. A major hurdle in the integration process is the provision of user interfaces (UIs) for applications based on SOA. A popular approach to this problem is to generate the UI whenever a user seeks to interact with an application. End users of applications are, however, increasingly different in their needs, capabilities and traits. Adaptive user interfaces (AUI) have been proposed as a means to cater for such differences. This paper outlines research undertaken to develop an AUI prototype using a SOA. A hybrid approach was used to analyse and design the prototype. An evaluation was conducted firstly to determine whether the components of the prototype adhere to established SOA principles by analytically evaluating the prototype based on these principles. Secondly, to determine the effectiveness of the prototype by evaluating the prototype and finally, to evaluate the effect the generated UI has on the performance of end-users by using a usability study. Results of the evaluation indicate that the prototype components indeed adhere to SOA principles, the prototype is effectively implemented and the UIs do not negatively affect the performance of end-users.

Keywords

Service-oriented architectures, adaptive user interfaces, web services user interfaces.

1. Introduction

Service-Oriented Architectures (SOA) is a computing and design paradigm as well as an architectural style which focuses on the design of computing systems by way of services (Oasis, 2006; Papazoglou, 2006; Josuttis, 2007; Shen, 2007; Erl, 2008). A major hurdle in the integration process when using SOA is the provisioning of user interfaces (UIs) for SOA based applications (Tibco, 2006). A popular method of integrating the UI in SOA, as a result of this challenge, is to generate the UI whenever a user seeks to interact with an application (Kassoff, Kato and Mohsin, 2003; Ellinger, 2007; He and Yen, 2007; Song and Lee, 2007; Spillner, Braun and Schill, 2007; Nestler, 2008; Gonzalez-Rodriguez, Manrubia, Vidau, and Gonzalez-Gallego, 2009).

The end users using these applications have different expertise and competencies and they have different needs, capabilities and traits. Adaptive user interfaces (AUI) have been proposed as means to cater for such differences; thus allowing users with different capabilities and needs to interact with applications. The provision of an UI, that could adapt, depending on the user's expertise and dynamic data obtained from user interactions, can improve productivity and task completion time. Jason (2008) indicated that novice users require a different UI from expert users, where expert users utilise short-cuts and control-keys more extensively.

This paper discusses key concepts such as SOA, Automated User Interfaces, Adaptive User Interfaces. This is followed by an overview of existing service-oriented (SO) analysis and design methods and the combination of two popular methods: SOMA by IBM and Service Oriented Analysis and Design Method (SOADM) by Erl (2008). The application of this method to an AUI is presented, and the outcome, a model for AUI services, is discussed. The implementation of a prototype as a proof of concept is presented and its evaluation to answer various research questions, as well as the results of the evaluation are provided. Finally, conclusions drawn from the research are presented.

2. Background

This section provides background discussions on SOA, automated user interfaces, adaptive user interfaces and service oriented analysis and design.

2.1. SOA

The most basic component of SOA is the service and the other components include the Service Provider, Service Consumer and the Registry. The Service Provider is the creator, owner or host of the service. Service providers register their services in registries which are repositories or databases with a list of services and their descriptions. The function of the registry is to keep a searchable list of services, in order to allow service consumers to find appropriate services for their needs and bind to them. Service Consumers are applications or other services looking to make use of the capabilities of a service. They are able to search the Registry for appropriate services and bind to them using a Universal Resource Locator (URL) provided in the Registry.

2.2. Automated User Interfaces

SOA, as an architectural paradigm, advocates encapsulating units of computation or capabilities and making them accessible via a defined interface. In practice, these capabilities may be written in a variety of programming languages, deployed on different platforms, and defined by an interface using WSDL. WSDL is an XML specification that defines the operation(s) of a web service; the input and output messages; the data types of input and output message; the messaging protocol (e.g. SOAP) and bindings of the web service. This level of detail provided in the WSDL provides limited information from which to generate a UI. Several authors have proposed methods for creating UIs for web services (He, Ling, Peng, Dong and Bastani, 2008; Spillner et al., 2007; Gonzalez-Rodriguez, Manrubia, Vidau, and Gonzalez-Gallego, 2009). Some approaches simply generate UI's from the WSDL of web services while others make use of additional documentation to supplement the generation of the UI (Kassoff et al., 2003). He and Yen (2007) propose an approach that uses an Object Layout Hierarchy (OLH) to define the layout of UI elements as nested groups.

2.3. Adaptive User Interfaces

AUIs use different techniques to achieve an increase in the flow of information between computers and users, and adapting the UI is one such technique. AUIs adapt the UI to match the needs of diverse users. AUIs consist of three components which work together in order firstly to capture user-interaction information and store this information in a meaningful way that models the user. This is achieved by using models of the user (User Model), the task (Task Model) and various other models of the AUIs environment (Jason, 2008). Secondly, the components analyse the stored information to make inferences about the user. Finally, the components are able to adapt the AUI by changing aspects of the UI to match the characteristics of the current user and thus facilitate the human-computer interaction between the application and the user.

2.4. Service Oriented Analysis and Design

A number of service oriented design methods exist for the analysis, design and implementation of SOA-based applications (Arsanjani, 2004; Zimmermann, Krogdahl and Gee, 2004; Mittal, 2006; Arsanjani, Ghosh, Allam, Abdollah, Ganapathy and Holley, 2008). SOMA is a popular method developed by IBM which provides details of the analysis design and implementation of SOA applications and systems (Arsanjani, 2004; Arsanjani et al., 2008). Erl's (2005) Service-Oriented Analysis and Design Methodology (SOADM) provides details that are not available in SOMA. Implementing SOADM, the analysis and design phase of a model includes three steps. The first step in system oriented analysis and design is to identify relevant services. This is followed by deriving specifications of the derived services. Lastly the realisation of the services involves decisions on how to implement, deploy and maintain these services.

3. Implementation of the prototype

This section discusses the implementation of an AUI prototype using SOA, based on an AUI services model (Figure 1). Firstly, the implementation domain is described in order to provide a background of the domain in which the prototype is implemented.

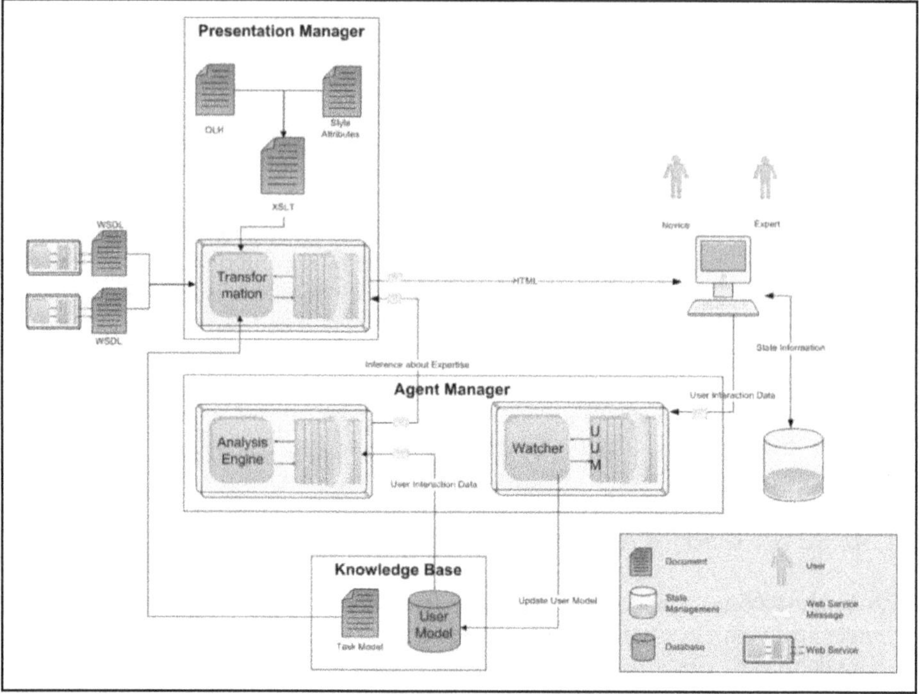

Figure 1: AUI Services Model

3.1. Implementation Domain

Contact Centres (CCs) are the main point of contact between companies and their customers. Contact Centre Agents (CCAs) are the personnel responsible for interacting with customers in a CC and they respond to customers' queries concerning company products or services. The query resolution process begins with logging the customer's query, followed by providing customer details, assigning the call and providing solution details. Jason (2008) implemented an AUI to improve the performance of novice CCAs by providing different UIs based on the user's inferred level of expertise. A prototype, consisting of two UIs was created. One UI caters for novice users and the other for expert users. For the current study, Jason's prototype was redeveloped within the SOA environment.

3.2. Prototype

An AUI services model (Figure 1) was defined after service identification and specification were conducted. The AUI services model using SOA, defines how the AUI services interact in order to provide adaptive functionality. The following sections discuss the implementation of the components of the AUI services model, as part of the service realisation phase.

3.2.1. Knowledge base

The knowledge base stores the user and task models. Both the user and task models are implemented using XML. These components are discussed further below.

3.2.1.1. User model

AUIs generally utilise a user model. The purpose of the user model is to store user-related information; which is used in the adaptation process. The user's unique characteristics are either stored or derived from the data stored within the user model. User performance data are stored as an XML document within a user's profile in a database. In addition, the user profile contains the user's log-in times, and the time taken to complete tasks. Every user begins as a novice regardless of expertise and experience. The Keystroke Level Model (KLM) is used to determine whether a user is an expert or a novice (Hurst, Hudson and Mankoff, 2007) and the low level behavioural data is obtained and analysed using Jason (2008) model. Once the performance matches the performance of predicted expert users, the prototype ceases to generate the novice UI and now generates the expert UI.

3.2.1.2. Task model

The task model maintains a model of a task or goal the user is trying to achieve. The model defines a task and its sub-tasks in a hierarchical structure. The sub-tasks are marked as being complete or incomplete as the user interacts with the UI and completes different sub-tasks. In this study, the task model is stored as an XML document. It is also exploited to provide additional capabilities, for example, element dependencies within the UI are addressed using the task model.

3.2.1.3. Agent Manager - Watcher Service

This research defines Informative Moments (IM) as UI elements with which users interact. For each IM with which users interact, various metrics, referred to as Predictive Features (PFs) are captured. A PF relates to a specific, measurable action (Hurst et al., 2007). It can be measured for any UI element such as a drop down list. The function of the Watcher component is to capture user-interaction information and store this information in the knowledge base. In order to achieve this as a service, the generated UI is created with JavaScript code to collect user-interaction information for each IM. An AUI object is created for each IM and updated if the user interacts with the IM.

The PFs that have time as a unit of measurement *(Dwell Time, Total Time and Selection Time*) are measured using the start-time and the end-time of the action. The *Dwell Time* measures the time (in seconds) during which a user was inactive for longer than 1 second while making a list selection. The *Total Time* measures the cumulative total time that a user has interacted with an IM. The *Selection Time* measures the time taken from when a user selects a list until an item is selected in the list. Jason (2008) identifies various other PFs such as *Mouse Velocity and Mouse Acceleration.* The KLM Predicted Time is a constant value (2.65 seconds) and is obtained from the design of a KLM (Jason 2008). The *KLM Difference* is obtained by subtracting the current *Selection Time* from the *KLM Predicted Time*. Experts are therefore expected to have a smaller KLM than novice users (Jason, 2008). The user model is updated when all the values for the PFs have been obtained, storing a separate record of each task performed.

3.2.1.4. Analysis Engine – Analysis Engine Service

The role of the Analysis Engine Service is to make inferences about users from the information stored in the user model. When invoked, this service uses statistical inference techniques to determine whether the current CCA's performance is equal to or better than the performance of previously defined (not part of this study) expert users, determining whether a user is classified as an expert or not.

3.2.2. Presentation Manager – Transformation Service

The Analysis Engine Service is invoked by the Transformation Service to determine which type of UI to generate for the user. The presentation manager, which satisfies the efferential component of adaptivity, specifies how an AUI should adapt. In this study, adaptation is provided by generating a UI for a user, based on the user's inferred level of expertise. The functionality of the presentation manager is provided by the Transformation Service. The appropriate UI for a user's level of expertise is generated once the expertise of the user is determined by using the Analysis Engine Service. The Transformation service performs its function by using Extensible Stylesheet Language Transformation (XSLT) (W3C, 2009) rules to combine information from the Task Model, the WSDL for the services that support Call Logging steps and the Object Layout Hierarchy to create the UI. The following sections discuss the elements used by the Transformation Service.

3.2.3. Object Layout hierarchy

The Object Layout Hierarchy (OLH) is an XML document which uses nested XML elements to define groups of UI elements in a UI and the layout that these groups have (He et al., 2008). This document is accessed with the Task Model and the XSLT documents to determine the UI layout during the generation process. Various horizontal and vertical groups (either sorted or not) can be defined. Figure 2 illustrates how the layout definitions are applied to the UI in order to achieve the layout of elements. Additional styling of the UI is required, however.

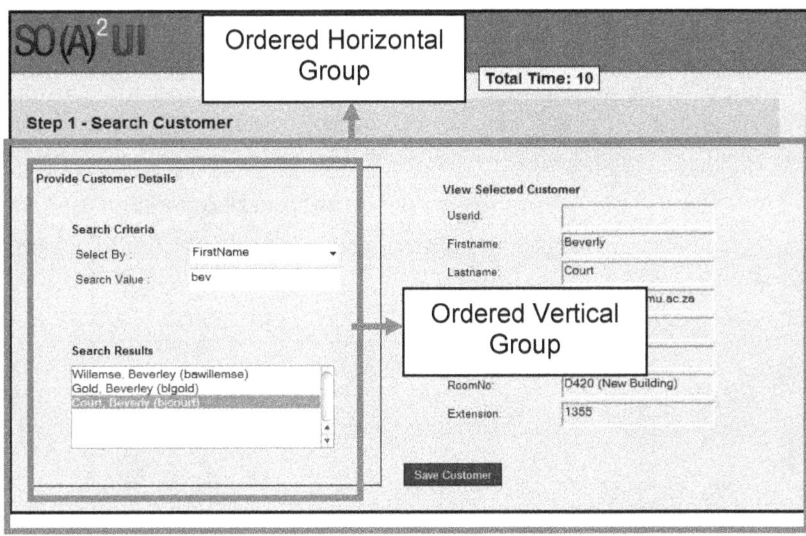

Figure 2: Example of the application of the layout groups to the Novice Step 1

4. Evaluation

The evaluation consisted of a three-component evaluation of the prototype, namely, an analytical evaluation, evaluation by software engineering metrics and finally, a usability evaluation of the generated UI.

4.1. Analytical Evaluation

Erl (2008) proposed a set of design principles to which application services for SOA applications should conform. An analytical evaluation was conducted to evaluate the prototype based on these principles:

A. **Service composability:** "*Services are effective composition participants, regardless of the size and complexity of the composition*";
B. **Service coupling:** "*Service contracts impose low consumer coupling requirements and are themselves decoupled from their surrounding environment*";
C. **Service abstraction:** "*Service contracts only contain essential information and information about services is limited to what is published in service contracts*";
D. **Service statelessness**: "*Services minimize resource consumption by deferring the management of state information when necessary;*
E. **Service re-usability**: "*Services contain and express agnostic logic and can be positioned as reusable enterprise resources*";
F. **Service autonomy**: "*Services exercise a high level of control over their underlying runtime execution environment*";
G. **Service discoverability:** "*Services are supplemented with communicative metadata by which they can be effectively discovered and interpreted*".

Table 1 provides a summary of the service evaluation using SOA design principles. The table shows the rating assigned to the AUI services based on the characteristics portrayed by the services. Green cells in the table represent full adherence to the design principle by the service. Yellow cells represent partial adherence. The information in Table 1 is evidence that the AUI services conform to SOA principles.

		TRANSFORMATION	WATCHER	ANALYSIS
A. SERVICE COMPOSABILITY		*COMPOSABLE*	*COMPOSABLE*	*COMPOSABLE*
B. SERVICE COUPLING		CENTRALISED	CENTRALISED	CENTRALISED
C. SERVICE ABSTRACTION		CONCISE	CONCISE	CONCISE
D. SERVICE STATELESSNESS		PARTIAL ARCHITECTURAL	PARTIAL ARCHITECTURAL	PARTIAL ARCHITECTURAL
E. SERVICE REUSABILITY	TACTICAL	HIGH	LOW	LOW
	ACTUAL	HIGH	HIGH	HIGH
F. SERVICE AUTONOMY		PURE (FULL)	PURE (FULL)	PURE (FULL)
G. SERVICE DISCOVERABILITY		*SUFFICIENTLY DESCRIBED*	*SUFFICIENTLY DESCRIBED*	*SUFFICIENTLY DESCRIBED*

Table 1: Summary of analytical evaluation

4.2. Software Engineering Metrics

A number of software engineering metrics was measured in order to evaluate how effectively the prototype was achieved. Decoupling metrics measured the level of dependency between the AUI services, while architectural metrics measured how effectively the prototype was architected.

4.2.1. Decoupling metrics

A single decoupling metric, the degree of coupling within a given set of services (DCSS) was measured. The formula for determining this metric is shown in Figure 3. This metric was first proposed by Quynh and Thang (2009) who state that a lower value DCSS value equates to a lower degree of coupling between services. Any result between 0 and 1 means that coupling for that set of services is low. The measured DCSS for the prototype in this study was found to be 0.33, thus showing that the coupling between services was indeed low. This means that services were developed with minimal dependencies in accordance with the loosely coupled principle of SO design.

$$DCSS = \frac{Max - \sum_{u \in V} \sum_{u \in V} d(u,v)}{Max - Min}$$

WHERE

1. U AND V ARE TWO SERVICES IN THE SET OF SERVICES
2. D (U,V) IS THE DISTANCE BETWEEN SERVICES U AND V
3. MAX = K*V*(V-1)
4. MIN = V*(V-1)

   WHERE,

   a. K = MAXIMUM VALUE BETWEEN ANY TWO SERVICES IN THE GRAPH
   b. V = NUMBER OF SERVICES (NODES IN THE GRAPH)

Figure 3: Formula for DCSS

4.2.2. Architectural design metrics

Characteristics of an application such as structural, data and system complexity can be measured by using software engineering metric models. High complexity values mean that complex code had to be written in order for the modules to function in an SOA, while low values mean that the complexity is low.

$$S = \frac{\sum f^2(i)}{n}$$

Figure 4: Structural complexity formula

Where, $f^2(i)$ is the fan-out of each class or module being evaluated and n is the number f modules in a system.

$$D(i) = \frac{v(i)}{f(i) + 1} \quad [A] \qquad D = \frac{\sum D(i)}{n} \quad [B]$$

Figure 5: Data complexity formulae

Where:

$v(i)$ is the number of input and output parameters passed to and from the module.

$F(i)$ is the fan-out of each class or module being evaluated

n is the number of modules in a system.

4.2.3. Structural complexity

Structural complexity measures the complexity of a module using the Fan-out approach (Card and Glass, 1990; Pressman, 2004). For the purposes of this evaluation, fan-out refers to procedural calls to dependent classes and web services, i.e. calls to other web services as well as subordinate classes (e.g. data access class for a service). Fan-out is calculated for each procedure in a module, and the sum of all procedures' fan-out values is the fan-out of the module. Figure 4 shows the formula used to calculate the structural complexity of a system S by adding up the fan-out for each module i (Kan, 2002).

Data complexity

Data complexity is a measure of the complexity in the internal interface for a given module (Card and Glass 1990; Pressman 2004). Figure 5 (A) shows how the data complexity is measured for each module of a system, while Figure 5 (B) shows how the data complexity of each module in a system is added up to get the average data complexity of a system.

System complexity

System complexity is a measure of the overall system complexity. Overall system complexity is affected when the structural and data complexity of components within a system change (Kan, 2002; Pressman, 2004). System complexity is measured by adding the structural and data complexity of a system.

4.3. Results from applying metrics

Table 2 provides a summary of the metrics when applied to the AUI services of the prototype. Increased structural complexity increases the problem and perceived complexity of a system (Bundschuh and Dekkers, 2008). A complex system requires more effort to implement. Low complexity values, therefore, indicate less effort in implementing a module. The values in Table 2 show the structural and data complexity for the AUI services. The transformation and expertise services have extremely low structural complexity values. This was done intentionally to decouple the services from their external environment. The watcher class, however, has higher level coupling and dependency as indicated by the complexity values. This indicates that complex code had to be written to perform the required functionality.

Service	Architectural Design Metrics		
	Structural Complexity	Data Complexity	System Complexity
Transformation	0	2	2
Watcher	9	1.43	10.43
Expertise	1	1.5	2.5
Overall	10	4.93	14.93

Table 2: Summary of Architectural Design Metrics for AUI services.

4.4. Usability Evaluation

The purpose of this section is to report on the evaluation of the generated UI by testing its usability using usability evaluation guidelines (Nielsen, 1993; Scholtz, 2000). The majority of the 30 participants were recruited from the NMMU Department of Computing Sciences Department. Thirty participants were recruited for the evaluation. Participants were required to have a high level of computer experience, a sound knowledge of IT and no application or domain experience. A role-playing scenario was used for the evaluation (Pretorius, 2005) and a simulated CC environment was created whereby the participant played the part of a CCA, while the instructor took the role of a customer calling into a CC with a query.

A test plan which provided instructions on how to complete the tasks and information on the tasks to be performed was created for the evaluation using the same set of heuristics as Jason (2008). The final task plan consisted of 7 tasks in total. The effectiveness and efficiency of the prototype was evaluated, which included eye-tracking evaluations (not included in this paper).

Effectiveness

Task success (or completion rate) can be used to measure how effectively a user is able to complete a given set of tasks on a UI (Tullis and Albert, 2008). Each task consisted of 4 steps, with each step contributing 25% to the task completion. Figure 6 shows the task success and failure rates for tasks 1 to task 7. Task one shows poor performance, with only 30% of the participants (n=9) completing the task with a 100% success rate and only 60% (n=18) completing more than 75% of the task successfully. Over the course of the evaluation, however, the task completion rate is observed to increase. Task 4 has 90% (n=27) of the participants completing more than 75% of the tasks and task 7 has 100% of the participants completing 100% of the task. Only five participants attempted task 7, however, since the UI was adapted for all the other participants before they attempted this task.

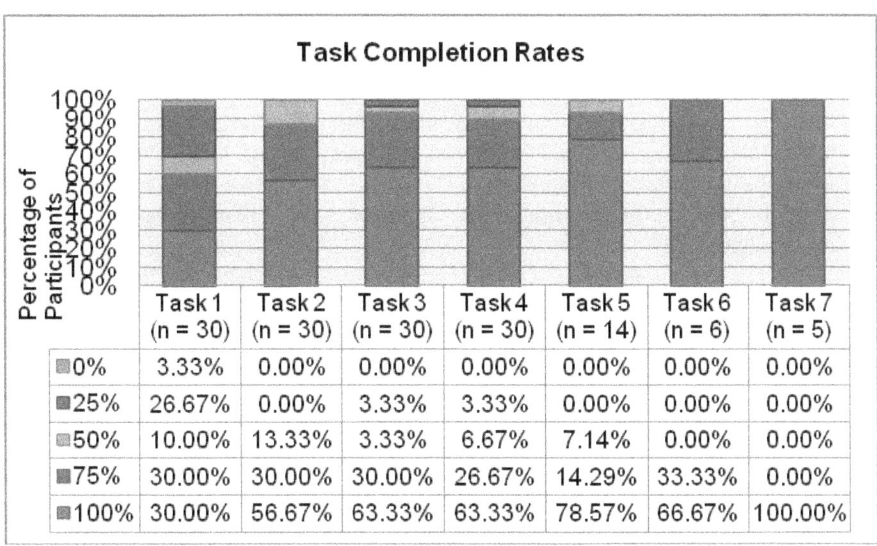

	Task 1 (n = 30)	Task 2 (n = 30)	Task 3 (n = 30)	Task 4 (n = 30)	Task 5 (n = 14)	Task 6 (n = 6)	Task 7 (n = 5)
0%	3.33%	0.00%	0.00%	0.00%	0.00%	0.00%	0.00%
25%	26.67%	0.00%	3.33%	3.33%	0.00%	0.00%	0.00%
50%	10.00%	13.33%	3.33%	6.67%	7.14%	0.00%	0.00%
75%	30.00%	30.00%	30.00%	26.67%	14.29%	33.33%	0.00%
100%	30.00%	56.67%	63.33%	63.33%	78.57%	66.67%	100.00%

Figure 6: Task Completion rates for Tasks 1-7.

Efficiency

Time-on-task is a metric that measures the length of time a participant takes to complete a task and thus user efficiency. Combining this metric with task success shows the participant's task efficiency as the completion rate per unit of time. Figure 7 shows the mean time-on-task achieved by all participants (n=30) for task 1 to task

7. The average time to complete tasks reduced drastically after the first task showing that users required only one task to familiarise themselves with the UI.

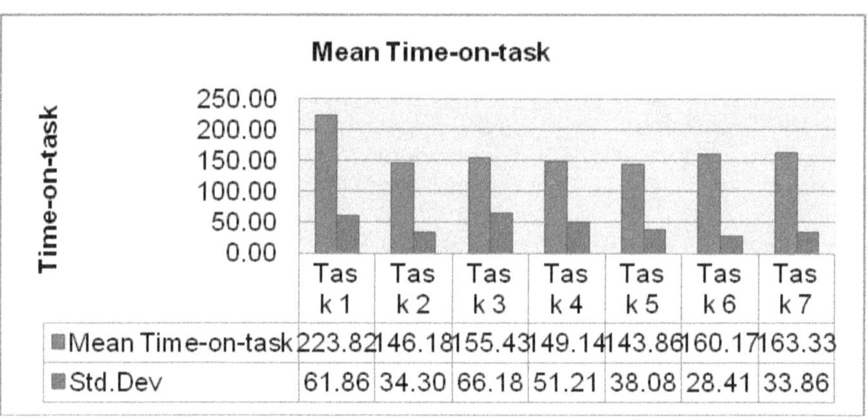

Figure 7: Mean Time-on-Task.

The success rate for each task was combined with the time-on-task to give a value for efficiency. CCAs from the NMMU ICT helpdesk are given approximately two minutes to resolve a query, after which the call must be assigned to a technician who can resolve the query (Vermaak, 2008). Efficiency was therefore measured as the task completion rate per two minutes, that is, how many calls an agent resolves every two minutes. Tasks 1-7 were typical tasks CCA's perform working at the NMMU helpdesk.

Figure 8 shows the efficiency rates for all the tasks completed by participants. This was done by measuring the efficiency as the completion rate per unit of time (two minutes in this case). Task 1 had the lowest efficiency rate of 37% which means that users were only capable of completing 37% of tasks every two minutes. This can be explained by the learning required to complete tasks. Task 5 has the highest efficiency rate of 77%.

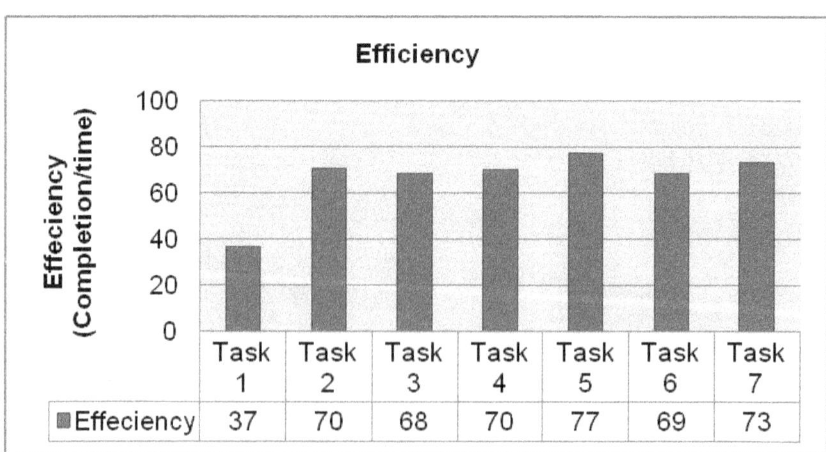

Figure 8: Efficiency rates.

These results indicate that the users could, effectively and efficiently, complete the tasks outlined in the task plan. By completing the tasks in good time, it can be inferred that the generated UIs did allow users to complete the tasks.

5. Conclusions and Recommendations

The aim of this research was to determine if an AUI could be implemented by using a SOA. In order to meet this objective, an AUI services model was designed and a proof-of-concept prototype was implemented and evaluated using an analytical evaluation and a usability evaluation. The evaluation of the prototype showed that users' productivity was not negatively affected by using a SOA. It can therefore be concluded that an AUI can be implemented effectively by using an SOA.

The scope of this research was limited to the use of AUI services in a controlled environment. Future work could involve a research study building on the work of Gonzalez-Rodrigues, et al. (2009) by implementing an adaptive user interface management system and comparing the results to the findings in this study. The envisaged benefits of this research would be increased by the availability of AUI services in organisations for improved UI usage by agents and for training purposes.

6. References

Arsanjani, A. (2004), Service-Oriented Modeling and Architecture (SOMA) (Online). Available at: https://www.ibm.com/developerworks/webservices/library/ ws-soa-design1/, Date Accessed: 20 May 2009.

Arsanjani, A., Ghosh, S., Allam, A., Abdollah, T., Ganapathy, S. and Holley, H. (2008), SOMA: A method for developing service-oriented solutions. *IBM Systems Journal,* 47, pp 377-396.

Bundschuh, M. and Dekkers, C. (2008), *The IT Measurement Compendium: Estimating and Benchmarking Success with Functional Size Measurement,* Berlin / Heidelberg, Springer.

Card, D. N. and Glass, R. L. (1990), *Measuring Software Design Quality,* University of Michigan, Detroit, USA, Prentice Hall.

Ellinger, R. S. (2007), Service Oriented Architecture and the User Interface Services: The Challenge of Building User Interface Services. *Technology Review Journal,* 15, pp 43-61.

Erl, T. (2005), *Service-Oriented Architecture: Concepts, Technology, and Design,* Upper Saddle River, NJ Prentice Hall PTR.

Erl, T. (2008), *SOA Principles of Service Design,* Upper Saddle River, NJ, Prentice Hall.

Gonzalez-Rodriguez, M., Manrubia, J., Vidau, A. and Gonzalez-Gallego, M. (2009), Improving accessibility with user-tailored interfaces. *Applied Intelligence, 30,* pp 65-71.

He, J. and Yen, I.-L. (2007), Adaptive User Interface Generation for Web Services. *In Proceedings of e-Business Engineering, 2007. ICEBE 2007,* pp 536-539.

He, J., Yen, I. L., Tu, P., Jing, D. and Bastani, F. (2008), An Adaptive User Interface Generation Framework for Web Services. *In Proceedings of the Congress on Services Part II, 2008. (SERVICES-2. IEEE)*, pp 175-182.

Hurst, A., Hudson, S.E. and Mankoff, J. (2007), Dynamic detection of novice vs. skilled use without a task model. *Proceedings of the SIGCHI conference on Human factors in computing systems*. San Jose, California, USA. ACM. pp 271-280.

Jason, B. A. (2008), An Adaptive User Interface Model for Contact Centres. *Department of Computer Science and Information Systems.* Port Elizabeth. South Africa., Nelson Mandela Metropolitan University.

Josuttis, N. M. (2007), *SOA in Practice: The Art of Distributed System Design,* Sebastopol, CA, USA, O'Reilly Media, Inc.

Kan, S. H. (2002), *Metrics and Models in Software Quality Engineering,* Reading, Mass, Addison-Wesley Professional.

Kassoff, M., Kato, D. and Mohsin, W. (2003), Creating GUIs for Web Services. *IEEE Internet Computing,* 7, pp 66-73.

Mittal, K. (2006), Build your SOA, Part 3: The Service-Oriented Unified Process (Online). Available at: http://www.ibm.com/developerworks/webservices/library/ws-soa-method3 /index.html, Date Accessed: 21 October 2008.

Nestler, T. (2008), Towards a Mashup-driven End-User Programming of SOA-based Applications. *In Proceedings of the 10th International Conference on Information Integration and Web-based Applications and Services*, pp 551-554.

Nielsen, J. (1993), *What is usability?,* San Francisco, Morgan Kaufmann.

Oasis (2006), Reference Model for Software Oriented Architectures (Online). Available at: http://www.oasis-open.org/committees/tc_home.php?wg_abbrev=soa-rm Date Accessed: 15 March 2008.

Papazoglou, M. P. (2006), Web Services Technologies and Standards. ACM Computing Surveys.

Pressman, R. (2004), *Software Engineering: A Practitioner's Approach,* New York, NY, USA, McGraw-Hill Science/Engineering/Math.

Pretorius, M. (2005), The Added Value of Eye Tracking in the Usability Evaluation of a Network Management Tool. *Department of Computer Science and Information Systems.* Port Elizabeth. South Africa, Nelson Mandela Metropolitan University.

Quynh, P. T. and Thang, H. Q. (2009), Dynamic Coupling Metrics for Service--Oriented Software. *International Journal of Computer Science and Engineering,* 3, pp 46-46.

Scholtz, J. (2000), Common industry format for usability test reports. *In Proceedings of the Conference on Human Factors in Computing Systems*, pp 301-301.

Shen, H. T. (2007), Service-Oriented Architecture *Future of IT: SERVICE-ORIENTED ARCHITECTURE.* University of Queensland, Australia.

Song, K. and Lee, K.-H. (2007), An Automated Generation of XForms Interfaces for Web Service. *In Proceedings of the IEEE International Conference on Web Services 2007*, pp 856-863.

Spillner, J., Braun, I. and Schill, A. (2007), Flexible human service interfaces. *In Proceedings of the 9th International Conference on Enterprise Information Systems*, pp 79-85.

Tibco (2006), Rich Portals: The Ideal User Interface for SOA. Palo Alto, CA, USA.

Tullis, T. and Albert, W. (2008) , *Measuring the User Experience: Collecting, Analyzing, and Presenting Usability Metrics,* Burlington, MA, USA, Morgan Kaufmann.

Vermaak, R. (2008), ICT Helpdesk Manager at the Nelson Mandela Metropolitan University. Port Elizabeth. South Africa.

W3C (2009) XSLT (Online). Available at: http://www.w3.org/TR/xslt. Date Accessed: 15 August 2009.

Zimmermann, O., Krogdahl, P. and Gee, C. (2004), Elements of Service-Oriented Analysis and Design. IBM developerWorks.

Efficient Resource Management based on Non-Functional Requirements for Sensor/Actuator Networks

C.Timm[1], F.Weichert[2], C.Prasse[3], H.Müller[2], M.ten Hompel[4] and P.Marwedel[1]

[1]Department of Computer Science 12, TU Dortmund, Germany
[2]Department of Computer Science 7, TU Dortmund,Germany
[3]Fraunhofer Institute for Material Flow and Logistics, Dortmund, Germany
[4]Chair for Materials Handling and Warehousing, TU Dortmund, Germany
e-mail: constantin.timm@postamt.cs.tu-dortmund.de

Abstract

In this paper, a novel resource management approach is presented for publish-subscribe middleware for sensor/actuator networks. The resource management was designed with the possibility to add non-functional requirements at runtime to subscription messages. This approach allows utilizing service level agreements that can then be employed in order to guarantee a certain quality of service or to reduce the energy consumption of a sensor node in a sensor/actuator network. As an example, a sensor/actuator network for facility logistics system (a conveyor belt system) is evaluated with respect to energy consumption. This sensor/actuator network is mostly controlled by image processing based sensor nodes. It is shown that an adaptive processing interval for these sensor nodes can reduce the energy consumption of the entire network. The utilization of non-functional requirements allows the system to adapt -- after software development -- to context changes such as the extension of the conveyor belt systems topology.

Keywords

Middleware, Non-Functional Requirements, Sensor/Actuator Network

1. Introduction

Web service based technologies are becoming a standard technique for connecting embedded systems. Especially the spreading of DPWS (Device Profile for Web Services) (Chan et al., 2006) in this field and its utilization of standard internet protocols shows that standardization is a major promoter of scalable and re-usable SANETs (Sensor/Actuator NETwork). SANETs provide the possibility to gather information from an environmental context via sensors and sensor nodes and to interact with the environment through actuator nodes without a central control infrastructure – often in a wireless environment (Akyildiz and Kasimoglu, 2004) but not restricted to this. The benefit of these networks is a high adaptation capability in terms of deployment and of failure recovery.

One of the major features of DPWS is the specification of a web service based publish/subscribe paradigm which is known from state-of-the-art automotive communication protocols or from factory steering components such as PLCs (Programmable Logic Controllers). The basic principle of this publish/subscribe paradigm is that there are service providers which push information about an event only to those service consumers that subscribe to the corresponding service providers in advance. Especially when processing capability and network bandwidth are scarce, publish/subscribe has an advantage in comparison to a polling-based communication because the transmission of data is only initiated when necessary. A state-of-the-art middleware which is based on DPWS is MORE (network-centric Middleware for GrOup communication and Resource Sharing across Heterogeneous Embedded Systems) (Wolff et al., 2007).

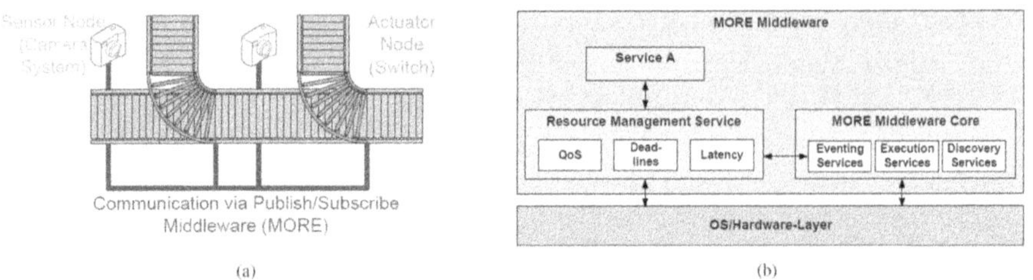

Figure 1: (a) SANET-based Conveyor Belt System and (b) Integration of Resource Management with Subscription Manager

According to (Pavlovski and Zou, 2008), "*non-functional requirements are ... referred to as constraints, softgoals, and the quality attributes of a system*". This non-functional "information" should be modeled in a middleware architecture to handle resource utilization efficiently. As stated in (Franch and Botella, 1998), software design comprises three non-functional core concepts. First of all, there are non-functional attributes which comprise certain attributes such as *time efficiency*. The second non-functional concept is a non-functional behavior which is the assignment of a non-functional attribute to a software component. The last non-functional core concept, is that of a non-functional requirement which is the actual assignment of a concrete value to a non-functional behavior. In many cases a non-functional requirements models a QoS (Quality of Service) requirement. The newly designed central point for gathering non-functional requirements and for controlling the adaptation to these requirements is the extended resource management, named NOFURES (NOn-FUnctional RESource management). In contrast to the original resource management service of MORE, NOFURES allows to assign non-functional attributes and requirements to the subscription mechanism of MORE. As opposed to other software design methods, the non-functional requirements from the actuator nodes are evaluated on each sensor node in a middleware environment at runtime.

In this paper, an exemplary SANET for a conveyor belt system from the field of automated facility logistics systems is the considered use case (Figure (a)). The SANET of the conveyor belt system comprises different sensor nodes and actuator nodes (Timm et al., 2011). The sensor nodes of the system (e.g. camera system or RFID readers) are directly connected to the actuator nodes such as a deflecting belt or switch employing publish-subscribe methods of MORE, as was presented in (Timm et al., 2011). This is fundamentally different – but more efficient – compared to traditional systems where there is only a central controlling instance. The functionality of NOFURES is employed and evaluated with respect to this exemplary

SANET. Constraints and non-functional attributes of the SANET controlling the conveyor belt systems can be, for instance: soft deadlines, analysis quality and input quality.

The most relevant resources at processing level are execution time and energy consumption. The first was already addressed in former versions of MORE (Alonso, 2010) while the latter is a new objective which is considered in this paper. One of the most critical parameters in terms of energy consumption of a service provider is the *update interval* in which events have to be processed and how often a service consumer needs that information. This *update interval* is directly connected to the QoS of a middleware service and therefore, this non-functional attribute is considered in this paper. The specification of a non-functional requirement allows to adapt the system behavior at runtime.

The major contributions of this paper can be summarized as follows:

- Non-functional requirements are taken into account in a publish/subscribe middleware at runtime.
- The specification of a central resource management enables controlling/observing the QoS of all middleware services.
- The energy consumption of sensor nodes is explicitly considered at runtime.

The paper is structured as follows: After this introduction, related work is presented in Section 2. The principles of embedding non-functional requirements to the subscription mechanism of a DPWS-based middleware are introduced in Section 3. In Section 4, the results are presented, followed by a conclusion in Section 5.

2. Related Work

In view of the enormous number of publications in the domain of SANETs as well as in the field of the SANET specification, the following presentation focuses on papers that are related to the approach presented in this paper. In (Sharaf et al., 2004), the authors presented an approach to reduce the amount of data which is transferred in a wireless sensor network over the course of time. The authors – in contrast to this paper – mainly focused on the routing in a network and on the aggregation of data inside the network to achieve savings in terms of energy. The authors of (Munir and Filali, 2007) described a routing and topology building methods for a wireless SANET. The proposed method models the end-to-end delay and the energy consumption as hard constraints which must not be violated. In addition to that, the topology of the network is constrained such that there is only one connection to an actuator node.

The methods proposed in this paper adapt the processing frequency of the sensor nodes in the network which can be seen as a type of Adaptive Sampling (Alippi et al., 2007). Within that work the authors proposed an adaptive sampling method that enabled the developer of a wireless sensor network to save energy. The approach took into account that some wireless SANETs, the energy consumption for processing is higher than for communication. This fact is also exploited by the methods in this paper. However, the work presented in (Alippi et al., 2007) does not focus on the same application environment which are Ethernet-based SANETs.

Another area of interest is the field of resource management (Alonso, 2010) and adaptive applications (Davies et al., 1996). In the latter work, the authors presented a framework for creating a sensor network with different QoS levels.

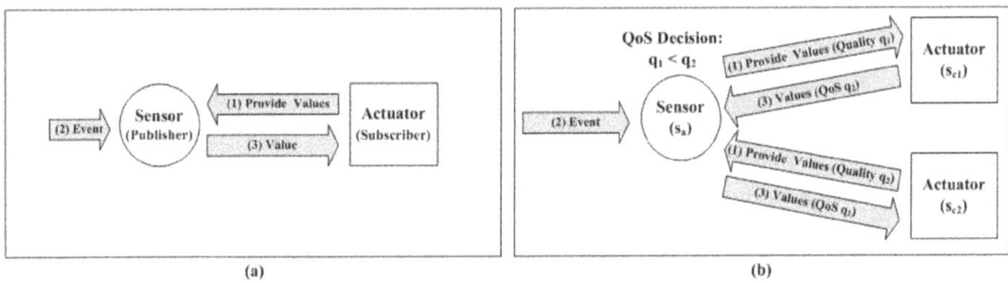

Figure 2: Publish-Subscribe-Mechanism without (a) and with (b) the ability to specify QoS requirements

The last areas of interest are business applications and software architecture. Several papers about non-functional requirements exist in these areas (D'Ambrogio, 2005; Pavlovski and Zou, 2008; Franch and Botella, 1998) but they are more software architecture related and do not focus on runtime adaptivity. Overall, it can be summarized that not all aspects of resource management in the area of SANET research are exploited.

3. Non-Functional Requirements Aware Middleware

The capability to adapt sensor node behavior in a system to non-functional requirements and its integration in a resource management (NOFURES) are the novelties presented in this paper (Section 3.2). Section 3.1 will summarize methods of the MORE middleware (cf. Figure (b)) which will be followed by the description of a exemplary implementation for a conveyor belt system in Section 3.3.

3.1. General Architecture

The design of the MORE Middleware (Schmutzler et al., 2008; Wolff et al., 2007) conforms to the paradigm of SOA (Service Oriented Architectures) by adopting it for external and internal communication to provide a high degree of flexibility. In terms of communication protocols, MORE satisfies a subset of the DPWS specification (Chan et al., 2006) including an ad-hoc service publication and service discovery mechanism which is specified in the standard WS-Discovery. The latter is a multicast-based approach which is well-suited for local area networks. For the use in wider network topologies, a concept called discovery proxy is described which hosts a directory service. The major contribution of the MORE middleware are the Added Value Services which offer common functionality like service orchestration, group and resource management services (refer to (Wolff et al., 2007) for more details). The two most important features of this middleware are the resource management – an extension of it is presented in the next section – and the publish/subscribe eventing services as specified in the DPWS specification (Chan et al., 2006). The latter extends web services by the possibility to subscribe to asynchronous event messages of a service and is based on the WS-Eventing standard. The use of the publish/subscribe paradigm (cf. Figure 2(a)) within the MORE Middleware is especially important for sensor/actuators networks and makes the design and deployment of such networks smarter. A polling-based approach is inappropriate in SANETs where nodes with low processing capabilities or with energy constraints can be found.

```
<SOAP-ENV:Envelope ... xmlns:nonfunc="...">
  <SOAP-ENV:Header>
    ...
    <nonfunc:Parameters>
      <nonfunc:item>
        <nonfunc:Nam e>notify_int_low</nonfunc:Name>
        <nonfunc:Value>490</nonfunc:Value>
        <nonfunc:Unit>ms</nonfunc:Unit>
      </nonfunc:item>
      <nonfunc:item>
        <nonfunc:Name>notify_int_high</nonfunc:Name>
        <nonfunc:Value>510</nonfunc:Value>
        <nonfunc:Unit>ms</nonfunc:Unit>
      </nonfunc:item >
    </nonfunc:Parameters>
  </SOAP-ENV:Header>
  ...
</SOAP-ENV:Envelope>
```

Figure 3: Integration of Non-Functional Requirements to Subscription Message

3.2. Non-Functional Resource Management – NOFURES

The novel resource management service has the ability to cooperate with the subscription management of MORE. The new functionality is summarized by the term NOn-FUnctional RESource management (NOFURES). A tight integration with the middleware core and the operating system enables the resource management service (cf. Figure (b)) to handle the non-functional requirements added to the subscription of a service. The specification of these requirements of the subscriber enables the resource management to adapt the behavior of the system towards a SLA (Service Level Agreement). NOFURES is designed to track several resources at runtime. The non-functional attributes are specified using the WSDL service description; analogue to the specification of performance qualifier for web services proposed in (D'Ambrogio, 2005). An example subscription message with non-functional requirements to the update interval of the service consumer is depicted in Figure 3. As one can see, non-functional information is added to the header of the subscription message. The integration was accomplished in a way that these messages can also be interpreted by DPWS devices which do not need non-functional requirements. A new namespace nonfunc was created in which the non-functional requirements can be specified. The non-functional requirements are listed in an XML sequence called nonfunc:Parameters which includes one or more non-functional items comprising a name, a value and a unit. The requirements listed in Figure 3 show lower (490ms) and upper bounds (510ms) for the update interval. The adaptation of the behavior of the service to SLA is controlled by NOFURES. In particular, the resource management service handles all accesses of a service to the underlying operation system and libraries and controls the execution of the service.

The control functionality can include features such as the (average and worst case) runtime of a service, the quality of the result of a service or service failures. This is needed in order to regulate the processing of a service towards a conformance to the specified non-functional requirements. The traditional publish/subscribe process is depicted in Figure 2(a). The actuator nodes subscribe to the sensor node events and get informed when new events of the subscribed type happen. In comparison to that, an example of how an SLA or QoS Decision can be used with NOFURES is depicted in Figure 2(b). For example, there could be service consumers s_{c1} and s_{c2} which are interested in a certain service s_a providing an image analysis with certain frame rates $x_1 < x_2$ with respective QoS of $q_1 < q_2$. With NOFURES s_{c1} and s_{c2} can now inform s_a with which particular QoS the results of s_a are required (e.g. s_{c1} needs q_1 and s_{c2} needs q_2). For the QoS, several policies could be applied, e.g. provide a service with a QoS that satisfies all requirements. If the latter is applied, the NOFURES service on s_a can choose q_2 for both services in order to satisfy the non-functional requirements of s_{c1} and s_{c2}.

3.3. Use Case: Camera-based Conveyor Belt System

As an exemplary system, a SANET controlling a conveyor belt is considered. The most important places within a conveyor belt system are the switches taking the decision to route a parcel to one or another direction. In the past, these switches were controlled by a larger number of sensors, such as light-barriers or RFID-readers and a central control instance that tracks all parcels on the conveyor belt and which is responsible for taking control decisions. This approach is inefficient, especially from the perspective of costs but also from the point of flexibility and scalability. A new approach was introduced in (Timm et al., 2011) which replaces light-barriers and RFID-readers at the switches by low-cost cameras and an in-situ marker detection system (as depicted in Figure (a)). The employed marker technology is called QR code (International Organization for Standardization, 2006). The image processing as part of the marker detection system was accelerated by a parallel processing hardware based on OpenCL (Khronos Group, 2010). The topology of the SANET is as follows (cf. Figure (a)): The sensor nodes observe one or more switches and the belt in front of them. The actuator nodes of the SANET are the switches which subscribe to the sensor nodes. All sensor nodes and actuator nodes are equipped with the MORE middleware and the new resource management NOFURES.

One of the most critical parameters in terms of energy consumption of a service provider is the interval in which events take place/have to be processed and how often a service consumer needs that information. If, for instance, the information (QR code) which is provided to the service consumer is not updated in consequent events, this information need not be transferred again. In terms of the conveyor belt, this could be a parcel which is still on the same trail towards a switch. The switch as a service consumer is only interested in the parcel's data if it represents new information and therefore attributes with the necessary update interval are added to the sensor node's subscription. The sensor node can then adapt to this requirement.

Therefore, the non-functional attribute which occurs on the sensor nodes and which is evaluated in this study, is the update interval. It describes the minimal and maximal time interval in which a sensor node has to provide data if events occur. NOFURES can actively restrain the events which are published by a sensor node. If more than one actuator node subscribes to a sensor node. The minimal update interval is chosen.

4. Evaluation

This section provides the basic requirements to evaluate the functionality and efficiency of the proposed resource management in real logistics system architecture and the corresponding results. First of all, the testbed for the sensor nodes is introduced (Section 4.1) and then the results are presented (Section 4.2). The evaluation shows how resources such as energy can be saved by providing non-functional requirements to the subscription process.

4.1. Testbed

Both, energy consumption and performance are measured with a performance and energy benchmarking testbed. The sensor node is powered via a 5V DV power supply connection. For measuring the power consumption of the sensor node, a power clamp at the 5V power line is utilized. The power clamp provides a voltage proportional to the current flowing through the probed lines which can be measured employing an oscilloscope (Sampling frequency: 10kHz).

The following tests were conducted: The energy consumption and the processing time were measured for two image sizes: 320×240 pixels and 640×480 pixels. After these initial tests, several update intervals were tested in order to determine the update interval with optimal energy consumption for the considered conveyor belt system. The update intervals of the sensor nodes are 250ms±10ms, 500ms±10ms and 1000ms±10ms. They are added as lower and upper bounds to the subscription messages as depicted in Figure 3. The maximal speed of the considered conveyor belt system is approximately 1 meter per second. Due to this and the architecture of the system, the largest possible update interval is 1000ms±10ms, otherwise not all parcels can be identified properly. This is the standard speed of conveyor belt systems.

The baseline system configuration is publish/subscribe SANET without any restriction in terms of detected QR codes. Every detection is therefore transmitted.

4.2. Results

The results in Figure 4 show the different processing phases of the sensor nodes and thereby prove that theses nodes can adapt to the desired update intervals. While waiting for the next image, the power consumption ranges from 3.5 up to 4.5 watts. During image processing, up to 6.75 watts are consumed by the sensor node. In this figure, only processing intervals are shown where a QR code was fully decoded. Therefore, the execution times for images with incomplete QR code detection are shorter. On the other hand, image processing methods and most of the detection-related algorithms are executed, regardless of the presence of a QR code in the image.

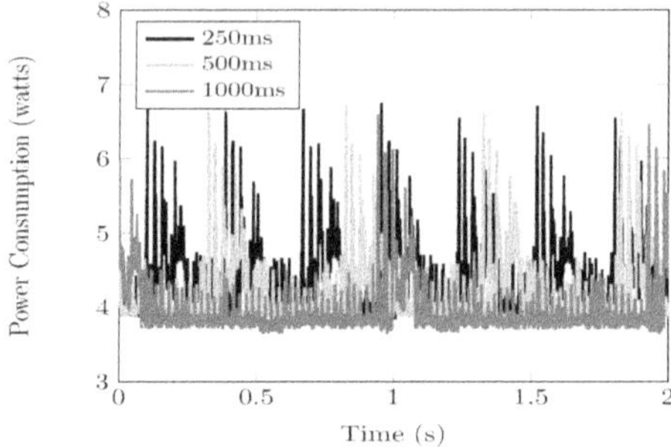

Figure 4: Power Consumption for Different Subscription Intervals

Table shows the results for energy consumption and the processing time for different image sizes. When an QR code is detected in a image, analysis required 88ms for a 320×240 pixels image and 291ms for 640×480 pixels image (energy consumption: 0.377 Joule, respectively 1.271 Joule). The lower bound for image processing (no QR code in an image) within the marker detection process for a 320×240 pixels image amounts to 36ms and to 132ms for a 640×480 pixels image. The minimal energy consumption for these lower processing bounds amounts to 0.152 Joule, respectively 0.574 Joule.

Image Size (Pixels)	QR code Detection		No QR code detected	
	Avg. Runtime (s)	Avg. Energy Consum. (J)	Avg. Runtime (s)	Avg. Energy Consum. (J)
320×240	0.088	0.377	0.036	0.152
640×480	0.291	1.271	0.132	0.574

Table 1:Energy Consumption for Analyzing a Single Image

The energy consumption results for the sensors nodes and the different update intervals are depicted in Table 2. The energy consumption values comprise a one minute time frame. Minimal energy is consumed when no QR code was processed in the specified interval and maximal energy is consumed in the specified interval when for each processed image a QR code was recognized. When no update interval was specified in a subscription message then minimal energy consumption for an image of size 320×640 pixels is 196 Joule and 211 Joule for an image of size 640×480 pixels. The maximal energy consumption for the same scenario is 212 Joule (320×240) respectively 225 Joule (640×480). These energy consumption values also characterize the system without NOFURES and therefore, they are used as the baseline for the evaluation. For an image size of 640x480 pixels and an update interval of 250±10ms, an evaluation not possible since the average runtime of QR detection exceeds this interval with 290ms. For the largest update interval (1000±10ms), the minimal energy consumption for an image of size 320×240 pixels is 183 Joule and 187 Joule for an image of size 640×480 pixels. The maximal energy consumption for the same scenario (1000±10ms) is 187 Joule (320×240) respectively 200 Joule (640×480). This means that, in total, 12% (187Joule/212Joule) energy is saved in a system working with images of size 320x240 pixels and an update interval of 1000ms±10ms, in comparison to a system without NOFURES. For 640×480 pixels sized images, there is a reduction of the energy consumption of up to 8% (200Joule/225Joule). Overall, it can be summarized that by extending the update interval of the sensor nodes energy can be saved.

Image Size (Pixels)	Interval (± 10 ms)	Minimal Energy Consumption (J)	Maximal Energy Consumption (J)
320×240	Without NOFURES	196	212
320×240	250	188	202
320×240	500	185	191
320×240	1000	183	187
640×480	Without NOFURES	211	225
640×480	250	-	-
640×480	500	194	218
640×480	1000	187	200

Table 2: Energy Consumption per Minute for Different Update Intervals

5. Conclusion

This paper described an enhancement of a publish/subscribe middleware by the utilization of non-functional requirements for enabling a more efficient utilization of resources such as energy in a sensor/actuator network. To this end, the resource management of a state-of-the-art middleware based on DPWS, called MORE, was expanded to control and track the behavior of running services. Furthermore, it was extended to evaluate non-functional requirements encapsulated in subscription messages. The subscription process of the MORE was modified to specify non-functional requirements by a service consumer and to interpret them on the service provider side. NOFURES was then applied on an automated facility logistics system. The SANET in this system was employed with MORE and NOFURES. It was evaluated towards it capability to save energy by specifying a certain event notification interval. For future work, several other QoS/non-functional requirements will be evaluated with NOFURES. Furthermore, it will be evaluated if it is even more beneficial for energy consumption of sensor nodes when they share information, e.g. a preceding sensor node can share information whether there are parcels on their way to succeeding sensor nodes.

6. References

Akyildiz, I. F. and Kasimoglu, I. H. (2004), "Wireless sensor and actor networks: research challenges", *Ad Hoc Networks Journal (Elsevier)*, Vol. 2, No. 4, pages 351 – 367.

Alippi, C., Anastasi, G., Galperti, C., Mancini, F., and Roveri, M. (2007), "Adaptive sampling for energy conservation in wireless sensor networks for snow monitoring applications", *IEEE International Conference on Mobile Adhoc and Sensor Systems*, pages 1 –6.

Alonso, A., Salazar, E., and Lo andpez, J. (2010), "Resource management for enhancing predictability in systems with limited processing capabilities", *IEEE Conference on Emerging Technologies and Factory Automation*, pages 1 –7.

Chan, S. et al. (2006), Device Profile for Web Services, OASIS Standard.

D'Ambrogio, A. (2005). "A WSDL extension for performance-enabled description of web services". *International Conference on Computer and Information Sciences*, pages 371–381.

Davies, N., Friday, A., Blair, G. S., and Cheverst, K. (1996), "Distributed systems support for adaptive mobile applications", *Mobile Networks and Applications*, Vol. 1, No. 4, pages 399–408.

Franch, X. and Botella, P. (1998), "Putting non-functional requirements into software architecture", *International Workshop on Software Specification and Design*, pages 60 –67.

International Organization for Standardization (2006), "Norm ISO/IEC 18004 2006. QR Code 2005 bar code symbology specification"

Khronos Group (2010), "OpenCL Specification"

Munir, M. F. and Filali, F. (2007), "Maximizing network-lifetime in large scale heterogeneous wireless sensor-actuator networks: a near-optimal solution", *Performance evaluation of wireless ad hoc, sensor, and ubiquitous networks*, pages 62–69

Pavlovski, C. J. and Zou, J. (2008), "Non-functional requirements in business process modeling", *Asia-Pacific Conference on Conceptual Modelling*, pages 103–112.

Sharaf, A., Beaver, J., Labrinidis, A., and Chrysanthis, K. (2004), "Balancing energy efficiency and quality of aggregate data in sensor networks", *VLDB Journal*, pages 384–403.

Timm, C., Weichert, F., Fiedler, D., Prasse, C., Müller, H., ten Hompel, M., and Marwedel, P. (2011), "Decentralized control of a material flow system enabled by an embedded computer vision system", *IEEE ICC RWFI*, pages 1–5.

Wolff, A., Michaelis, S., Schmutzler, J., and Wietfeld, C. (2007), "Network-centric middleware for service oriented architectures across heterogeneous embedded systems", IEEE *EDOC Conference Workshop*, pages 105–108.

Wikipedia-Based Efficient Sampling Approach for Topic Model

T.Zhao, C.Li and M.Li

School of Software, Tsinghua University, Beijing 100084, China
e-mail: zt882001@hotmail.com; cli@tsinghua.edu.cn; imyli1024@gmail.com

Abstract

In this paper, we propose a novel approach called Wikipedia-based Collapsed Gibbs sampling (Wikipedia-based CGS) to improve the efficiency of the collapsed Gibbs sampling(CGS), which has been widely used in latent Dirichlet Allocation (LDA) model. Conventional CGS method views each word in the documents as an equal status for the topic modeling. Moreover, sampling all the words in the documents always leads to high computational complexity. Considering this crucial drawback of LDA we propose the Wikipedia-based CGS approach that commits to extracting more meaningful topics and improving the efficiency of the sampling process in LDA by distinguishing different statuses of words in the documents for sampling topics with Wikipedia as the background knowledge. The experiments on real world datasets show that our Wikipedia-based approach for collapsed Gibbs sampling can significantly improve the efficiency and have a better perplexity compared to existing approaches.

Keywords

Gibbs sampling, Latent Dirichlet Allocation, Wikipedia, Topic Model

1. Introduction

The Latent Dirichlet Allocation (LDA) model, a general probabilistic framework for topic modeling, has been widely used for topic modeling and other related fields since it was first proposed by Blei et.al, 2003. The key idea of LDA model is to assume that a document is a mixture of topics, and words in the document have a distribution over these topics. Actually, these topics are represented as a multinomial distribution over the words. Based on these assumptions, the LDA model takes Bayesian framework as learning model by executing Expectation-Maximization algorithm from data iteratively. In 2004 Griffiths and Steyvers proposed a Markov-chain Monte Carlo method called Collapsed Gibbs Sampling (CGS), which has been widely used in LDA variants. From then on CGS becomes a straight-forward approach for LDA and rapidly converged to a well known ground-truth.

Based on LDA model, further ideas and techniques have been widely applied in LDA variants and other research fields. For example Author-Topic model (Steyvers *et al.*, 2004) uses the CGS to discover author's topics among documents; Joint Sentiment/Topic model (Lin and He, 2009) combines topic model with sentiment analysis to find topics with sentiment information by using CGS. All these works need to employ LDA or its variants to generate topics from large amounts of documents automatically. However, since CGS views each word as the same status when sampling a topic for each word in the documents during each iteration, its performance seems far from satisfaction, especially on large textual corpora.

Therefore, to speed up the estimation procedure of LDA, we propose a novel sampling approach for topic modeling called Wikipedia-based Collapsed Gibbs sampling (Wikipedia-based CGS). We use the Wikipedia concept as background knowledge to distinguish words in the documents with three different statuses according to the meaningful case of the words. Then we assign different sampling times for these statuses. Experiments on real world datasets show that our approach presents a significant improvement for efficiency and a satisfied perplexity performance. From the experiment results, we also conclude that our approach focuses more sampling times on those meaningful words and less on other words to extract meaningful topics compared to other existed approaches.

2. Related work

Previous works on optimizing or parallelizing CGS have been explored in different implementations to improve the efficiency and overcome the scalability limitation. The first implementation of LDA is GibbsLDA. This standard LDA implementation has been widely used as a baseline model. Porteous et al. proposed FastLDA (Porteous *et al.*, 2008), considering that the posterior distribution is sparse for most words w and topics z. They exploited an upper bound of the posterior distribution and divided it into segments. Thus, FastLDA could sample the topic assignment for words without computing all $p(z_i \mid w)$, which means it improved the efficiency by executing less than K operations per iteration. Yao et al. proposed a SparseLDA (Yao *et al.,* 2009) to further improve the efficiency of CGS by dividing the full conditional probability mass into three parts and using an original approximate sampling scheme for document-topic count matrix and topic-word count matrix. Both FastLDA and SparseLDA require sampling for each word in the documents. Han Xiao *et al.* assumed that the same words in a document represented partly the same topics, so they considered to reduce sampling times for the same words in one document and proposed an Efficient Collapsed Gibbs sampling strategy (ECGS) (Xiao and Stibor, 2010). This paper described two optimization strategies for the ECGS algorithm. One is shortcut-ECGS, which assumes that the same words in one document have the same topic distribution. Though the shortcut-ECGS contributes to the efficiency improvement, the perplexity performance is unsatisfied. The other strategy is Dynamic-ECGS, which introduces a sampling-time vector for the same words in documents to decide the word's sampling times per iteration. In this strategy, the sampling-time of the type is a random variable and Dynamic-ECGS draws it from a multinomial distribution with the parameter vector Γ_{di} with a damping variable γ in iterations to gradually reduce the sampling-time for the same words over iterations. The vector is updated due to the unique drawn topics in each iteration. On the other hand, some parallelization works have also been proposed due to the high computational complexity of training LDA by using CGS. Newman et al. (Newman *et al.*, 2007) presented two synchronous methods, AD-LDA and HDLDA, to process distributed CGS algorithm. By straightforwardly mapping LDA to a distributed processor setting, AD-LDA is easy to implement and can be viewed as an approximation to Gibbs-sampled LDA. While HDLDA is a model that uses a hierarchical Bayesian extension of LDA to account for distributed data directly. This model has a theoretical guarantee of convergence but is more complex to implement. In 2009, Wang et al. (Wang *et al.*, 2009) used the map-reduce framework and MPI to implement the AD-LDA, which is called PLDA.

However, all these works we mentioned above sample topics for all words, which takes considerably computational cost. Although the ECGS algorithm has reduced the sampling times of the same words, it does not distinguish status of the words in documents which could further reduce the sampling times per iteration.

3. Wikipedia-based CGS approach

Wikipedia-based CGS Algorithm

In the rest sections of this paper, we use token to represent the occurrence of a word and use type to represent the unique words, e.g. "the cat and the dog" has five tokens but four types. The important notations in this paper are demonstrated in Table 1.

Notation	Description
N_d	Number of types in document *d*
N_{di}	Number of the i_{th} type in document *d*
w_{di}	The i_{th} type in document *d*
z_{di}	The topic assignment for i_{th} type in document *d*
S_{di}^{t}	The sampling rate for w_{di} in iteration *t*
α, β, ω	Dirichlet priors

Table 1: Notations used in this paper

As mentioned above, Dynamic-ECGS algorithm is proposed to reduce the sampling times of repetitive words. However, not all types in documents should be reduced to a lower sampling rate. For instance, given a document with eight tokens “take” and three tokens “algorithms”, we naturally care more about the topics on “algorithms” rather than “take”, so the algorithm should take a relatively higher sampling rate for type "algorithm" than that of "take". Accordingly, we consider to employ higher sampling rate on those particularly meaningful words and lower sampling rate on others due to the theoretical reason that higher sampling rate for the type contributes to a more focused topic distribution. Here the sampling rate is formally defined. Sampling rate in CGS iteration *t* for type *w* is defined as the ratio of sampling times of the type to the number of occurrence of the type in a document as follows.

$$S_{di}^{t} = \frac{\square_{di}}{N_{di}}$$

where $S_{di}^{t} \in (0,1)$. $\square_{di}$ is defined as the sampling times in *t* iteration for the type w_{di}. Based on these, we propose a Wikipedia-based CGS algorithm. We consider to distinguish the statuses of types in a document into three statuses (*concept type*, *meaningful type* and *general type*) according to its meaningful statuses based on Wikipedia background knowledge. The concept types are the words in vocabulary that can be matched by Wikipedia concepts and the concept types are constant. E.g., "algorithmic" is a concept type for that it can be matched by the Wikipedia concept "Algorithm". Assuming that some words that are not matched by Wikipedia are also partly meaningful, we divide the non-concept words into two statuses: meaningful type and general type. Actually, we view the non-concept word as a dynamic status between meaningful type and general type. Whether the non-concept type in a document is a meaningful type or a general type is determined by an indicator variable y drawn from a multinomial distribution π. The decision is made during the sampling process for the type of each document in each iteration, which means that a non-concept type in a document can be viewed as a meaningful type in this sampling process and then treated as a general type in the next sampling process. The distribution π is affected by the proportion of the concept types' number to the size of vocabulary and takes the proportion as its priors. Then we assign a higher sampling rate strategy for the concept type, a common sampling rate strategy for the meaningful type and a lower sampling rate strategy for the general type.

In order to evaluate the performance of our approach, we employ three sampling strategies as follows. 1). *Standard CGS strategy*: this sampling strategy does not reduce the sampling rate for the type in documents. 2). *Dynamic ECGS strategy*: this strategy has been illustrated in Section 2. We follow Dynamic-ECGS with different γ to be sampling strategies for our Wikipedia-based CGS strategies. A larger γ leads to relatively larger sampling rate in Dynamic-ECGS. 3). *Shortcut sampling strategy*: this strategy samples each type in a document only once in each iteration. The order of these strategies according to the decreasing order of sampling rate is shown as follows:

$$\text{Standard CGS} > \text{ECGS-}\gamma \sim 10 > \text{ECGS-}\gamma \sim 1 > \text{Shortcut CGS}$$

The reason we choose these strategies is that these strategies own different sampling rate which we need to assign a higher one for concept type and lower one for general type. We take experiments of choosing three different sampling strategies from the fours for the three statuses of types we defined to evaluate the performance of Wikipedia-based CGS approach.

3.1. Wikipedia-based CGS Framework

Wikipedia-based Collapsed Gibbs sampling algorithm assigns different sampling rate to different statuses of types as what we defined in Subsection 3.1. Concept types are constant during the sampling procedure, while meaningful types and general types are dynamic. We introduce a random variable y for each non-concept type to decide whether the type is meaningful or general. For those non-concept types in each document in each iteration during sampling process, if y =0, the type will be viewed as a meaningful one in this iteration; and if y=1, the type will be considered as a general one. Figure1 (b) shows the graphical model of Wikipedia-based CGS framework for LDA. The generative process is formulated as follows.

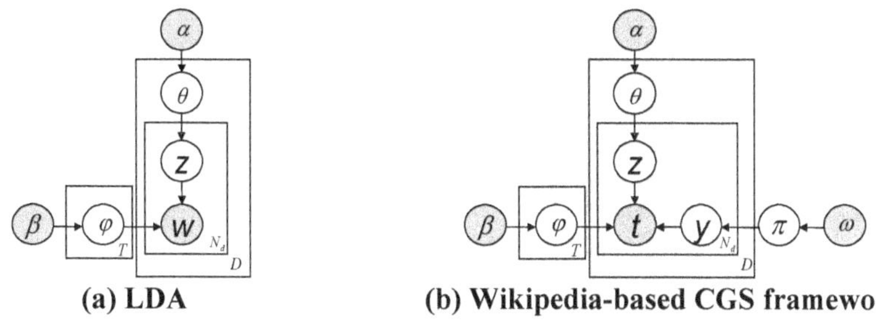

(a) LDA (b) Wikipedia-based CGS framework

Figure 1: the graphical model for LDA and our proposed method

1. Draw a multinomial distribution $\pi \sim Dir(\omega)$
2. For each topic, draw a multinomial distribution over words, $\varphi \sim Dir(\beta)$
3. For each document, draw a multinomial distribution over topics, $\theta \sim Dir(\alpha)$
4. For each type *t* in each document
   a) Draw a topic $z \sim Multi(\theta)$
   b) For each type t' matched by Wikipedia concepts
      i. Draw $t' \sim Multi(\varphi)$ with a higher sampling rate
   c) For each type t'' non-matched by Wikipedia concepts
      i. Draw $y \sim Multi(\pi)$
      ii. Draw $t'' \sim Multi(\varphi)$ with a common sampling rate if $y = 0$
      iii. Draw $t'' \sim Multi(\varphi)$ with a lower sampling rate if $y = 1$

Due to the random variable *y*, the decision of meaningful type and general type is dynamic during the sampling process, and is affected by the number of concept words in vocabulary. Thus, as we employ a higher sampling rate for concept types and a lower sampling rate for general types, the total sampling times of Wikipedia-based CGS algorithm are reduced but focus more on both the concept types and meaningful types, which demonstrates a significant improvement for both the efficiency and the generalization performance.

4. Experiments

As is shown in Table 2, the experiments are conducted on three real world data sets: KOS blog entries (from dailykos.com), NIPS full papers (from books.nips.cc), and Enron emails (from www.cs.cmu.edu/~Enron).

	D	**W**	**V**
KOS	3,430	0.4×10^6	6,906
NIPS	1,500	1.9×10^6	12,419
Enron	39,861	6.4×10^6	28,102

Table 2: Details of three datasets used in experiments, D is the number of documents, W is the total number of words in the collection, and V is the size of vocabulary.

The experiments aim to demonstrate the speedup of Wikipedia-based CGS approach against the standard CGS and Dynamic ECGS algorithms and to show the better leverage of both improving efficiency and optimizing the topic extraction. We present the results of the experiments from three perspectives. We use perplexity curve to validate the convergence of Wikipedia-based CGS. Then, we measure the execution time of Wikipedia-based CGS algorithms by setting different number of topics under fixed iterations. Finally, we detect the proportion of sampling times for concept types to total sampling times over iterations to validate that Wikipedia-based CGS algorithm focuses more on those meaningful words. All the experiments are compared with standard CGS algorithm and Dynamic-ECGS algorithms. Wikipedia-based CGS algorithm requires us to know which words in vocabulary of the dataset can be matched by Wikipedia concepts. Here, we first briefly introduce the web service we use for matching Wikipedia concepts -- Wikipedia Miner.

4.1. Wikipedia Miner

Wikipedia Miner (Milne, 2009) is a toolkit for tapping the rich semantics encoded within Wikipedia. Here we use the search service to detect the concept types in vocabulary. We call the search service to find if there are any concepts that correspond to the word in vocabulary. E.g. given a query word "ai" for this service, the XML file returning from search service demonstrates "Artificial intelligence" as most related concept for this word. In KOS dataset, the proportion of the number of concept words to the size of vocabulary is 52%, which means that 52% words in KOS vocabulary can be matched by Wikipedia concepts. In NIPS dataset, the proportion is 54% and in Enron dataset the proportion is 24%. The proportions will affect the decision of a non-concept type whether to be set as a meaningful type or a general type during the sampling process.

4.2. Experimental setup

We implement the standard CGS, Dynamic-ECGS and Wikipedia-based CGS algorithms in JAVA. All the experiments are run 500 iterations. And we set the Dirichlet parameter α =50/K, β=0.02 proposed by Griffiths and Steyvers; Dirichlet parameter ω is set by the proportion of the number of concept words to the size of vocabulary. All models are training on 500 iterations. Due to the definition that Wikipedia-based CGS algorithm requires different sampling strategies for concept types, meaningful types and general types respectively, we experiment with different strategy combinations for Wikipedia-based CGS algorithm as is shown in Table 3.

	Concept type	Meaningful type	General type
Strategy 1	Standard CGS	ECGS $\gamma\sim10$	ECGS $\gamma\sim1$
Strategy 2	Standard CGS	ECGS $\gamma\sim10$	Shortcut CGS
Strategy 3	ECGS $\gamma\sim10$	ECGS $\gamma\sim10$	Shortcut CGS
Strategy 4	ECGS $\gamma\sim10$	ECGS $\gamma\sim1$	Shortcut CGS

Table 3: Different strategy combinations for Wikipedia-based CGS algorithm.

4.3. Convergence Analysis

We use perplexity value to measure the convergence of Wikipedia-based CGS algorithm. Given test dataset D, the perplexity can be calculated as follows.

$$Perplexity(D) = \exp\{-\frac{\sum_{d=1}^{M} \log(p(w_d \mid D_{train}))}{\sum_{d=1}^{M} N_d}\}$$

We present the perplexity of the experiments for Wikipedia-based CGS, standard CGS and ECGS algorithms on KOS dataset, NIPS dataset and Enron email dataset. For each dataset in the experiments, 3/4 data is used for training, 1/4 data is used for testing. For NIPS dataset and KOS dataset, the number of topics is set as 40, and for Enron dataset, the experiments run with the number of topics as 100. Perplexity over iterations for Wikipedia-based CGS, standard CGS and ECGS algorithms is depicted in Figure 2. Due to the fact that a lower perplexity value indicates better generalization performance, we can observe that shortcut CGS algorithm converges to a suboptimal high perplexity value on all datasets, which makes it difficult to infer on new dataset. The reason that can be attributed to the assumption of the sampling strategy is that all repetitive tokens in a document represent the same topics. We can also observe that all the results of Wikipedia-based CGS approach show a better perplexity performance than that of Dynamic-ECGS with γ =10 on all these three datasets. The reason that we choose Dynamic-ECGS with γ =10 as a baseline is that we find out that a larger γ contributes to a better perplexity value but shows unsatisfied performance on efficiency. Even that Dynamic-ECGS with a larger γ can not show the efficiency improvement compared to standard CGS. From the experiments, we can see that our Wikipedia-based CGS approach converges as rapidly as standard CGS and has a significant improvement for efficiency. Moreover, Wikipedia-based CGS approach distinguishes the statuses of types in a document. Therefore, although the total sampling times of Wikipedia-based CGS strategies reduce, all the different settings of Wikipedia-based CGS strategies show optimized effects on perplexity performance.

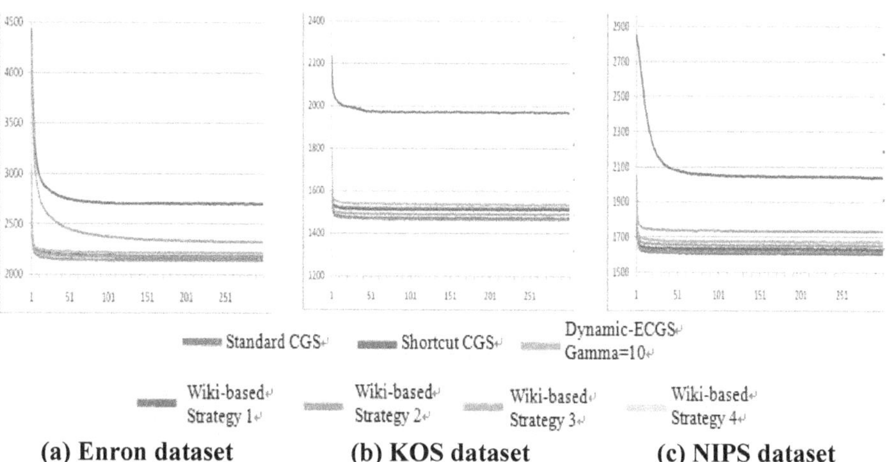

(a) Enron dataset **(b) KOS dataset** **(c) NIPS dataset**

Figure 2: perplexity value versus number of iterations on three datasets. Y-axis represents the perplexity value and X-axis represents the number of iterations

4.4. Speedup Results

The speedup results are evaluated by runtime of the different Wikipedia-based CGS strategies, Dynamic-ECGS and standard CGS algorithms in 500 iterations on both KOS and NIPS datasets. We experiment with different number of topics for these sampling strategies and depict the results in Figure 3. As for the poor performance of shortcut CGS in perplexity, we assume that shortcut CGS algorithm is just designed for speedup but not suitable for using on the real world datasets. Therefore, we do not make comparison with shortcut CGS algorithm. Runtime of standard CGS increases linearly with *K*, so we use standard CGS strategy as baseline to investigate the efficiency improvement of Wikipedia-based CGS approach. In Figure 3, we can see that with the increasing number of topics, Wikipedia-based CGS strategies show a remarkable efficiency improvement. The standard CGS strategy samples every token in a documents and Dynamic-ECGS strategy samples all types in a document with the same strategy. In contrast, Wikipedia-based CGS strategies separate the types in a document into three statuses. These strategies highlight the concept types and save sampling times from general types. This biased view for types makes the sampling process more efficient than other sampling strategies. From the result on KOS and NIPS datasets, we can also see that the improvement of efficiency on NIPS dataset is more outstanding than that on KOS dataset. The reason we analyze is that KOS dataset is collected from blog entries which have less redundancy repetitive tokens, while NIPS dataset is a collection from science papers including more repetitive words in document for clarifying the main idea of the paper and more official and scientific words that can be matched by Wikipedia concepts. Wikipedia-based CGS approach can use an equivalent sampling strategy as the standard CGS or Dynamic-ECGS strategy for concept types and employ other sampling strategies with lower sampling rate for those meaningful types and general types to improve the efficiency. From the experimental analysis, we can see that Wikipedia-based CGS strategies provide a subtle way to leverage the efficiency improvement and the goal of extracting meaningful and focused topics.

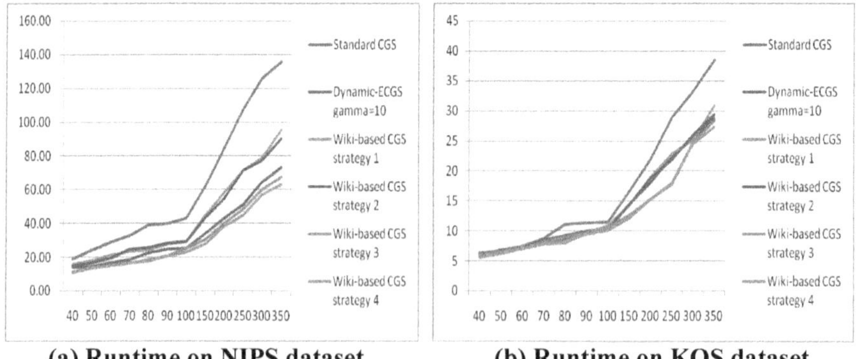

(a) Runtime on NIPS dataset **(b) Runtime on KOS dataset**

Figure 3: runtime results on KOS and NIPS datasets. Y-axis represents the runtime (minutes) of training model and X-axis represents the number of topics

4.5. Sampling Proportion of Concept Types

The main difference among Wikipedia-based CGS strategies and other sampling strategies is that the former ones emphasize the concept types and focuses more sampling times on them. In this subsection, we will calculate the sampling times for the concept types to validate our main idea of Wikipedia-based CGS strategies over iterations. We record the proportion of sampling times for concept types to total sampling times over 500 iterations with different algorithms by setting the number of topics K=40 on NIPS and KOS datasets and K=100 on Enron dataset. We depict the curves in Figure 4.

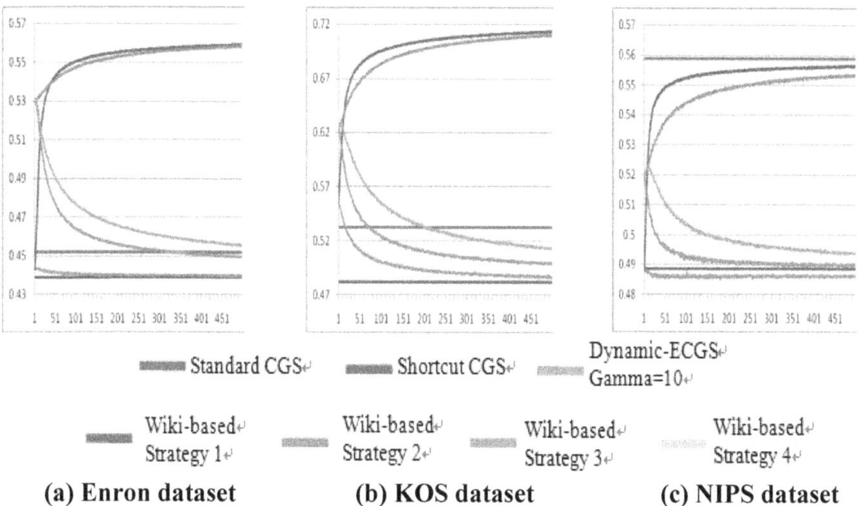

(a) Enron dataset **(b) KOS dataset** **(c) NIPS dataset**

Figure 4: Sampling proportion of concept types over iterations on three datasets. Y-axis represents the proportion and X-axis represents the number of iterations

From the experiment results, we can observe that standard CGS algorithm has a fixed lower sampling proportion for concept types for that it does not reduce any sampling rate for all tokens in documents. Dynamic-ECGS algorithm has an even decreasing trend to a lower sampling proportion over iterations for concept types due to its non-biased sampling strategy. For Wikipedia-based strategy 3 and 4, we can see that due to the chosen strategies for the three statuses of types, which remarkably reduce the sampling rate of types, the sampling proportion of concept types decreases over iterations. However, the sampling proportion of concept types in Wikipedia-based strategy 3 and 4 are still higher than Dynamic-ECGS and Shortcut CGS algorithm, which means Wikipedia-based CGS algorithm focuses more on concept types than other algorithms when sampling. For Wikipedia-based strategy 1 and 2, we assign high sampling rate strategy for concept types, common sampling rate strategy for meaningful types and lower sampling rate strategy for general types, so we can see that the proportion of sampling times for concept types to total sampling times is increasing over iterations, which shows that Wikipedia-based CGS strategies focus more on those meaningful concept words than others, making it achieve the improvement for both the efficiency and accuracy.

5. Discussion and Future Works

Although we distinguish the words in documents into three statuses, we ignore the relatedness between the concept types and the document in this paper. Indeed, the relatedness between concept types in a document should also be considered to further improve the efficiency of sampling approach. We mark all these ideas to our future works.

6. Conclusions

In this paper, we present the Wikipedia-based Collapsed Gibbs sampling approach for improving the efficiency of LDA. This novel sampling strategy bias the types in a document to three statuses including concept type, meaningful type and general type according to their meaningful status by using Wikipedia concept as background knowledge. Instead of taking an equivalent sampling rate for all types in a document, Wikipedia-based CGS strategy incorporates three sampling algorithms with different sampling rate for the three statuses we define in order to sample more times on concept types and save sampling times from general types. We evaluate the experimental results from three aspects with different settings and validate that our approach obtains promising speedup and shows a better generalization performance.

7. Acknowledgements

This research work was supported by TSINGHUA National Laboratory for Information Science and Technology.

8. References

Blei, D.M., Ng, A.Y. and Jordan, M.I. (2003). "Latent dirichlet allocation", in *J. Mach. Learn. Res.*, 3:993–1022.

Griffiths, T. and Steyvers, M. (2004). "Finding scientific topics", in *Proceedings of the National Academy of Sciences,* 101(90001):5228–5235.

Lin, C. and He, Y. (2009). "Joint Sentiment/Topic Model for Sentiment Analysis", in *CIKM.*

Milne, D. (2009). "An open-source toolkit for mining Wikipedia", in *Proc. New Zealand Computer Science Research Student Conf., NZCSRSC*'09, Auckland, New Zealand.

Newman, D., Asuncion, A., Smyth, P. and Welling, M. (2007). "Distributed inference for latent dirichlet allocation", Volume 20, pages 1081–1088.

Porteous, I., Newman, D., Ihler, A., Asuncion, A., Smyth, P. and Welling, M. (2008). "Fast collapsed gibbs sampling for latent dirichlet allocation", in *SIGKDD*, pages 569–577. ACM.

Steyvers, M., Smyth, P., Rosen-Zvi, M. and Griffiths, T.L. (2004). "Probabilistic author-topic models for information discovery", in *SIGKDD*, pages 306–315.

Wang, Y., Bai, H., Stanton, M., Chen, W.Y. and Chang, E. (2009). "Plda: Parallel latent dirichlet allocation for large-scale applications", in *AAIM*, pages 301–314.

Xiao, H. and Stibor, T. (2010). "Efficient Collapsed Gibbs Sampling For Latent Dirichlet Allocation", in *JMLR.*

Yao, L., Mimno, D. and McCallum, A. (2009). "Efficient methods for topic model inference on streaming document collections", in *SIGKDD*, pages 937-946. ACM.

Author Index

www.ingramcontent.com/pod-product-compliance
Lightning Source LLC
Chambersburg PA
CBHW051049050326
40690CB00006B/655

* 9 7 8 1 8 4 1 0 2 3 1 5 1 *